STOCK CAR RACERS

The history and folklore of NASCAR's premier series

"Tail straight out and belly to the ground"

Allan Girdler

Motorbooks International
Publishers & Wholesalers Inc
Osceola, Wisconsin 54020, USA ®

First published in 1988 by Motorbooks International Publishers & Wholesalers Inc, P O Box 2, 729 Prospect Avenue, Osceola, WI 54020 USA

Motorbooks International is a certified trademark, registered with the United States Patent Office

Printed and bound in the United States of America

The information in this book is true and complete to the best of our knowledge. All recommendations are made without any guarantee on the part of the author or publisher, who also disclaim any liability incurred in connection with the use of this data or specific details

We recognize that some words, model names and designations, for example, mentioned herein are the property of various manufacturers. We use them for identification purposes only. This is not an official publication

Library of Congress Cataloging-in-Publication Data
Girdler, Allan.
    Stock car racers.

    Includes index.
    1. Stock car racing—United States—History.
2. NASCAR (Association)—History.   I. Title.
GV1029.9.S74G57   1988   796.7'2'0973   88-8898
ISBN 0-87938-316-X (pbk.)

On the front cover: Davey Allison in the number 28 Havoline Ford. *Bill Warner*
On the back cover: Marshall Teague in a fabulous Hudson Hornet on the Daytona Beach race's north turn, circa 1951. *Daytona International Speedway* The author, Allan Girdler. *Bill Warner*

Motorbooks International books are also available at discounts in bulk quantity for industrial or sales-promotional use. For details write to Special Sales Manager at the Publisher's address

Contents

Dedication and appreciation

We all have dreams and ambitions, usually involving becoming rich and famous, but when we get serious what we really want is to make a difference, to leave the world a different and better place.

Big Bill France is one of the few who will do just that, a man who needs no introduction. This book is dedicated to him.

No less important to my job were all the people who helped me, especially when they knew they would get little in return. My thanks to the Mauks father and son, the Daytona Speedway staff, the Elliott team, the Skoal Bandit crew and to Elizabeth Baker, Smokey Yunick, Richard Petty, Tom Tucker, Tom Cotter, Terri Boyce, Humpy Wheeler, Jan Jones, Otis Meyer and Bill Warner.

Allan Girdler

Introduction

Flip the switch and the screen is packed with racing cars. They are averaging better than 200 mph and they look it when suddenly a car in mid-pack veers and kicks sideways. It becomes a 3,500 lb. four-wheel Frisbee, soaring into the air and into the catch fence, then settling back to earth still spinning like a top as other cars arrive, darting and jinking and slamming into the stalled car and each other.

When the dust settles, the drivers emerge with grim nods to the crowd. They stalk away, unhurt, a bit shaken, feeling lucky only if the car will make the restart. While the crew repairs the fence we watch the instant replay of the spin and crash from several angles, then switch to the in-car camera to see what it's like to roar into the smoke and debris, miss the looming hazards and then get rammed from behind, live on camera.

Welcome to NASCAR, where, as the poet says, you have to see it *not* to believe it.

Stock car racing, or to put it more properly, Grand National Winston Cup racing, the nationwide professional championship series for late model domestic sedans, under the auspices of the National Association for Stock Car Auto Racing (NASCAR), is so unique, so ferocious and so successful that no cliche is strong enough, no contradiction contrasting enough.

One of the tenets of automotive enthusiasm in the United States has for generations been that the domestic product is too big, too simple and too slow, yet racing stock cars routinely run longer and faster than do the high-tech Grand Prix cars.

NASCAR rules are invented, applied and enforced with what can at the very least be described as authoritarian practices, yet the rules are as fair and equitable as any in racing.

The legends have grown around backwoods builders, moonshine runners and guys who are brave because they're not quite smart, but Grand National cars are at least as sophisticated as any vehicle on any track anywhere. The commercial success of NASCAR has ensured good racing because the top twenty teams can make a good living, which means close racing, which means commercial success. No other form of motorsport handles nearly as much money as fairly.

Running through all this, on all sides, is the cheerful willingness of all parties to pretend that we're building and driving and promoting and watching something called stock domestic sedans—which of course we aren't. Not by hundreds of horsepower and tens of thousands of dollars and about 100 miles per racing hour.

NASCAR is beyond unique.

It's also worth long, intensive study, which is what this book is.

There's history, as in how and why stock car racing began, how it evolved and why we are where we are now.

There's technical brilliance, all the work and study and creative interpretations of rules that have given us those 200 mph laps.

There are people who are just as brave as legend holds, while at the same time they possess heaps more smarts than they like the outside world and each other to know they have. (Some of this research will shatter several of the better known myths, but that's not bad, because in NASCAR the truth is much more interesting than any fiction.)

And of course there's racing, how they do it, who does it and why.

That last, the why, is the key to everything else. NASCAR isn't like other racing. It's safe to say that if this form of stock car racing hadn't begun where it did, when it did, none of this would have taken place.

Chapter 1

Early days

Make Tracks, Not History would have been the slogan on the bumper sticker back when the motor vehicle was invented—if there had been bumpers to put stickers on. But there weren't, and the pioneers were too busy making their devil machines run while everybody else knew the contraptions would never amount to much.

While the world was busy being changed beyond imagination, the right people didn't take the right sort of notes and claims are conflicting as to exactly who did what first.

With due respect to various claimants elsewhere, the first motor vehicle meeting most of the clauses in the definition, and the first to be officially recognized, was constructed in 1886 by Gottlieb Daimler near Stuttgart, Germany. It had two big wheels like a bicycle, with outriggers. We can consider it a motorcycle because Daimler waited until his wife was out of town before letting his teenage son take the first ride. Naturally the kid went the fast way and just as naturally his mom caught him and was so angry that Daimler father and son had to put the rig back in the garage, grounded, so to speak, for months. If that isn't a motorcycle story, mothers aren't mothers.

Then came Karl Benz and his self-propelled buggy and we were, to coin a phrase, off and running. The motor car filled a basic human need—never mind that until it was met, we didn't know it was there. Motion equaled freedom. The more ground we could cover in a given length of time, the better. Speed freed, so to speak, and it followed from that that going fast was good. So naturally the faster the car, the better the car. We settled that question with racing. As with the first car, nobody can precisely prove the date and time of the first contest of speed, but the poets who say it happened when two motor vehicles met for the first time are probably as correct as possible.

We are dealing here with one branch of the racing family so the full story can't be told. For our purposes, the record begins in 1904, with the formation of the Automobile Club of America (ACA).

Grand name aside, this was a New York club. It was also the first sanctioning body for races and other variations of motorized competition. The ACA set the rules, enforced them and laid down the law. Nobody liked them very much and they didn't last very long.

Prior to 1910 there was no such thing as a stock car or a racing car, at least not in terms we'd accept today. The men who built cars, built them. They used the best engines and parts they could make or buy and equipped the car for what it was going to do, be that town duty or the Paris-Madrid sprint.

By 1910 Henry Ford was making history at one end of the spectrum and there were genuine full-race machines, good only for racing on closed circuits, at the other end. It became obviously unfair for the chap in the racer to run against the man with the family runabout. Further, cars were still suspect in terms of durability and performance, as in climbing the demon hill outside of every town. So there were commercial reasons to have contests of what we'd call stock cars, production vehicles sold to the public and used for daily transportation.

The idea was obvious.

It didn't work.

In hindsight, the idea had several immediate drawbacks, not the least of which was democracy. In

The car is a Model T Ford, the time is 1910 and all the details have been lost. But look at the expressions: the mixture of honest confidence, hard-won pride and innocent enjoyment of the challenge. Everything about stock cars and racing has changed since this picture was taken . . . except for the spirit and enthusiasm shown here, which is why we care so much about it. Henry Ford Museum

America the people rule and have rights, including those of access and freedom of movement. Public roads were just that and there were darn few places where the town fathers could get away with shutting down the roads for the weekend while the racers made dust and upset the cows and chickens. (In Europe they used to hand complete islands—the Isle of Man and Sicily to name two—over to the racers.)

There was also the spirit of free enterprise. The spectator watching the race from the side of the road, or from his or her own backyard, isn't a spectator who has bought a ticket.

We didn't have access to public roads. Instead we had access to a network of fairgrounds—state, county and local—with racetracks already in place. These tracks were ovals for horse racing, built on a packed dirt surface. We expanded onto other ovals, Indianapolis being the one that worked, and for many years we had board tracks, half a mile, one mile or even

more in diameter. Steeply banked, dangerous and thrilling.

For reasons of speed, scale and showmanship, the cars that raced on these tracks were as small as they could be. They were as light, slender and slick as the science of the day would allow. They had every feature—independent suspension, multiple valves, supercharging, overhead camshafts and so on—that we know today. They were wonderful devices.

They had little in common with the cars folks drove to and from the races. America developed its own forms of motorsport, in a natural sort of pyramid. At the top was the Indianapolis 500, held once a year because the organizers realized that if they acted as if the race was special, it would become so, and it did. The Indy cars had a national circuit, pure racing machines driven by professionals. Then there were sprint cars for the dirt, sometimes with racing engines, more often powered by modified production engines. And in the corners of the racing world were the

The original form of competition for stock cars—when there was such a thing as a stock, catalog-version of a production car—were runs like this: part tour, part rally, part reli- *ability run and part hillclimb. Any event more serious or more professional fell victim to the lack of rules or enforcement.* Henry Ford Museum

homemade jalopies engineered by hammer and driven for fun.

About two laps back, stock cars were mentioned and then left behind.

The first rules

The idea of racing stock cars was never forgotten. About the time the Indy 500 was getting started, there was so much dispute over stock car rules that forty of the top US factories—yes, we had that many makers then—got together and formed the Manufacturer's Contest Board (MCB). They asked the American Automobile Association (AAA), at that time a network of local clubs, to administer the rules the members of the MCB had drafted and agreed to abide by. The arrangement lasted as long as it took the ink to dry.

Hindsight again, but each and every one of the members wanted to win more than they wanted to be fair. The AAA had no power of enforcement; it hadn't asked for the job in the first place and racing wasn't what they'd set out to do anyway.

A production model was supposed to be one of which at least fifty examples had been made. That was OK until the others learned that one make built fifty disguised racers and tucked forty-five of them away in the warehouse, so the rule became fifty made and sold during the preceding twelve months. That meant manufacturers couldn't improve the design or fix flaws without being banned from the race.

The winners were being declared in the hearing room, not on the track. The manufacturers' group lapsed into record trials and economy runs. The races—minor ones, at that—were held for stock chassis cars, ones that looked stock but had freely improved engines (don't forget that idea).

The notion of stock car competition never disappeared. In 1927, the AAA's own contest board began a stock car racing circuit, sort of, on the banked tracks. Stutz, Auburn, Studebaker et al. fielded teams of 120 mph roadsters, which weren't stock but had begun life that way. Stutz and Chrysler competed in France's famous twenty-four-hour endurance race of Le Mans in 1928 and 1929, and did fairly well. Chrysler and Studebaker used the board tracks for record runs, and one of those funny Chrysler Airflow sedans even held the mile record at 95.7 mph in 1934.

California's second Ascot track, also known as Legion Ascot, northeast of Los Angeles and a long way from the present Ascot, had an event race officials mislabeled the Targo Florio, in which stock roadsters were driven off the track and through the surrounding foothills, up hill and down dale, for a total of 200 miles. In Elgin, Illinois, site of classic road races in the teens, there was a revival meeting, and in 1933 and 1934 they raced stripped roadsters. Almost all of them were Fords, zipping around an 8.5 mile course of mixed dirt and pavement. Winner Fred Frame *averaged* 80 mph for 200 miles. These cars, as well, were not as stock as they looked.

But that was that. The principle of racing stock cars—cars just like the ones people bought and drove—to see which was the fastest and the best and would hold up longest under the hammers of speed, was sound. It had been sound since the first time it didn't work.

Deciding why it didn't work is sort of like deciding why this or that team didn't win the World Series. But without giving the game away, we can look back from the advantage of knowing how stock car racing has worked and we can make some good guesses. Maybe watching the stockers wasn't as exciting as watching Indy or sprint cars. Maybe it was too darn hard to keep the rules fair enough, for long enough. Or maybe not enough of the audience was able to make the connection between what they drove to the race and what they saw on the track.

Having said that, we reverse direction and move to one of the world's least plausible success stories.

And those who didn't know how to make stock car racing work needn't brood over it, because the man who did it, didn't know how to either.

An uncanny forerunner of stock car racing was the Elgin, Illinois, road race of 1933 and 1934, in which stripped roadsters ran a road course, part paved and part dirt. The races drew top drivers and beautifully prepared cars. The winner averaged better speeds than a really stock car could reach in a straight line, but as this scene shows, you can't collect money from folks standing alongside a public road. Henry Ford Museum

Chapter 2

On the beach

One subtle benefit to harsh economic times is that you don't have to be dumb to be poor.

When times are good and the living is easy, just about anybody can make a good living. But when the going is tough, when the game of economic musical chairs means ten players for every eight places, there's no stigma attached to having to scratch for a living. In fact, there's a lot of progress that comes out of having plenty of people with plenty of ambition and not much raw material.

Bill France wasn't rich in 1934. Nor was he dumb.

He was born in Washington, D. C. in 1909, the son of a bank clerk. He wasn't much for books, but he did like mechanical things. He and some pals built race cars—not terribly good ones, but fun. In 1931 he made the best move of his life, as he himself said and nobody

The cars, a selection here of Ford roadsters, weren't quite as stock as they looked in those early beach–road races, but the sand in the turns was as loose and treacherous as this picture hints, even after they added clay to the stock (so to speak) sand. Daytona International Speedway

argued with, when he married Annie, a nurse with her head properly attached to her shoulders. France was working in a gas station in Washington when he simply got tired of the cold. He, Annie and Bill, Jr. loaded the family car and headed south.

It was the fall of 1934, not the best time to take chances, but France, who was six-foot-five and had a manner that could be winning or intimidating depending on what he had in mind, wasn't afraid to bet on himself.

They pulled into Daytona Beach, Florida, on a perfect day, so perfect they stopped and went for a swim and simply unpacked for good.

In later years there was a legend that they'd run out of money. Not true. Annie was too good a manager to allow that to happen. Nor did their car break down. "I was a mechanic," France would say later, with a touch of asperity. "If the car had broken down, I would have fixed it."

No, he said, Daytona Beach was a beautiful place. He could get a job at a car dealership and the fishing was terrific, so that's where they settled. And as a side issue, a completely lucky accident, in 1935 France went out to the beach and watched Sir Malcolm Campbell make the last world record run on the beach.

To deal with that, however, and to start at the beginning of this saga, we go back to 1902. Or perhaps to the dawn of our present geological age. Florida is mostly beach, in the sense that it's sand, a peninsula that looms a hundred feet in the air, but no more. There is a swamp, an east coast and a west coast, and the east coast is real beach, all the way up and down.

Some unique circumstances of tide, geography, and wind and wave action have caused one stretch of east coast beach to become flat and firm at low tide. This stretch begins at Ormond Beach, north of Daytona Beach, and runs south to the outlet of the river that separates the beach strip, a long island, from the mainland proper.

By 1902 Florida was the home of alligators, Seminole Indians, pioneer orange growers and a handful of resort hotels, made possible by the extension of railroads from the chilly north and by the desire of the rich to escape the cold.

The manager of the Hotel Ormond had noticed what a flat, firm and isolated place the beach was, and he invited two of his guests to make use of the spot. The guests were Alexander Winton and Ransom E. Olds. By no coincidence, they'd brought their motors south for the winter, and one day they went on the beach, opened the throttles and let 'em rip. This was sport and they were gentlemen; they looked the press and the other guests straight in the eye and said it had been a dead heat, 60 mph.

The actual speed didn't matter, nor did the winner. The point was, the beach in front of and south of the hotel was a fine place to go fast—if not safely, then safer than just about any place else. The times

were perfect: there were flocks of cars and motorcycles, steam, gas and electric, looking for a place to run, set records and establish reputations. To top it off, Florida was all beach and the east coast was mostly resort hotels, all the way south to Miami.

But only Daytona had the wide, straight stretch of sand that made itself flat and firm every time the tide came in and went out. The city fathers and businessmen naturally did all they could to encourage these record runs and the money they brought into the city and surrounding areas.

The speed records were good sport and good business. They made Daytona Beach world famous. But as the cars got faster the beach got shorter, so to speak, until the machines had plainly outgrown the sand. France enjoyed watching the record runs, but as he said later, the beach wasn't flat at 276 mph, the wind wasn't calm and Campbell had earned the knighthood his record brought in.

Campbell's record was the last set on the beach and everybody knew it would be. By that time the Bonneville Salt Flats, which were as poor a place for tourism as Daytona Beach was good, had become the

The program for that inaugural beach–road race shows first that art directors were as keen on style and careless about legibility then as they are now, and that not even the sponsors knew what sort of cars to expect. National championship status was obtained simply by being the only such race in the nation. Daytona International Speedway

record-setting center. The speed guys could keep on going fast.

For love or money

What couldn't go on was Daytona Beach's income unless something was done—which, obviously, it was. Very early in the beach's speed history there had been a mass race. Everybody lined up in the same direction and charged down to the finish line at the other end of the beach. But that clearly couldn't be done anymore. Instead, a promoter named Sig Haugdahl dreamed up a new and different format.

It would be called a beach-road race, and as the name implies, it would be a race with a mix of surfaces. (As mentioned earlier, this was an accepted style of racing, using both dirt and pavement.) The cars would race down the highway that paralleled the beach south of town, then they would swing onto the beach itself and race back, another wide U-turn and so on.

Next, it would be a stock car race. Nobody knew how to make that work right, nor were there any rules, so the stock portion was equalized by being a handicap race: each car was timed, and a handicap assigned on the basis of that time. If a car went faster in the race than in qualifying, it would be called into the pits. If that happened three times, the car would be disqualified.

Further, this completely different race would have the sanction and approval of the AAA's contest board as the AAA had—in a way—endorsed stock car racing in other forms. The race was, no kidding and quoting from the program, a "250 Mile National Championship Beach-Road Race."

As a topper, the field was star-studded. Goldie Gardner, the English speedster, had a Lincoln Zephyr. Bill Cummings, winner of the 1934 Indy 500, drove a supercharged Auburn Speedster. There was Sam Collier, one of the brothers whose private sports car club formed the basis for the later Sports Car Club of America (SCCA). AAA midget ace Bill Schindler had a Dodge. There were twenty-eight entries, in seven makes. Cummings was fast qualifier, 70.39 mph, and Collier's Willys 77, at 58.60 mph, had the slow time, which meant Collier got half an hour start on Cummings.

Also in the field was a Ford driven by pro Milt Marion. It was the first sponsored stock car, in a sense, because it was backed by Permatex Corporation, makers of gasket shellac; the car itself boasted sealer in place of gaskets. The car's mechanic was none other than Bill France—who just to keep busy, also drove a 1935 Ford owned by a friend.

In a surprising link between beach eras, honorary grand marshal for the first national beach-road

ENTRANTS

CAR NO.	MAKE	DRIVER	ENTRANT	QUALIFYING SPEED
14	FORD	WALTER JOHNSON	O. L. MOODY	63.92
5	DODGE	WM. SCHINDLER	H. ATKINSON	59.65
22	FORD	"HICK" JENKINS	H. R. DIXON	67.95
19	FORD	SAM PURVIS	SAM. PURVIS	67.25
15	FORD	DAN MURPHY	CARL PURSER	63.96
17	FORD	ED. ENG	DON SUTTLE	64.25
29	AUBURN	JOHN RUTHERFORD	JOHN RUTHERFORD	65.97
16	FORD	ALBERT CUSICK	ALBERT CUSICK	64.25
9	FORD	WM. LAWRENCE	WM. LAWRENCE	62.81
11	FORD	LOU CAMPBELL	L. S. CAMPBELL	63.32
21	FORD	BILL SOCKWELL	BILL SOCKWELL	
3	CHEVROLET	B. J. GIBSON	B. J. GIBSON	61.47
1	WILLYS 77	LANGDON QUIMBY	LANGDON QUIMBY	58.71
4	WILLYS 77	SAM COLLIER	SAM COLLIER	58.60
24	FORD	DOC. MACKINZIE	G. D. MACKENZIE	67.92
18	FORD	BEN SHAW	ED. PARKINSON	66.01
6	FORD	BOB SALL	RUDY ADAMS	61.51
26	FORD	TOMMY ELMORE	THOS. ELMORE, JR.	62.30
20	OLDSMOBILE 8	KEN. SCHROEDER	FLOYD A. SMITH	66.32
2	AUBURN	BILL CUMMINGS	M. J. BOYLE	70.39
25	FORD	AL WHEATLEY	AL. WHEATLEY	65.23
12	FORD	AL PIERSON	AL. PIERSON	63.54
27	FORD	JACK HOLLY	JACK HOLLY	68.94
28	FORD	VIRGIL MATHIS	DAN H. STODDARD	66.28
8	FORD	GILBERT FARRELL	C. A. HARDY	62.71
7	LINCOLN ZEPHYR	MAJOR A. T. G. GARDNER	A. T. G. GARDNER	61.76
10	FORD	WILLIAM FRANCE	ISAAC BLAIR	63.02
23	FORD	MILTON MARION	MILT MARION	66.16

—FLAG SIGNALS—

GREEN — Start of Race; Course is clear.
YELLOW — Caution; Bring car under control and reduce speed to 50 miles per hour.
ORANGE with BLUE CENTER — Competitor is attempting to overtake you
WHITE — Report at your pit on the next lap.
RED — Danger; stop.
BLUE — You are entering your last lap.
CHECKER — You have finished.

1936 NATIONAL CHAMPIONSHIP
BEACH AND ROAD RACE
DAYTONA BEACH, FLORIDA

The official entrants' list for the first race includes some household names—in racing households, at least. Major Gardner was an English contender for the land speed record. Cummings and Schindler were top pro drivers. Collier was a wealthy sportsman and pioneer sports car enthusiast. And William France was a mechanic with an interest in driving and maybe getting into the business. Daytona International Speedway

Goldie Gardner's Lincoln wasn't one of the fast cars, but it was heavy and bogged down in the deep sand, leading one to guess, as his expression here hints, that he really raced on the beach because he was there and so was the race. Daytona International Speedway

Having just as much fun in a borrowed Ford was Big Bill France, who was credited with fifth place in the first race although he said officials really never did get the lap charts straight and fifth seemed fair enough to him. Daytona International Speedway

championship was R. E. Olds, the man behind Oldsmobile and REO, and the man who'd scored that gentleman's tie in the beach's first race way back when. He had two homes in the area and he still liked cars.

So did the public, who turned out by the uncounted thousands.

The race itself wasn't a total success. The road part was firm and as fast as expected, as was the hardpacked sand below the tide line. But the turns were on the sort of beach we think of as beach, that is, fine, loose sand in heaps and dunes. Most of the cars got stuck at least once, the big fast jobs like the supercharged Auburn and the Lincoln sank into the ruts and the race wasn't as fast as qualifying had predicted.

It was so much slower, in fact, that the tide came in before the full distance was run and the checked flag waved at the waves.

It then took a few days to figure out the lap charts and penalties. The official winner finally was declared to be Marion and his Ford, followed by four other Ford V-8s. Bill France was in fifth place.

The bad part was that the crowd was uncounted because some paid for tickets but many more didn't. There might have been 20,000, or perhaps it was 30,000, but the bottom line here was that the promoters, the Daytona Beach Chamber of Commerce, paid a $5,000 purse and all expenses. When the counting was complete, they'd lost a lot of money.

The idea seemed too good to pass up, however, so in 1937 the promotion was handled by the Daytona Beach Elks Club. The AAA had lost interest and did not sanction the event, nor was the race a national championship, nor were quite so many stars involved.

But people were learning. Florida has a clay known as marl, which sets soft when wet and then hardens as it dries, so the promoters mixed marl with the sand on the turns and solved that problem.

They also shortened the race to fifty miles so they could count on the tide staying out. The race was supposed to be a stock car competition but the lesson of the first race was clear and most of these cars were Fords. The race was won by a local bar owner with a V-8 coupe.

The Elks Club lost money on the race, too.

About the cars. As movie fans know, the Ford V-8 was the choice of chaps like Clyde Barrow, Bonnie's friend, who stole Fords for business use and wrote Henry letters of thanks, which Mr. Ford was canny enough to leak to the press.

The Ford was the fastest car most people could buy. Not as fast as the high-priced jobs like the Auburn, Stutz or Duesenberg, but much quicker than the Chevy or Plymouth of the day.

Next, there was a lot of jalopy racing, especially in the South. They didn't call it stock car racing because the cars weren't stock. They weren't terribly fast or sophisticated, either, mostly because the guys who built them didn't have much money for equipment, but they still weren't strictly stock.

And it's time to mention another factor that has been overdone ever since Hollywood discovered racing: bootleggers. It is true that in the rural South there were people making whiskey out in the hills and other people hauling the stuff into the cities. They used cars with beefed-up engines and suspensions and, yes, they did get real good at driving fast on dirt and, yes, they had some mighty fast motorcars and, yes again, they were brave and daring highwaymen, no question. And some of them did get into racing, as we'll see.

But the main force behind pre-stock car racing was concentrated on the dusty tracks, the bull rings around which semi-pro drivers raced in stripped and battered Ford V-8 coupes.

France was one of them. He'd opened his own gas station, for Pure Oil (we'll hear that name again, too), and he was driving a 1937 Ford coupe owned by Charlie Reese, who had what France said was the best restaurant in town. There were dirt tracks in the area; France worked during the week and raced on weekends.

A will and a way

France's gas station was informal headquarters for the racers in town in 1938. When the chamber of commerce didn't want to do the race and the Elks Club said ditto, some businesspeople dropped in and asked France if he knew anybody who'd like to handle the promotion—that is, be responsible for profit, or loss.

This sounds too pat to be true, but France said years later that his first choice was a man in a nearby town, who had promoted some races in the area. France called collect, but the guy wouldn't accept the fifteen-cent charge.

France mentioned this to Reese, the car owner and restaurant man. Reese asked if France had any interest himself and France confessed that yes, he'd been intrigued by the idea of promoting. He knew the racers and how to actually put on a race, but he didn't have the cash or the credit. OK, said Reese, you do the work and I'll put up the money.

Which is what they did, and France surely filed away one of the secrets of successful investment: use other people's money.

They only sold 5,000 tickets to the 1938 race. They didn't have a sanction, nor stars, but they kept the purse aligned with the ticket price and split a profit of several hundred dollars. If, as it happened, the winner didn't stop at the flag but roared on up the beach, where they found him trying to remove the high-compression cylinder heads from his, um, stock engine, well, nobody was terribly surprised, nor upset. When no two sets of rules were alike it wasn't surprising that no two stock cars were alike, either.

France took another big step in 1939. He kept everything else much the same, but doubled the price of the ticket, from fifty cents to one dollar.

Even Mrs. France questioned that one, but as France said, if you have a good show, people will pay to see it. That year France and Reese split $2,000, after donating ten percent of the profit to Bundles for Britain, a charity tied to the war that arrived all too soon.

France promoted the beach races through 1941, with stock cars and without any sanction except his own. The only real sanctioning body, AAA, had no stock class, nor any races, although their contest board would certify some types of record runs.

Racing was suspended for the duration of the war, of course. France was a middle-aged father by then and did his stint in a Daytona Beach shipyard. He had lots of time to think about racing, when he wasn't able to do it.

After the war it was back to the beach. He—and Mrs. France, as well—promoted the races. He was learning, he said later. For example, there was the time he tried to sell tickets at the track but cars came faster than they could make change. The police stopped in to mention the ensuing traffic jam and the cars were waved through. That happened only once.

There were races in most sections of the country, with different rules and interpretations of just what

Television and commercial breaks can be timed to suit the races, but time and tide . . . no. The sand was at its firmest, and therefore fastest, close to the water. But if a driver got too close to the ocean he could bog down or drown the engine.

In later years officials shortened the races so the racers could finish before the tide came up. Daytona International Speedway

stock meant. For instance, there was the race France won in Pennsylvania after staying up all night modifying his car to match the rules for stock in Pennsylvania instead of Florida.

At the beach, they had the same problem. There was the man with the 1939 engine in a 1934 car, with a 1935 flywheel. He was disqualified, but he would have been legal if the flywheel had been the same vintage as the car *or* the engine. And there was the driver ruled out because his car had valve springs painted a different color than the other racers had. They were sure he was using stiffer springs. Years later, France said, they learned that spring color actually identified the plant where the springs came from and had nothing to do with stiffness or power.

Throw in the time France tried to bill a race as a national championship, only to be told by the news-papers that you couldn't claim such a thing unless you had a complete set of rules, kept point tallies and had an organization that crossed more than one state line.

It all went into the hopper for France to think about, make plans to cure and use in a speech.

But before that, a quote. The program issued by the Daytona Beach Chamber of Commerce asked, "Who can foresee what miracles this road-beach stock car race may bring?"

Well, nobody could do that. In light of what happened in 1936, whoever wrote that question probably wished they had phrased it differently.

In the long run, however, nobody could have guessed what would come from that beach-road stock car race.

But Bill France would come the closest.

Obviously the races were popular. France provided bleachers, and he solved one of the original problems by moving the course down the beach as the town grew, keeping it on private property and thus making it possible to collect money from the spectators. This shows the original north turn, now completely hidden and built over. Daytona International Speedway

15

Chapter 3

The birth of NASCAR: 1948-1954

On December 12, 1947, William H. G. France stood at the head of the table in a conference room at the Streamline Hotel in Daytona Beach and gave one of the most effective speeches of his life.

Like most such speeches, it was effective because first, he was preaching to the converted, an audience already firmly on his side and, second, because he told his listeners things they already knew.

He told them automobile racing was on the verge of unparalleled popularity and financial success, and that at the same time racing was in chaos and confu-sion. There were too many conflicts of interest. The rules weren't uniform, they weren't fair and the promoters couldn't be trusted.

This wasn't news. Everybody who'd been in racing longer than a week knew about getting cheated out of a win, swindled out of the purse, or tricked in one way or another.

The news was that Bill France reckoned to do something about it. He'd been thinking about this since the first beach race, and he knew firsthand about all sides of the questions, having been driver,

Marshall Teague, NASCAR's pioneer professional, in the north turn at Daytona Beach, 1951. As the car clearly states, he's driving the Fabulous Hudson Hornet powered by a big six. Teague was a gifted driver, a hard worker and *the man who persuaded Hudson to introduce the factory-backed team. Note the classic, rear-wheels-out dirt track stance, and the packed stands. Daytona International Speedway and Mitzi Teague*

mechanic and promoter, sometimes all at the same time.

He didn't begin by thinking big. In fact he had approached the AAA in hopes they'd provide a structure within which he could simply promote races, but the AAA had outgrown the minor leagues and brushed France off.

Meanwhile France and Bill Tuthill, a New England promoter, had been working out ways to swap drivers, to have the stars from North and South compete with each other. And as mentioned, France had been told (and obviously agreed) that truly national racing meant just that.

So France issued an invitation to drivers, promoters and car owners. He invited them all to Daytona Beach, to meet and see if collectively they could hammer out some form of national organization and set of rules.

They could and they did.

Jerome—who reasonably enough preferred the nickname Red—Vogt, was a tuner from Atlanta, known for building racing cars and, OK, whiskey cars as well. His garage was where the Atlanta racers started toward the beach from every year; folks say the race to the race was sometimes better than the formal event.

In this case, Vogt suggested naming the organization the National Association for Stock Car Auto Racing, shortened ever since to NASCAR. There was some worry that NASCAR sounded too much like Nash Car, Nash being a make since departed (ask your dad about Nash). But nobody figured Nash would care, so NASCAR it would be. Then they worked out committees for the rules and the championship points and so forth, and the club was in business.

Mark that, in business. France had created the foundation for a new sport. He'd done it with the help and cooperation of his peers. NASCAR would have memberships and dues, just like a club. But at the same time, it was established as a corporation, a privately held corporation, with the France family, Tuthill and Ed Otto as the partners and owners.

NASCAR was brand new and neither the organization, the name or the principals were known outside racing's small and friendly circle. So France did another smart thing and enlisted world-famous Erwin "Cannonball" Baker, record-holding endurance and race driver. Baker became NASCAR's Commissioner of Racing, the referee and final vote on disputes. Baker was still keen on racing machines. He was known, and known to be fair, and he did in fact do the job he was appointed to do.

Worth noting here, however, was that NASCAR wasn't a Southern operation, not by intent at least. There were founding members from New England and the Midwest as well, and if the West wasn't present it was because distances were much farther than they are now.

Bill France, left, and co-founder Ed Otto hard at work when NASCAR's headquarters consisted of some rented offices. The pile of mail is supposed to show the public that the club is going great guns, which of course it was. Daytona International Speedway

Equally, this was a racing crowd. It wasn't a bunch of moonshiners or hillbillies fresh from the backwoods. The founders were racers and businessmen and they knew what they were doing.

The first "stock" cars

Perhaps the oddest point of departure was that NASCAR—with the words stock car racing right there in the name—didn't begin by racing what we'd now call stock cars.

They were stock-based cars, built with parts from mass production and virtually all Ford. They were known as Modifieds.

In brief, those early NASCAR racing machines were Ford coupes, 1937 or newer. They were supposed to have full fenders and windshields, stock tanks and ignition, but engines could be exchanged (for example, a 1939 engine in a 1937 body), as well as bored and stroked to as large as the engine block would take. Racers could run different carburetors, or multiple carbs, high-compression heads, reground camshafts—all the way through the hot rod catalog.

That catalog, by the way, was virtually all Ford as well, for reasons listed earlier. But that was about to change.

The horsepower race begins

There's a saying in racing, and maybe in real life as well, that it's better to be lucky than smart.

France was smart, but he was also lucky. One major factor for the success of stock car racing—which can be defined here as equal competition among makes and models, as sold to the public—had to be the availability of such makes and models.

As noted, that wasn't the case during the thirties or early forties. Just about all cars sold were sold for transportation and while there were cars with big engines, they usually were in big cars. Superchargers and overhead camshafts were reserved for the rich. Everybody else, which in the thirties was just about everybody, drove a slow car or a Ford.

This changed and it changed overnight, and neither NASCAR nor racing had anything to do with it.

Ralph Nader will flinch to hear this, but Detroit's horsepower race didn't begin with a quest for speed, or even for horsepower. Efficiency was the watchword and World War II was the prime mover.

War accelerates research. While working on airplanes, tanks, boats and so on, the engineers at the car factories and oil companies learned a lot about fuels and combustion. They came to an informal agreement that after the war they would work on refining better gasoline—better meaning higher octane—and on building more efficient engines that would produce more power for the same fuel. They would do this with higher compression ratios, and such gains in com-

pression would come about because there would be better fuel. A closed loop, but a sensible one.

Some basics here. The tighter one squeezes the air-fuel mixture before setting it on fire, the more the mixture expands as it burns and the more power one gets. This power comes at both low and high speed. It's a power gain that comes directly from more torque, while a tuning gain, the hop-up stuff, usually comes when one takes power from the low end of the scale and moves it to the top. Hopping up the engine adds power but can hamper daily operation; increasing the compression ratio is, in a way, free power.

The first problem is that if the mix is squeezed too hard, it goes off by itself, preignition, ping, knock and so forth. This hurts power, annoys the driver and destroys the engine if left unfixed. It can be cured with better gas, but making that higher octane was the oil company's problem.

The car companies' part wasn't exactly a problem but it was an obstacle. Engines in the forties were as strong and reliable as they could be made, within cost limits, and were no more powerful than they had to be. For cost reasons most engines were side valve, valve in block or flathead. The valves were parallel

In the early days NASCAR was mostly a promoter of races. The races were on dirt, the cars were rough and the racing was tough. Slam-bang fatalist action, somebody wrote, and *the name on the sun shade of the sedan still in action bears this out.* Daytona International Speedway

with, and next to, the cylinder bores. The cylinder head was above the bores, and the combustion chamber was above the bores and valves.

When compression ratios were five and six to one, this was no problem. But increasing compression means reducing the volume of the chamber. If you reduce it above the bore, you hamper the expansion of the burning air-fuel mixture. If you reduce it above the valves, you limit valve opening, shroud the valves, block passage of the charge from ports to cylinders or all three.

The obvious, natural cure is to go to overhead valves, with the camshaft in the block, operating lifters, pushrods and rocker arms to the valves, which are in the cylinder head above the bores and pistons.

This was no big secret, nor until the late forties was it much of an advantage. Chevrolet used an overhead-valve six and Buick had an ohv eight, while the fabled Ford V-8, the humdrum Plymouth six, and the luxurious Cadillac and Lincoln V-8s were all side-valve. It didn't matter much—when the average family car had some 200 cubic inches and 80 or 90 bhp—how they got that power.

There had been other engines, sure. Duesenbergs came with straight eights, double overhead cams and even supercharging. There had been V-12s and even sixteens from Lincoln and Cadillac and in one odd

According to the fine print, this is Hoyt Moore of Buford, Georgia, with a sponsor who liked art more than commerce, or with no sponsor at all. Daytona International Speedway

Moving upscale, this gentleman is running a truly stock car, backed by a dealership. Or, more likely, he owns the   *store and likes to drive in races and tells his tax man it's a business venture. Daytona International Speedway*

coincidence, Buick offered compound carburetion for a few years just before the war. But in general all the cars on the market had enough power, it didn't matter how they got it, and Ford was the fastest car most people could buy.

That changed in a hurry. General Motors had five divisions and each division had an engineering staff. Each engineering group was told to design new, better engines and they all set to with a will.

On the other side of town Chrysler Corporation, a smaller organization, had the same general assignment. Ford was last off the mark.

This wasn't a race in the formal sense, but GM was the first with a new engine. The Oldsmobile and Cadillac had brand new powerplants for the 1949 model year.

The new engines had overhead valves, which was the obvious choice. The logical extension of the overhead valves was that the new engines were going to be strong and run at higher rpm, which calls for a short stroke. The bigger the bore, the bigger the valves you can have above the bore, and the new engines had larger bores than the old style called for.

There was more. The war put the economy back on its feet and the family car could go upscale, with eight cylinders rather than four or six. The older style was for inline engines, as in the Duesenberg or Buick straight eights.

But a shorter engine put the passengers within the wheelbase for a smoother ride, a shorter engine was stiffer and stronger, and improved production techniques—another war benefit—meant the more intricate castings of the vee cylinder block wasn't the

challenge it was when only Henry Ford was willing to tackle it.

In short (excuse the play on words), the new engines were all going to be ninety-degree, short-stroke, big-bore, overhead-valve V-8s.

Adding to that, while the Cadillac was a big, expensive car, the Olds line overlapped the other divisions, a GM trademark, so the smaller Olds shared bodies with the Chevrolet, except that the Chevy still had the Stovebolt Six and the Olds had the Rocket 88. The 88 truly was a rocket. It displaced 303 ci, developed 136 bhp at 3600 rpm and would run all day at 4500 rpm.

One other change heralded a hint of things to come. The new V-8s used hydraulic valve lifters. These were two-piece assemblies, usually a sleeve and collar, with a hollow center that was pressurized by engine oil. The idea was to keep the required clearance between the valve and the valvetrain, so the valves closed firmly on their seats, using the oil as a cushion. (Previously the clearance had been mechanical, with threaded adjustment, but the factories knew people didn't like to maintain their engines, so they were working to reduce maintenance.) The hydraulic lifters were quieter than mechanical lifters, especially now that the valves were in the head and not tucked away in the block.

The lifters worked fine in daily service but if the engine was revved to its limit, the lifters would pump up, fill with oil under pressure and not bleed down. The lifters expanded and the valves didn't quite close, which combined to confuse the engine.

Now we're getting serious. This is Curtis Turner, at Hillsboro, North Carolina, in a 1949 Olds 88, the fastest of the true production models at the time. The car had been prepared for racing; notice the removal of the lights and the gas *filler door, and the taping over of the chrome trim and bumpers. When the car has been raced enough, it will be put back in street trim and sold. Driven only on Sunday, as they say. Daytona International Speedway*

Some of the guys quickly figured out that if they used lighter, thinner oil and shimmed back the pressure at the pump's relief valve, they could turn the Rocket V-8 tighter, longer. And it was still stock . . . sort of.

Chrysler Corporation took a little more time, until 1951, to introduce their new big-bore, short-stroke V-8. They also took a different path.

The classic engines, and the racing engines of the past and the 1951 present, used a hemispherical combustion chamber. As the name implies, the chamber is half a sphere, an orange divided right down the middle. The chamber contains two valves, set at right angles to each other and at a forty-five-degree angle to the top of the piston and cylinder. This set of angles lets the valves be as large as possible for the given bore. The larger the valve, the more airflow. The more flow, the more power.

This is both easy and expensive to do when you use twin overhead camshafts. The cams, driven by chain or gears from the crank below, sit side by side in the head, working exhaust valves or intake valves.

The hemi makes room for the largest valves, but has a drawback; this combustion chamber, the half an orange shape, has a higher octane demand than the more conventional chamber. This works in two direc-

tions. You can get equal power with a lower compression ratio, or you can use better gas, higher octane, with the same compression ratio.

Either way, Chrysler decided to go the hemi route, and introduced hemi-head V-8s for Dodge, DeSoto and Chrysler in 1951. They wouldn't make the opening round of the horsepower race but they would surely be heard from in due course.

Meanwhile, over at the logical contender, Ford, nothing was happening. Well, a lot was happening but in the engine department Ford was sticking with the old, reliable flathead V-8s for Ford, Mercury and Lincoln. The engine revolution wouldn't arrive until 1952 for Lincoln and 1954 for Ford.

The shocker, the rival, came from another quarter entirely.

Hudson was always the odd firm out. They did their own thinking, and used stuff like a cork-lined wet clutch when all the other factories had conventional dry plates. Their postwar car was a beauty only to some beholders, as it was long and low and enclosed the wheels . . . it looked strange, OK? But while the conventional makers had frame rails down

Red Byron, center, was the first NASCAR national champion, in 1949. He was aided, here and elsewhere, by master mechanic Buckshot Morris, on the right. Daytona International Speedway

Bill Rexford was the second driving champion, in 1950. Byron was one of the original group, while Rexford came from up north. He had one good year, helped a lot by NASCAR's feud with Lee Petty, which cost Petty most of his points that season. Then Rexford faded away, and retired to California. Daytona International Speedway

the middle and the floor above the frame, Hudson ran the frame outboard of the floor—the step-down design, as they said in their ads. The Hudson was lower than the others and had an advantage when cornering.

Like Nash, Studebaker and Willys (which won't be heard of much after this), Hudson was an independent, struggling to compete against GM, Ford and Chrysler. Hudson didn't have a lot of money, so they kept costs down by using a sidevalve six, a giant at 308 ci. It couldn't match the Olds V-8 for peak power but it could offer massive torque.

The stage was set.

The engineers in Detroit were busy in the lab and on the proving ground. They didn't know Bill France from Paris, France, and he in turn was forming his sanctioning body, promoting races, driving now and then, and still running the neighborhood gas station.

Detroit had introduced a new element, with cars that were a fair match for each other and faster than ever before in the bargain. NASCAR, while they had no idea that these new cars were going to invent the horsepower race, was working out ways to offer fair and public confrontation. Not that they knew this at the time.

NASCAR opened an office, hired clerical help and began signing up racetracks to run their sanction, in competition with the scores of other clubs, promoters and sets of rules. The races NASCAR organized or sanctioned or both were for modified cars, usually the familiar Ford coupes, known as late models if they were postwar. And they were still not strictly stock, or not yet anyway.

The original cast

While France, Tuthill and Ed Otto, the third shareholder in NASCAR and like the others, a promot-er, were working out the rules and procedures for their group, there were already plenty of racers hard at work, or even at play. Some of the heroes and legends-to-be are chosen at random here to illustrate what a variety there would be in this new form of motorsport.

The Flock family

As the folk singers said about another group, this was a wild old family, with eight children and a widowed mom. The father was a bicycle daredevil and tightrope walker. He died young, not of accidental causes, and the widow took her children from rural Alabama to the big city of Atlanta. It was a tough life and the kids helped their relatives, the bootlegging side of the family.

Four of the children, Tim, Bob, Fonty and Ethyl, drove racing cars. Another sister, Reo, was a skydiver and wing walker. The oldest Flock of that generation, Carl, raced boats. Must have been something in the genes. Before anybody asks, Tim Flock says his sister Reo was named after the REO Speedwagon and Ethyl for high-test gasoline.

The brothers hauled whiskey in and out of Atlanta, and drove the modified and jalopy races there. In his excellent history of Ford's racing efforts, Leo Levine says stock car racing was born in Atlanta. That may be stretching things, as we've seen earlier stocks in California, Illinois and even on the beach, but Atlanta was a hotbed—and yes, there were days when the moonshine haulers and bootleggers raced on dirt tracks for prestige and side money.

The Flocks were more interested in the racing than in the whiskey business and in the end, gravitated naturally to the modifieds and NASCAR.

Curtis Turner

This is where the original legend began. Turner was a timber cruiser, a man who prowled the South-

Illustrating the wide range of machines in the early days, we have Marshall Teague on the high line, with an obscure Nash from Pennsylvania in the middle, and then the plain *little Plymouth with which Johnny Mantz won the first 500 mile stock car race. Daytona International Speedway*

Fast women

If the sage is correct and if nothing on earth can resist the power of an idea whose time has come, then it's also true that few things have less impact than an idea whose time isn't quite yet, an issue for which there isn't a constituency.

For example, the history of women in stock car racing.

This is an especially odd set of facts. First, the Old South is famous for being socially a few steps behind the rest of the United States. Second, women were banned from most forms of auto racing in America all during the thirties and forties and well into the fifties.

The AAA rules, at Indianapolis and elsewhere, specifically banned women from behind the wheel, and even from the pits. Folklore had the gentler sex rated as bad luck, right along with peanuts in the pits and cars painted green. Professional motorcycle racing not only didn't allow women to ride, there were cases of discipline meted out against riders whose machines had been pushed, yes pushed, to the starting line by a woman. An entrant got free tickets to the grandstand and that's where his womenfolk were supposed to be, period.

Things were a bit different in Europe, where people were always allowed to do anything they could pay for, and there was a history of wealthy women having the occasional fling behind the wheel; several of them were competitive drivers in fact. When the sports car movement came to America, it brought with it the European attitude and women were allowed in the amateur races as well as in separate races: Powderpuff class as they were innocently named.

That's where things stood when NASCAR began to make sense out of the low-buck, low-tech turmoil that until then was stock car racing: modified production cars on dirt tracks.

One could assume that because women were banned from the professional branches of racing in America, and because the South was famous for defending womanhood as the sheltered sex, the new club would have the most stringent objections.

Nope. The new NASCAR rules made no mention of gender. "Drivers" is what the rulebook said and drivers is what women got to be, if they so chose.

That may have been the secret here. Perhaps the power of custom, strong in the Old South now as well as then, made women's role so clear and defined that it was safe to not follow along. That is, neither men nor the other

Good old girls Louise Smith, left, and Sara Christian were racing long before they even suspected that someday female drivers would be news. And they gave as good as they got. *Daytona International Speedway*

women, the wives and mothers, felt threatened by a woman racing.

Slotting right into that is another tradition, what used to be called tomboys (before our language became politically polarized). There's a history of Southern women who rode horses, hunted, shot, flew airplanes and the like. For instance, the Flock family's son who didn't race cars, raced boats. And then there were three Flock sisters as well. Ethyl (named from the gasoline) drove stock cars. Reo (for the truck) was a sky diver. The only sister who wasn't a daredevil broke another mold and became a barber.

Or it may have simply been that dirt tracks and modified cars were a tough, rough place to make a living so it followed that people who did it had no regard for the other rules, either. If being seen at the stock car race was going to destroy your reputation anyway, you might as well *drive* the cars.

At any rate, when NASCAR began putting on races, there were three women who turned up in Grand National events: Ethyl Flock, Louise Smith and Sara Christian. And they didn't drive Powderpuff, because there was no such class. Everybody was equal, to the extent that Curtis Turner would—and did—lure Louise Smith into following him too deep into a turn, watched in his mirror as she went over the wall, and went on to win the race.

Turner, that is. Statistician Greg Fieldon says that from 1949 through 1987, fourteen women drove in Grand National races, but no woman has ever won a major championship NASCAR race.

Nor was this remarked about at the time. As noted elsewhere, good drivers can run Grand National for years, earning a living and a reputation, and still not win a title race. By the evidence, the women were good enough to be taken seriously and treated as equals, which they accepted as being fair.

Then the factories and teams and big money arrived and the women disappeared. Sara Christian, declared the best of her sex by those who were there, was hurt and her husband/car owner took advantage of that—he'd never been happy to have her at risk anyway—so they became co-owners and Fonty Flock drove their car. Ethyl did the same with her husband and Louise Smith became a pilot.

Meanwhile, when road racing became national, women were part of the package and several of the better road racers promoted themselves into USAC and NASCAR rides. They didn't do well on the track but they did OK in the press room. They presented themselves as pioneers; for all we know they really believed they were, and they were accepted on their own terms. Then as now, the public figures there were not liberated women until there was Women's Liberation. (Then as now the public doesn't think for itself much.)

Two ironic facts: one, the best known woman who tried NASCAR was Janet Guthrie. A large share of her support came from an oil company promoting an all-female team, that is, men were excluded on sexist grounds. One would like to hear Louise Smith or Ethyl Flock on that issue.

Second, if you go really deeply into history, the first woman racing driver did so in 1898, driving a De Dion tricycle in the Marseille-Nice race of that year. She finished second in class, fourth overall and two places ahead of her husband.

ern foothills looking for stands of wood. Then he'd try to buy it cheap and sell it expensive.

One day in 1946, the legend begins, Turner went to watch a race at Mount Airy, North Carolina. He saw a few cars practice, but then the racers pulled off the track. The announcer said the race was canceled because there weren't enough entries or spectators to make it worthwhile.

Turner climbed into his own car, a 1940 Ford coupe, roared onto the track and put on a show of powerslides, cutting doughnuts and what later would be called brodies. The crowd stayed in their seats, and when Turner slid to a stop and passed his hat, they filled it.

Turner next entered a real race, and was eighteenth out of eighteen cars. But the one after that, he won. He was a big man, a backslapper, womanizer and two-fisted drinker, a combination of several Southern types. He was also a natural driver, famous for his ability to go faster and farther sideways than anybody else of his day.

Lee Petty

If Curtis Turner was rough, which he was, Lee Petty was tough. Petty was another classic mountain man, but of a different ilk. He lived in the North Carolina hills, as had his ancestors for uncounted generations. He had a small trucking business, with most of the jobs coming from his father-in-law's lumber business.

Petty was a born mechanic. He didn't make whiskey, haul it or drink it—in public at least. He modified cars in his backyard, for fun. And when the time and chance arose, he raced on the street, against the homemade cars from shops like his. When the dirt track boom began, Petty started driving his car to the track, and racing legally, for whatever prize money was offered. Usually it wasn't enough to pay expenses, but Petty was primed for real professional racing when it arrived.

As soon as racing began, and as soon as sons Maurice and Richard were old enough, Petty and his wife and sons went to the races as a family. A closely knit family, and one that didn't share in the ribaldry of the time. Turner and Joe Weatherly, a motorcycle racer and Turner's best drinking buddy, might be whooping it up in the pits, but the Petty family was having a picnic, homemade fried chicken with all the trimmings, in the infield. The other racers weren't excluded. Those who walked over would be welcomed and fed. But the others went to Lee Petty, he didn't come to them.

And Petty was the strongest man in racing. Fighting in the pits was common in the early days. Once Turner and Petty had a disagreement, but it lasted until Petty aimed well, swung once and knocked Turner flat.

Marshall Teague

A hometown boy, graduate of Daytona Beach's Seabreeze High, Teague was another professional racer, with experience in Indy cars as well as late model stocks and modifieds. He owned a garage in Daytona Beach; even the winners in the late forties didn't earn enough to not need weekday jobs as well.

Teague was a skilled mechanic and an organized man, with a knack for business and promotion, which in due course got him what may have been the first factory backing.

Banjo Matthews

The nickname replaced his given name, which was Edwin, in childhood and came from the shape of his gold-rimmed glasses.

Matthews was a driver from Miami. He raced modifieds and open-wheel racing cars there and followed the circuits when they were developed. Matthews was an aggressive driver, and in his career would be suspended for overdoing things in the heat of battle.

He was also a born, intuitive and creative mechanic. He was most at home in the shop, building cars for himself and later for most of the NASCAR circus.

Ralph Moody

If the war exposed Southern men to the rest of the world, so did it expose the rest of the world to the South. Moody came from Massachusetts, where he had been a top driver, mostly in open-wheel midgets when that form of racing was at its peak.

He liked the South and could see the opportunities, so he moved south after the war and switched to driving stocks and modifieds, later becoming a car owner and builder. He was in the right place and time when the factories got into stock car racing.

Fireball Roberts

A hero, mostly pure and not at all simple, Roberts was also from Daytona Beach. His nickname preceded racing; he earned it on the diamond in high school with his fastball.

Marshall Teague and crew, at the beach, 1952. (Teague is the tall man in the helmet, standing at left.) The beach can be very cold in February at night, as the layers of clothes indicate. And a lot of people were needed to change tires and fill the tank. Daytona International Speedway

Roberts had what's now called charisma. They didn't have the term back then, so everybody simply liked the guy. He was a born driver, while at the same time the nickname lent itself to headlines.

This sample is mostly a slice across the program of the day, included here to show that the first people in the new form of racing came from different places and had different levels of experience. What they had in common was hunger and skill, especially when concerning mass-produced engines and cars.

Grand National begins

The original meeting was held in December 1947; NASCAR was incorporated early in 1948, but the first strictly stock car race held by the new organization, and the first in the championship series happily named Grand National, didn't take place until June 19, 1949.

That stock cars were raced was an act of faith, and an enactment of vision.

Perhaps inspired by those first races on the beach, France had the idea that the paying public would enjoy and appreciate comparison racing, brand versus brand, with no advertising claims to muddy the water. His partners were experienced promoters. They knew about racing from what they'd learned, but

they weren't men of imagination. (This isn't to criticize: few of us can imagine what we haven't seen.)

To the average thinker, racing was thrills, and thrills came from speed, so the faster the cars went, the more fun the spectators would have and the more people would buy tickets.

So that's the way NASCAR began. Jumping ahead in time for a comparison, NASCAR sanctioned the races at Daytona Beach. In 1949 the winter race, the one for tourists and during the busy season, was for modifieds. The stock car race was held in July, the hot and humid season. This was conventional wisdom.

In 1950, both beach races were held in the winter, but there had been a switch. The modified race was run on Saturday. The fast qualifier turned 114.43 mph and the race was won at an average speed of 93.19 mph.

The Grand National race was run on Sunday, and the fastest stock car was a 1950 Olds, clocked at 98.84 mph, and the winning average was 81.75. So the modified, in the form of a 1939 Ford coupe, was heaps faster than the stock 1950 Olds, but the new car got to be the star. The other guys were smart men and had no problem with telling France—while they counted the receipts, one likes to think—that he'd been right.

Meanwhile, back to that first stock car race, held at Charlotte, North Carolina, but far removed in time

NASCAR tried the first of many experiments in racing classes at Daytona Beach in 1952. They created a class of sprint cars, single seaters, but powered by stock-blocks. The idea was, there would be more speed for less money than the

Offenhauser-powered AAA cars cost. It didn't work, mostly because the fans didn't want to watch what they didn't drive, but also because sponsors didn't care about cars they couldn't sell. Daytona International Speedway

The other side of racing, as seen at Martinsville, West Virginia. Teague used to go through several cars each year; *they were driven hard and they did push each other around.* Daytona International Speedway

and physical features from the splendid facility now known as Charlotte Motor Speedway.

Nobody really knew what to do, because the rules were new. In the milling around for practice and qualifying, a journeyman driver, Glen Dunnaway of Charlotte, was without a ride, and there was a local car owner who was without a driver. The racer and the owner didn't know each other when they first teamed up that day, and the driver had never seen the car before. Keep that in mind.

A clue: the car was a prewar Ford coupe.

Dunnaway won the race, in a mixed field of new cars and old Fords. But after the flag there was a careful inspection and the winning car was found to have been modified. Fords then used a single, transverse spring in front, and another in back. These springs bolted to the center of the car's frame, and attached to the axles with shackles. The shackles moved back and forth to let the spring go up and down. But on the winning car somebody had snubbed the shackles. The spring was stiffened and wouldn't

roll as much under cornering loads. It wouldn't sag under extra weight, either. The wedging to stiffen the springs was a whiskey runner's trick; the car was a whiskey car, in fact.

It wasn't legal because it didn't meet NASCAR's new rules defining stock. Dunnaway was disqualified, and the first Grand National race was officially won by Jim Roper of Great Bend, Kansas, in a 1949 Lincoln.

The warm, human part of the story is that the guys who'd been moved up, guys like Tim and Fonty Flock and Red Byron, who drove for Red Vogt out of the famous Atlanta racing shop, knew that Dunnaway hadn't seen the car before and didn't know it wasn't legal. By the rules, he was responsible for the car, but he hadn't actually cheated. The other drivers chipped in part of the purse and Dunnaway went home with more than he'd have collected if his win had held up.

The cold, equally human part of the story is that the car's owner went to court, claiming that his car was stock and demanding the prize money. NASCAR

27

Another legend—make that two legends. The driver is Fireball Roberts and the car is a highly modified Ford coupe known to fans as the Florida Hurricane. *Obviously, it was a winning combination.* Daytona International Speedway

won the case. The judge was shown the car and the changes. He read the rulebook and he upheld France's call.

The car owner wasn't a bad man. On his side were years of precedent, with many clubs and groups each claiming to have the correct definition of stock. There had also been years of racers not following the rules and getting away with it, through popularity or even intimidation.

NASCAR's rules served notice but the court ruling really made it clear that these were going to be the rules, and they would be enforced, even if the winner was tossed out. There were some who said the judge had been more interested in ruling against a bootlegger than for a racing club, but that didn't matter. Houston Lawing, who was a newspaper reporter and later did public relations and press for NASCAR, said that day in court was the day people began to take the new group seriously.

That first race paid a total purse of $6,000, and was watched by 13,000 paying customers, so NASCAR was also beginning to prove that racing could pay its own way, and that people did want to watch new cars race. And as noted, it didn't hurt a bit that there were really new cars, the hot Olds and the challenging Hudson in particular.

Nine Grand National races took place in 1949, with less than $50,000 paid in prize money. A total of 875 people—drivers, mechanics, car owners, promoters and a few fans—joined the club. The first Grand National series title went to Red Byron.

France wasn't the only brave man in racing. Two years after that original meeting, some businessmen in Darlington, South Carolina decided to build a new, paved track. The group's leader, Harold Brasington,

was an Indy 500 fan. The track was half that circuit's distance, 1¼ miles around, but banked more steeply than the original was. It wasn't quite an oval, as one end was wider than the other—sort of an egg shape. Legend says this was because one of the owners of the land on which the track was built didn't want to lose his fish pond, so they kept that end narrow. True or not, Darlington was an unusual track.

NASCAR had just begun when the track was taking shape, and the owners went first to AAA. Like France, they were told to go away; AAA wasn't interested in any racing except that for open wheel, single seaters. But the Darlington people and the NASCAR people got together and came up with another milestone, the world's first 500 mile race for strictly stock cars.

They posted a $25,000 purse and mailed out entry forms. The limit was seventy-five cars, but 100 showed up. Nobody knew what to do, or what to expect. The smart money, the drivers like Red Byron, did the logical thing and entered Cadillacs, Lincolns and Oldsmobiles, the biggest and most powerful cars on the market.

Others were doing some different thinking. Richard Petty wrote years later that his dad could see that a light car would hold up better than a heavy one, and bought a new Plymouth club coupe, the kind used by salesmen of the day.

Legend says that NASCAR owned a similar Plymouth, bought for use by the staff, and it was borrowed by Johnny Mantz, an Indy car driver who'd met France in Mexico and been invited south for the races.

In fact, Mantz had driven a Lincoln in his first NASCAR race, then an Olds, but that car was damaged. While he watched Darlington practice, Mantz realized that a light car was the answer, so he persuaded the NASCAR owners to buy him a Plymouth coupe. He then carefully broke in the engine and checked out the car. For his secret weapon, Mantz had Indy-type Firestone tires, the only racing tires in the field. And his crew had air wrenches, while the other helpers had tire irons. Mantz made three tire changes and won easily against teams that used twenty and thirty tires. The winner collected $10,000. (But there was a catch. The AAA considered NASCAR an outlaw club, and levied a fine of $2,500. Mantz paid that out of his $10,000 winnings and went home happy.)

More important, all the other guys had learned something, while a capacity crowd saw just the sort of show they'd hoped for. The track made a profit on the day, the fans went home to tell their friends and the Southern 500 was off to a grand start.

The Grand National series was also starting well, although rule enforcement was part of the learning curve.

The 1950 Grand National champion was Bill Rexford. He was from rural New York state, a quiet driver who didn't mingle much, and only won one race in his

Much less common was the Plymouth as the basis for a modified racer. But the driver and builder here is Cotton Owens, who went on to do great things for Chrysler Corporation. Daytona International Speedway

NASCAR career. He didn't make much of an impression; there are no anecdotes about Rexford and the portrait printed here is the only one in NASCAR's files.

The story is behind the story. NASCAR and its rival groups were fiercely devoted to their own interests and in those days the antimonopoly and restraint of trade rules didn't apply to professional sports.

The best actual record compiled in 1950 was Lee Petty's. But at mid-season he drove in a non-NASCAR race and was stripped of the points he'd won thus far. He began again, with a vengeance, and his total from eleven of the year's nineteen Grand National races still put him in third for the year, behind Rexford and Fireball Roberts. If Petty ever forgave NASCAR for that ruling, he didn't say so.

Domestic use for export kits

The next step in the learning curve was mechanical. The original 500 mile race was one of attrition. There were literally heaps of cars on the sidelines, victims of broken wheels, hubs, axles and the like. The need for change was obvious, safety would be the excuse and there were people waiting for just such an opportunity.

The opportunists were in two camps—Olds and Hudson. The Oldsmobile engineers later said that yes, they had realized the potential of their new engine, and the even better potential that came when they put the semi-Cadillac V-8 into the nearly-Chevrolet lightweight coupe. By no chance, Oldsmobiles turned up in the hands of the Flocks.

Hudson had no such raw material; that is, their engine wasn't modern. But it was big, they had the best handling car on the market and, somehow, they were aware of the opportunity offered by racing.

Hudson seems to have been the first factory sponsor, in that they came through with help for Marshall Teague.

In 1950 Hudson introduced their Heavy-Duty Suspension Kit. This kit was supposed to be intended for export, the premise being that other countries didn't have our superb highways and needed extra strong components. The kit contained heavy-duty wheels and hubs, revalved shock absorbers, stiffer springs, and shotpeened axles, spindles and steering arms.

Hudson offered two engines, the 308 ci Hornet straight six and a smaller inline six for the Wasp. The smaller engine came with an aluminum head. The parts books said you could order a Hornet engine with the Wasp head, for a compression ratio of 9:1. A hotter camshaft, also optional, claimed power of 200 bhp at 4000 rpm.

During the 1951 model year Oldsmobile came out with its export kit as well. This kit included heavy-duty hubs and wheels, stiffer springs, heads with

NASCAR was always careful to stretch the time and the use of Daytona's beach to the maximum, so the local business people would do well in exchange for the noise and the use of the public beach for private purposes. Here scores of cars have been lined up for timed runs down the beach. The early Corvette in the middle is sort of a pace car, provided by Pure Oil Company. Daytona International Speedway

higher compression ratio, camshafts with more lift and duration and valve lifters that were solid; that is, they didn't use oil pressure and couldn't pump up or bleed down, so the engine could be revved faster. The heat risers in the intake manifold, where the exhaust heat warmed incoming air, were blocked off. This meant rougher warm-up, but denser intake charge and was clearly a racing modification, as opposed to (chuckle) equipping the car for use in foreign climes.

Hudson countered with more of the same, in the form of dual carburetors. The inline six lent itself more to twin carburetors on a log manifold than to the centered four-barrel carburetor that would soon be obligatory for the compact V-8. Hudson called the system Twin H-Power; their ad-writers called it a miracle.

The two contenders were close, and dominant. In 1951 there were forty-one Grand National races. Olds won twenty of them, and Hudson won twelve. Studebaker, also with a modern V-8, albeit a small one, had three wins; Plymouth and Mercury had two each; Chrysler and Nash had one each; and Ford, Pontiac, Packard, Lincoln, Cadillac, Buick and the Henry J went down swinging. Hudson driver Herb Thomas won the driver's title, followed by Fonty Flock, Tim Flock and Lee Petty—Olds, Olds and Lincoln or Plymouth, depending on the event.

Another step in the legend—Curtis Turner has bought the Florida Hurricane *from Fireball Roberts.* Daytona International Speedway

Another aspect of racing ran parallel to the Grand National history. In 1951 NASCAR put the official stamp of sanction on 585 races; along with Grand National, there were races for modifieds, late models and so on. The group had races at ninety-one tracks and paid out $779,589 in prizes and $40,000 in points money.

This was growth beyond everybody except France's wildest dreams. And it was acceptance, in the sense that there were scores of other clubs, promoters and literally hundreds of tracks, all ready to do business. But NASCAR had quickly become *the* power in the South, which was also where stock car racing was the most popular.

How did they do it? One distinction might have been the points system. It wasn't only that NASCAR paid points money, as opposed to event money. Unlike all the other forms of racing, where first place is best and the rest don't matter, France had worked out a system that was complicated, with points for winning, leading, qualifying, all the way up and down. It was also supposed to reward effort. A racer could get points for leading; thus, even if the car broke down his day had been worthwhile. And points were paid for finishing, so when the star was twelve laps down, he'd still go out there and race and the fans got to see the guys they'd paid to see.

The fans were there—new kinds of fans. Until the early- and mid-fifties, remember, there were two kinds of cars in the South, Ford and Chevy. The Chevy was slow and the Ford was fast, and there wasn't any point in arguing about it.

But now the Fords were in the modified class and the other brands were winning races. An American racing magazine, *Speed Age*, ran a correspondence column jammed full of wonderfully illogical and heated debate. One chap wrote that if the Chrysler had two carburetors the way the Hudson does . . . Another man said if the Hudson had the overbuilt V-8 like the Chrysler . . . And a third chap said his little Plymouth had shown its taillights to countless overrated Chryslers and Hudsons . . . Strictly stock was selling lots of tickets, lots of cars and generating lots of bench racing, never mind street racing.

These lessons were not lost on the racers, or the factories. The Hudson and Oldsmobile so-called export kits were joined by similar gear from Lincoln, Dodge and Nash, while Plymouth announced an "export" (their quotation marks) aluminum cylinder head. It had a compression ratio of 8.5:1 and a parts number 868456 in case an owner wanted one and his dealership hadn't heard about it yet.

(As another sidelight here, the first recorded use of two-way radio in racing came at Daytona Beach

Little Joe Weatherly, ex-motorcycle racer, hard charger and Curtis' best drinking buddy. The Fish Carburetor Company was an early NASCAR backer and so got to run the M-4 designation years after everybody else was required to use numbers only. *Early aerodynamic work here includes replacement of the window glass with riveted plastic, and openings cut into the rear fenders and running boards.* Daytona International Speedway

Speed Week in 1951, when a modified driver named Al Stevens installed one in his Ford. In real life Stevens operated a wrecker service so he knew about radios. He was third in the sportsman class; the radio might have been useful but did not make up for other shortcomings. Three years later Tim Flock was given credit for coming up with the idea.)

Hudsons won twenty-seven of the thirty-four Grand National races in 1952, the closest thing to a sweep in modern times. This sweep didn't set well with NASCAR or the fans, never mind that Tim Flock was national champion, leading Thomas and his Hudson and Petty and his Plymouth.

Boilerplate rules

Here begins another NASCAR invention, the revision of the rules to make sure one make or model doesn't have a lock on the races. (Never mind what would have happened if the rules hadn't been revised.)

The 1953 Grand National rules were done in the style that came to be known as Boilerplate: If the rules don't say you can do it, you *can't* do it. And although the rules take only one page, they do allow such things as beefed-up wheels and hubs, so safety and durability are taken care of without export or heavy-duty kits.

Herb Thomas won the national title again in 1953 with Lee Petty second on consistency. Note here that Lincoln got its overhead valve V-8 in 1952; that make was ready to make a run for it. Buick had also acquired a V-8. Buck Baker told the press that his Olds 88 had the factory cam, solid lifters, 8.5:1 compression ratio cylinder heads and a big gas tank for the Southern 500, in which he averaged 115 mph for fifty-six laps. Then the engine blew. Bill Blair drove an Olds to win the Daytona Beach Grand National race at 89.5 mph, while the top speed on the beach that year was another Olds at 113.38 mph. Olds was in the hunt.

Baker's car owner spent $17,000 for the season. He collected $13,000 in prize and points money and was happy to get that much, proving first that car owners need to be sportsmen, and second that sponsors were required early in the sport's history.

Fonty Flock, left, and brother Tim engage in mock debate with Curtis Turner and Billy Myers, far right. NASCAR publicity campaigns have always been heavily weighed on *personalities, and hardly mention the machines at all.* Daytona International Speedway

Grand National circuit specifications 1953

The following is a reprint of NASCAR's rules for 1953, short and sweet.

In all specifications the word "stock" shall be defined as meaning any part which is listed in the manufacturer's catalog for the year, model and type car entered, as designated by NASCAR.

1. No jeeps, suburbans, station wagons, pickups or convertibles will be permitted.
2. All cars must have complete bodies, hood, fenders, bumpers and grilles.
3. Roll-over bars inside car are optional but recommended.
4. Roll-over bars are compulsory in hard top model with no center door support to roof.
5. Headlight lenses must be removed or covered with masking tape. Hole must be covered.
6. Chrome or other parts may be protected by masking tape.
7. Windshield may be protected by celluloid or cellophane covering.
8. Rear seat cushions must be removed. Front cushion must be intact and not altered.
9. All doors must be securely fastened in an approved manner with either cable with clamp or metal strap with nuts extended to outside for quick removal. Suggest a "U" bolt with clamp at least ³/₁₆ths inch thick. Suggest two on each door.
10. Radiator dust screens will be permitted.
11. Muffler must be removed.
12. Hub caps must be removed.
13. Wheel and tire size must be for make and model as catalogued.
14. No special racing tires allowed.
15. Wheels may be reinforced in any manner provided general appearance is not changed.
16. Stock hubs for make and model only, may be reinforced. Steel hub allowed is same type and design.
17. Only stock radiator and cooling system will be permitted.
18. Water pump impellers may be altered.
19. Transmissions must be stock for model car used.
20. Differential must have stock catalogued gears for model car used. NASCAR reserves the right to list allowable gear ratios for any make or model automobile.
21. Locked rear-ends will not be permitted.
22. Overdrives and two speed rear axle will be permitted.
23. Complete motors must be in chassis and body for which they are catalogued.
24. Stroke must be stock, as catalogued. Reboring of block is allowed to compensate for normal wear up to an absolute limit of .033 oversize, measured at base of cylinder.
25. Valves, valve springs, cylinder heads and manifolds must be stock.
26. Altered or special camshafts will not be permitted.
27. Ignition system must be stock. Automatic advance in distributor may not be altered and must be in complete working condition.
28. Flywheels must be stock. No alterations permitted.
29. Carburetor must be listed for make and model car, but jets may be of any size.
30. Heavy duty shock absorbers and springs may be used if listed for make and model. No other changes permitted unless approved by NASCAR.
31. Only gasoline may be used as fuel.
32. Any oil is permissible.
33. Pickup in fuel tank may be moved to right side.
34. Any type spark plugs will be permitted.
35. Self starter must be in working order. All cars must start under their own power. (Cars may not be pushed from motor pits but may be pushed or towed into pits. Any motor started by either pushing or towing will automatically cause car to be disqualified).
36. Generator must be in working order.
37. Stock exhaust manifold only. No alterations or changes permitted.
38. Motor mounts may not be altered or changed, but a safety bolt may be used.
39. Motor parts may be polished, providing dimensions are not altered. Porting and/or relieving are prohibited.
40. Removal of fan or fan belt or air cleaner is not permitted.
41. Straight exhaust pipes extending past rear of body are recommended.
42. Hoods must remain in original locked position and closed.

NASCAR was operating as a club from its first day, and the club started a newsletter in 1951. The newsletter held family stuff, as in the notes about the co-owners of a car that came in second in a modified race who were badly hurt later that night driving the car home from the track. (Oh yes, they were still driving their racers home, not for sporting reasons but because many of the drivers didn't own any other car, never mind a tow truck or flatbed.)

This newsletter is a valuable, if surprising, source of information, especially if one reads between the lines. NASCAR had problems with education and enforcement of the rules. The newsletter warned against the use of "oversized" shock absorbers, uncatalogued wheels or additional antiroll bars. It mentioned rumors that some brands of cars supposedly sold in Canada had aluminum cylinder heads. If so, said the newsletter, "these will not be allowed."

There's an item reminding everybody not to use the higher compression ratio cylinder heads for the 1953 Olds 88, or thin head gaskets for the Buick Century or Special, or a 1954 230 ci Plymouth six in a 1949-1953 Plymouth, which came with a 213 ci engine. The bulletin was used to alert builders and

Lee Petty survived his fights with NASCAR and went on to make racing into a family business. He had help from Chrysler-Plymouth, as the paint here shows, and from other sponsors. His cars were always clean and properly prepared. Daytona International Speedway

The fastest cars in those early beach days were the modifieds, later known as late model sportsmen. This is Gober Sosebee, who was probably the best driver and builder in the class; at least he won the fastest races. The sad surprise here was that the modified class guys didn't always make the switch when the pure stock cars proved to draw the crowds. Sosebee dropped out and went back to his repair shop when the modifieds were given reduced billing. Although the car says Soseby, Gober's name was really Sosebee; we can guess the signpainter had it wrong all those years ago. Daytona International Speedway

inspectors that the combustion chamber for the Hudson alloy head must displace 92.5 cc, while the iron head must have chambers displacing 100 cc; other sizes would mean that the chamber had been modified, and thus illegal. It fell upon the newsletter to detail these rules because the factories didn't always bother. Or care.

Rule enforcement was a delicate matter. It began with a strength. Bill France had worn every hat in racing. He knew what it was like to be a driver, a mechanic, a car owner, a promoter and a referee. So he understood all sides and could speak for all sides.

This also led to awkward problems, inside NASCAR and outside. Just because France knew all sides to a question didn't mean the various factions accepted his views. Just about the time the club was beginning to take hold, the drivers decided they weren't getting their share of the money, and they began talking strike.

The luck or foresight of appointing the legendary Cannonball Baker as NASCAR's first commissioner of racing soon became evident. Baker, who was then in his seventies but with his forces unabated, called a meeting and gave a speech.

Marshall Teague said it was quite a speech. Baker cited the glory of racing, the value of sportsmanship, the matter of men of honor keeping their word. And he reminded everyone present that if the club didn't succeed, they'd all be out of work as well.

The strike was canceled. Teague said that if the court ruling that established NASCAR's right to make rules made the organization a reality in the eyes of the business world, Baker's speech made the club worthwhile for the racers.

And France did in fact keep Baker's word. The money has been fairly apportioned ever since.

But things got tougher. In the beginning France, Tuthill and Brasington simply assumed racers were all pals together. They offered to work with the AAA. They were rejected, and came to learn that professional racing was bitter rivalry. Sanctioning bodies considered themselves their players' keepers. Each group acted as if it were the only legitimate power and proclaimed the others to be outlaws.

This situation could be awkward. In 1950, Mexico put on a road race. It was a lark, in the beginning at least, and France co-drove with Curtis Turner. It was France's last race as a driver and he had a wonderful time.

But the race got serious. It got full sanction from elsewhere and the NASCAR newsletter for November 7, 1951, carried the notice "Any member who enters the Mexican race will be subject to a fine of $579.50, which is equal to the entry for the race. This fine will

The north turn again, for the 1954 Grand National. This is what the crowd has come to see: late model cars carefully prepared and well driven, in close quarters. Also worthy of comment is the improvement of the actual beach surface.

This is much more of a dirt track than the lumpy and rutted sand of the original circuit. Daytona International Speedway

The Mexican rehearsal

There's a character in *Alice In Wonderland* who says he not only believes in impossible things, he makes it a point to believe in at least three impossible things every day before breakfast.

Even somebody like that, from the vantage point of 1987, would have trouble believing there ever was such a thing as the Mexican Road Race.

But there was, and it provided some wonderful raw material for stock car racing even if nobody expected anything like that at the time.

The Carrera PanAmericana, to give the race its right name, began with a highway: Mexico's share of the route that was supposed to join the Americas, from Alaska to the tip of South America. When Mexico finished their portion of the highway, it had been quite a job. They were proud, and they decided to celebrate with a race, from one end of the country to the other, with classes for sports cars and stock sedans. (The young will be surprised to hear that at one time highways were consi-

dered improvements, that people actually wanted to build them and use them. Hard to imagine, but once you accept that, you can accept the use of public roads for racing.)

This was real road racing on real roads, with hills, ditches, curves and blind corners, much too long a race to be learned beforehand. It was a classic, in the tradition of the Mille Miglia in Italy, the Targa Florio in Sicily and the Tourist Trophy motorcycle events on the Isle of Man.

Everybody liked the idea but nobody knew what to expect and it seems to have begun as a busman's holiday. The winner of the first race, in May 1950, was Hershel McGriff with co-driver Ray Elliott, in a 1950 Olds 88. McGriff was a true amateur, a driver with professional talent but a man who liked to earn his living in the lumber business and drive for fun. The first race was tough, with 132 entrants and fifty-eight finishers. McGriff beat Cadillacs, Lincolns, Delahayes and Alfa Romeos, among others.

In with those others were Bill France and Curtis Turner, driving a Nash. They had a wonderful time scar-

The Mexican Road Race became a breeding ground and training camp for stock car builders from all parts of the United States, but it began as a strictly stock race *from one end of the newly finished cross-Mexico highway to the other. Here a brand new Cadillac sedan gets the starting flag.* Daytona International Speedway

The down side of the Mexican race was the series of fatalities that marred—and finally ended—what had become a classic event. The driver of this Guatemalan-entered Lincoln was killed, and a crowd has collected instantly, as one often does in Mexico. Daytona International Speedway

ing each other and the onlookers. It was France's last race as a driver, and he and Turner had a good chance to do well—until the next to the last day. They raced all day, parked for the night, then started again the next day, keeping score with elapsed time from point to point. France went off course and put a hole in the radiator. Turner was offered another Nash and won the last leg— except that the switch was noticed and he was disqualified.

But that's a sidelight. What mattered here, or came to matter later, was that the race came to the attention of the California hot-rodders.

The term isn't powerful enough. By this time, the late forties, California had a professional roadster racing circuit backed up by a vast number of gifted amateurs racing on the dry lakes and, yes, on public roads. They had been modifying Fords since the teens, and some of the West Coast guys were second generation, learning from their fathers before the NASCAR crowd even became fathers. The whiskey cars and New England Ford-powered midgets were fast, but the best engines and equipment came from California and everybody knew it.

Two of the top builders there were Bill Stroppe and Clay Smith. Odd though it sounds, they came to the attention of Ford through their achievements with a Ford six-cylinder-powered hydraplane. When Johnny Mantz, whom we met earlier in this account, winning NASCAR's first strictly stock 500, heard about the Mexican race he asked Stroppe and Smith to prepare his car. The car would be the best one they had, Mantz's personal transportation, a new Lincoln.

Mantz, Stroppe and Smith thought it would be useful if Ford or Lincoln came through with backing. Ford Motor Company didn't think so, although the team did persuade a Lincoln-Mercury dealer to chip in $500.

The fastest truly stock car of 1950 was the Olds 88, so it was only fair that the race was won by McGriff, in an 88. Then came a Cadillac 62 driven by a Cadillac dealer from Texas, another Cadillac 62 and then an Alfa Romeo 6C 2500 sedan at the hands of the Italian star, Piero Taruffi. Mantz and Stroppe were ninth, after everything in the book went wrong or fell off.

In 1951 the race was a real race, with a class for sedans and one for sports cars, and the rules were loosened some. Smith figured the best car would be a Chrysler, or so Leo Levine's account in *Ford: The Dust and The Glory* tells it. But the local Chrysler dealer wouldn't contribute a new car. He did donate a used car, a 1948 Mercury coupe.

This was right down Smith's alley. The flathead V-8 received everything the book allowed and maybe things the books hadn't thought about prohibiting. For Troy Ruttman, an AAA driver who came up the hard way via ashcan derbies and Ford roadsters, it was a comfortable return to roots. The used car was fourth, behind Taruffi and Alberto Ascari in Ferrari 212 E Inters, and four minutes behind a new and prepared Chrysler Saratoga.

This race set the stage for 1952. Smith and Stroppe made their approach to Benson Ford, of the family whose name was on the factory, at Indianapolis in 1952. Their reputations had preceded them, and when Smith showed more concern for a rival driver who crashed than for his own chances to move up, Ford approved the man's character as well as his talent. Further, Lincoln had a brand-new car coming for model year 1953 and this race, held in the fall, would be timed perfectly.

There are more heroics and details than can be covered here. Most important, this was Ford's first official venture into racing since an ill-fated stock-block try at Indy in 1935.

Smith and Stroppe had Ford's full backing. They needed some parts certified for the race, and the factory came through. In return, the Lincolns finished one, two, three in the 1953 Turismo class: Chuck Stevenson, AAA national champion; Mantz; and Walt Faulkner, a West Coast driver. As another hint to the future, in fourth was a private Lincoln, driven by Bob Korf and entered by Carl Kiekhaefer, whom we'll meet again.

The race escalated in 1953. It became part of a world championship and had classes for big and small sedans, and big and small sports cars.

There was also a tremendous increase in entries: there were eighty cars from Argentina alone. This was a trick, in fact, as Argentine dictator Juan Peron had exempted racing cars from the whopping import tax imposed on new cars coming into the country. Thus, everybody who had the money for a new car had it shipped to Mexico, where it flew the Argentine flag but motored sedately across the country and then went home, virtually unraced.

In the real 1953 race, the class finishing order was Stevenson, Faulkner, Jack McGrath (another West Coaster) and Mantz, all in Lincolns, followed by Tommy Drisdale in a Chrysler.

Just as it happened up north, the Mexican Road Race stock cars were edging into race car territory. Oldsmobile was involved at the factory level, for instance, and had come out with the first J-2 option: a heavy-duty package with engine and suspension parts (don't get confused here just because the factory later billed its three-carburetor option as J-2). Despite all this, Olds finished behind the Lincolns, Cadillac, Chrysler and

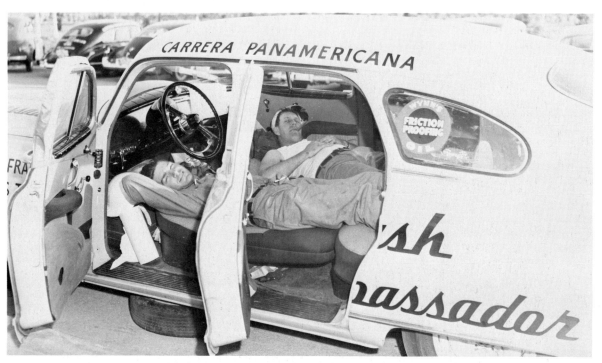

The two gentlemen of leisure here are Curtis Turner, foreground, and Bill France, with cigar. Their car is a Nash and they are sprawled so comfortably because one of Nash's sales pitches of the day concerned seats that converted into a bed (radio comedians had a lot of fun with that). Turner and France made good time in the 1950 race but when it became a sanctioned event, NASCAR refused to let its drivers take part. After that, France barred Turner from NASCAR events because the latter tried to organize the drivers into a union. You could say that bedfellows make for strange politics. Daytona International Speedway

Hudson. The best Olds, driven by Jim Rathman, was disqualified for having reworked heads.

The rules were tightened for 1954. Export or heavy-duty kits were banned, and the stock cars had to be current or from the two previous model years. There had to have been at least 600 examples of the model made. Straight pipes, roll bars and big fuel tanks were allowed, but they were supposed to have been the only modifications (chuckle).

Lincoln entered another team, backed by privateers, for a total of nine. There were five Buick Centuries from a team in Mexico. Chrysler was now taking an interest at the factory level and built fifteen optional equipment models for Daytona that year so some of that knowledge went to Mexico, too.

Tragically, Smith was killed in a pit accident at an AAA dirt track race. Stroppe and Don Francisco, another California hot-rodder, took over the team and the preparation. They had learned a lot, but so had the other racers. Ray Crawford, a private driver with help from the factory, won the class for Lincoln. He was followed by Faulkner in a team Lincoln, two Caddies and two Mexican Buick Centurys. Crawford's Lincoln was ninth overall behind several Ferraris, Porsches and an OSCA.

By the end of 1954, the PanAmericana had become a world championship event, a legend, an epic—and a liability. Too many people had been hurt and killed. Mexico was by then too modern to allow the government to simply shut down the country's major highway so a few score of foreigners could conduct a contest. The 1954 race was the last one.

The legacy, however, is still with us.

Ford Motor Company had become officially and thoroughly involved with racing. Not just racing, but stock car racing. There was a cadre of talent at Ford, trained by Smith, on the payroll and in need of work to do. When you're a hammer, as the saying goes, everything looks like a nail.

NASCAR people had learned about road racing. They'd met racers, mechanics and managers from all over the world. Levine's Ford racing history mentions that Alfred Neubauer was the godlike overseer of the Mercedes-Benz racing team, and that Clay Smith's results and techniques were just as good, something neither party could ever have known if they hadn't met away from home.

The West Coast hot-rod crowd had also been exposed to new influences. They too had gained some skills and would now need a place to exercise them. Like the factory men, they would find it.

In the long run, this race series was a combination of a meeting of minds and a war of the worlds, old and new. The American drivers and mechanics and engineers met their counterparts from Europe, one of the few times and places this had happened, and something that wouldn't happen on this scale again for a generation. All parties had their eyes opened, and all the people who'd been there took their knowledge home. It's fair to say that these races, which began just to celebrate a new road, had an influence on car design worldwide.

Stock car racing in the United States surely would have become important without the Mexican Road Race. But it wouldn't have been the same, and one can wonder if it would have been as good.

The winner of the first Mexican Road Race was Hershel McGriff, here with co-driver Ray Elliott. As the photo hints, they treated the race more like a holiday, right down to the funny hats. McGriff went on to be a top West Coast racer for better than thirty years. Daytona International Speedway

be placed in the NASCAR points fund. In addition, the Mexican jumper will be subject to losing all his points."

Printed in the letter for January 31, 1952, was a copy of a check from Marshall Teague, who had entered the race. The check was for $574.50; presumably the exchange rate between peso and dollar had affected the entry fee and thus the fine. The newsletter said this amount "was the fine assessed (sic) all NASCAR members who participated" and added that Teague "is back in the good graces with (sic) the association."

Obviously there there were no favorites. Well, there might have been; some guys said the enforcement of NASCAR rules was uneven, but even Banjo Matthews, who would go on to become *the* builder, was suspended for rough driving. In this case, he says he probably deserved it. In the same vein and at the same time, Herb Thomas was fined $100 for not appearing at Palm Beach Speedway "as he signified he would."

Later that year Tuthill levied a punishment against Teague, in a letter beginning, "We would like an explanation as to why you allowed your car to race in the late model event in Tampa at Speedway Park without receiving permission from NASCAR headquarters.

"If you fellows want to continue to run for cut-rate purses when we are keeping the minimum for this type of race at $4,000, I think you are doing yourselves and racing a good deal of harm . . . In view of the fact that you violated Rule #2 under Section #2, there is nothing we can do but subject you to a loss of points up to that date."

Never mind here that the trial seems to have been held in the middle of the letter. NASCAR was keeping a close watch on the drivers and the other clubs, and was willing to enforce the rules. It used the newsletter to let everybody know that this was being done, and would be done against or for them if they didn't act right.

Drivers were suspended for running in unsanctioned events, were put on probation and fined for things like unsportsmanlike conduct and illegal equipment. One track's sanction was revoked because its insurance wasn't up to NASCAR standards. When the 1952 steel strike reduced the supply of new cars, 1950 models were allowed into the 1952 Southern 500 to fill out the field.

Modified rules and stock cars

All of these rules and regulations worked two ways. Humpy Wheeler, president of Charlotte Motor Speedway now but a promoter then, says that the rivalry among the clubs and tracks got down to genuine fisticuffs at the grass roots.

And the newsletter quotes an official opinion from the AAA: "The contest board is bitterly opposed to what it calls 'junk car' events and believes the fad for such hippodroming is dying out."

For the record, hippodroming was a thirties practice in which the winners of the race were known before the start of the race. Fixed racing, in other words, done during those tough times because it was easier on the equipment and a better show than honest racing. But skip that, the fad isn't going away.

Instead, we are at the next watershed with the rules.

Until this point, say 1953 and just before that, car preparation meant exactly what the term implies. Marshall Teague explained, in *Speed Age* and *Motor Trend*, just how he did it. The cars were carefully broken in on the way home from the factory, then they were dismantled and all tolerances and clearances brought to maximum or evened up or both. Teague used one of the three rear axle ratios in the catalog, either the three-speed stick or the automatic, and spent extra time getting the carb jets, ignition setting and advance curve just right. The cheating in those days was honest cheating. The cheaters used milled cylinder heads, reground camshafts or overbored cylinders.

Then came the factory export and heavy-duty kits; things appeared to be getting out of hand. Late in 1953, NASCAR announced the 1954 rules. Roll bars would be required rather than encouraged. Beyond that, the general outline was as before, except that "No extra cost parts or options to boost power are permitted."

No factory kits, in short. No export, mountain or heavy-duty gear.

Early in 1954 NASCAR officials announced that the Hudson factory option for the Twin H-Power dual carbs was under review. A review committee went to the Hudson factory.

Their findings, duly published in the newsletter, were first that Twin H-Power was a genuine option, installed on cars moving down the assembly line. Second, Hudson had kept one step in front, by incorporating some of the former optional parts into regular production. Therefore, the ruling read, the dual carbs will be permitted in the Grand National class during 1954.

The kicker here was that any and all cars so-equipped were required to proclaim that fact, in letters painted on the side of the car, with a minimum height for said letters.

That was unique. At first one would think they'd do the reverse, and hide the equipment. But no, they'd read the letters from Chrysler, Plymouth and Ford owners, and they must have known the dual carbs would be seen as an unfair advantage.

Beneath that, there was a canny recognition of politics and balancing of the system.

This is how NASCAR learned. By 1954, Hudson was way behind. Buick had its V-8, and had put the big engine in the smaller body, creating the Century, and one of the first supercars. Olds listed its J-2 option for 1954, with four-barrel carb, stronger rear axle, heavier suspension components, oversized radiator and beefed steering linkage, engine mounts and wheels, high-compression heads, solid lifters and high-lift camshaft. Lincoln, Cadillac and Chrysler enlarged and modified their V-8s. And Ford and Mercury now had real V-8s, overhead valves and all. So Hudson got to keep its dual carbs and alloy head and stay in the running for a while longer, despite the out-of-date engine design.

The actual racing was in fact balanced, except perhaps that Ford's engine wasn't an especially good design and Ford was still far from being a performance car. Lee Petty, driving a Chrysler, was named winner of the 1954 Daytona Beach race, named in this case because the first man across the finish line was Tim Flock in a Super 88, with what were revealed to be modified parts in the carb. The Olds team took this hard. They had factory backing and had equipped six cars with what were later declared illegal parts. Olds withdrew from stock car racing well before the AMA ban on factory involvement and stayed out of racing for the next twenty-five years. Their cars, meanwhile, did well in private hands.

Why did they pull out? Oddly, the men at the factory and in the sales office had been keeping track and had learned that for Oldsmobile, winning on Sunday didn't translate into sales on Monday. It did for Ford, Chevy and Plymouth, but not for the others, although winning may have improved public awareness or generated a reputation for engineering.

And then we come to Hudson, winner of the manufacturer's title in 1951, 1952 and 1953, the inventor of the racing option, and the first beneficiary of NASCAR's selective approval.

Hudson's peak and finest hour came in 1954. Teague had quit NASCAR by then, partially because his ambition was to win the Indy 500 and he couldn't do that unless he joined AAA. The battle over various fines and rules may have contributed as well. The Hudson flag was now flown by Herb Thomas, with the connivance of a guy named Smokey Yunick. Yunick was a self-taught practical engineer and former bomber pilot, who'd settled in Daytona Beach at the end of the war and opened what the sign proclaimed "The Best Damn Garage in Town," as it may in fact have been.

The ban on factory speed equipment led to a mass impound just prior to qualifying for the Southern 500 at Darlington. There were seventy engines inspected; twenty-one were declared illegal. Thomas's Hornet was among them, and NASCAR inspectors locked the engine away. Yunick had three days to build a new engine, more or less in public. Yunick worked for two days straight, around the clock, chewing cigars and setting off firecrackers to keep awake— or so everybody said later, and Yunick never minded having people talk about him.

Thomas started the race with an untried, untested engine declared stock and legal, no question. He started in twenty-third, his car not having been allowed to qualify. It was a four-hour race, through dense traffic. A few laps from the end he'd worked up to second, behind Curtis Turner in an Oldsmobile.

Then Lady Luck blew a kiss and real life acted like Hollywood. Turner's fuel pump failed, and Thomas won.

But that was the end of the legend. Later in 1954 Hudson merged with Nash in a vain attempt to keep the smaller firm in business. The step-down design was outmoded, while the strange old flathead six was replaced with a normal V-8. Much later, drag racers armed with the Hudson police package, the optional 7X engine with carbs, alloy head and cam, and so on, turned times that indicated the Teague and Yunick Hornets probably had close to 200 bhp. The record shows Hudson with seventy-nine Grand National wins, also an indication they had at least as much power as the early ohv V-8s.

Meanwhile, Olds withdrew, Hudson faded, Lee Petty won the national championship in a Chrysler, Ford's new V-8 didn't make much of a splash . . . and NASCAR took a giant step forward and an equally big step in a new direction.

Chapter 4

The Hot Ones: 1955-1958

Richard Petty doesn't use the term, but when he talks about how racing got to where it was in 1955, he's talking about what social scientists call the New South.

Richard Petty: "All the boys went off to war and they saw what the world was, away from the South. They wanted to see more of it but the South was such a rural area, no trains or airplanes—the only way they could go anywhere was in a car.

"Everybody went in cars, so racing was a natural situation. Everybody drove a car; if they drove a Pon-tiac, they pulled for Pontiac. If they drove a Ford, they pulled for Ford.

"In the South there were no major league teams, no baseball or football or hockey or anything. When people were talking around the gas stations or beer joints, it wasn't if the Yankees won or Boston won, we didn't worry about that. We wanted to know who won the race."

Humpy Wheeler adds another ingredient. "In the Piedmont, along what's now I-85 north of Atlanta through to Richmond, Virginia, the land is gifted with

Late model stocks—really stock—quickly became the popular form of racing. This is Darlington in 1955, packed to the rafters. A Mercury Outboard (Kiekhaefer) Chrysler is about to pass a new ohv Ford V-8. Daytona International Speedway

a great resource, a wonderful soil called red clay, the greatest natural racing surface in the world." The only requirements for a racetrack were a farmer with land he wasn't using and a contractor with a bulldozer that wasn't on a job. A couple of hours and there it was, a half-mile dirt track, ready for the racers.

Becoming a racer was just as informal. Wheeler and his peers scoured the farms and hollers, armed with fifty dollars in crisp one-dollar bills, looking for Ford coupes. "You know that car that doesn't work, the one down by the creek," they'd say to the farmer. "We'll give you $50 for it."

They'd tow the car home, make it run, race it into the ground and go get another. Wheeler: "In the fifties we could have had our choice of fifty racetracks within fifty miles of Charlotte. If we drove a triangle from Charlotte to Bristol to Richmond thirty years ago we probably would have seen three or four

It was Daytona Beach speed week, so here's a crowd of racing fans, with their hot Lincolns, Oldsmobiles, Buicks and more, lined up for a drive down the sand. The cars raced were the cars driven to the races. Daytona International Speedway

Double meaning here for racing what you drove. This hapless victim is a 1955 Chevrolet, by happy accident a natural short track car. It even has a license plate, so the car surely was driven to the races. Guys like this won a lot before the factory even knew they were racing, never mind how this poor devil got home. Daytona International Speedway

hundred race cars parked alongside a shack or a filling station.

"Those were the roots. And it was tough. Your mother and father didn't want you to listen to hillbilly music, live in a log cabin because they'd just gotten out of one, wear overalls or go to stock car races. Those were the harsher things of the South and they were trying to pull their families up."

Races were not a place for dates or families. The Petty women and children were kept as apart as Lee Petty could keep them, while at the same time when things did get physical Mrs. Petty waded into the battle at least once.

Wheeler compares the racing crowd in the South after World War II to the young men of the post-Civil War South, the men who went to Texas to become cowboys, cattle barons, gunfighters or sometimes all three.

"The boys came home to the cotton mill, the furniture mill or the farm. There were some smart, aggressive people. The ones that couldn't go to college lived a tough existence, but they wanted to do something with themselves."

Car racing was a natural outlet. NASCAR and the rival sanctioning groups created a vast, brawling network of tracks and races. While NASCAR invented and began to promote the strictly stock late model class, the real stars of the show were the modifieds, usually prewar Ford coupes or sedans with ohv V-8s and all the speed equipment California could devise.

Then Detroit arrived on the scene.

This was close to being an accident. When the overhead-valve, short-stroke, stiff-block, high-compression V-8 was designed, the goal was efficiency. That was achieved, and the car factories then moved to using that added power to drive assists for steering and brakes, automatic transmissions, air conditioning and so on.

But some of the power went to speed. There was the Mexican Road Race, and speed week at Daytona

The photo is posed but the meaning is accurate. This is Carl Kiekhaefer, the inventor of the stock car racing team, at Daytona Beach in 1956. He is telling the drivers what to do. The drivers, from left, are Charles Scott, Tim Flock, Fonty Flock, Frank Mundy, Buck Baker and Speedy Thompson. They look as if they're suppressing grins and scorn, and they probably are. But they also knew Kiekhaefer would spend the most money, build the best cars, fight for his team and pay them a fair wage, so they put up with it. Kiekhaefer won a lot of NASCAR races and taught the factories how to organize a team. Daytona International Speedway

Beach, and the factories learned that people were paying attention, thus the involvement of Hudson, Oldsmobile, Buick and Lincoln.

The horsepower race speeds up

The next step began in 1951, with Chrysler's V-8. The goal was the same as at General Motors, but the design was different.

The hemispherical combustion chamber design was used by racing engines since before World War I. It worked for simple reasons: there was a lot of wall in the combustion chamber and when you put two valves directly opposed to each other in the chamber, it left lots of room for the valves to be large. In the conventional design, the valves were side by side. In theory, the hemi could have both valves as wide as the bore, while the wedge or pentroof chamber could only have valves half as wide as the bore. The next theory states that the bigger the valves, the more power.

There's a drawback, however. These V-8s all had the camshaft, singular, in the vee of the block, parallel with the crankshaft. Everything had to be at right angles: the pushrods from the cam to the rocker arms, the rocker arms on their shafts (which were also perfectly parallel with the crank and the camshaft) and the valve stems to the rocker arms.

Chrysler didn't solve this problem so much as they overcame it. They put two rocker shafts on each head; the intake valves were above the bore, the exhaust valves were below it. The valves were forty-five degrees to the bore, and ninety degrees to each other.

The Chrysler hemi was a classic design. It was also more expensive to produce and install, and it was bulky, heavier than the rival V-8s of the same displacement. Chrysler believed in the principle, however. They were willing to spend the money on the engine and on promoting and extolling its virtues, at least for the Chrysler, DeSoto and Dodge lines—Plymouth not being included due to its rank as the lowest priced make and thus price sensitive.

Ford came next in sequence, as Henry the Younger, his relatives and the new executive team had so much to do with keeping the corporation alive when the old man died, they were the last of the majors to have an ohv V-8, never mind independent front suspension or even hydraulic brakes.

The Ford got its V-8 in model year 1954. It was a normal, even dull, version of the cast-iron block, two-valves-per, camshaft in the vee with pushrods and rocker shafts. It displaced 292 ci and boasted some 160 bhp. The new engine came in a body that was three years old. It wasn't much peppier than the flathead it replaced and nobody paid much attention.

Then came the Chevrolet V-8 and *everybody* paid attention.

Cost was also important to Chevrolet, which is probably why that division was the line in General Motors to get a modern V-8 in the model year 1955.

But the timing was quickly forgotten. The Chevy V-8 was rated at 164 bhp with a two-barrel carburetor and it displaced only 265 ci, smaller than the rival Ford.

The Chevy engine had several advantages, some spotted right away and some more subtle and not appreciated until the V-8 had been in service for a while.

The quick and easy parts were first. The engine was smaller and lighter than the new Ford V-8 or the older engines from Cadillac, Olds, Dodge, Studebaker, Buick and so on. You could use the new Chevy powerplant in an early Ford or Austin-Healey and the car weighed less than it did stock, something that didn't apply with the Caddy and Chrysler engines.

Next, the cylinder head design was superior; the Chevy engine breathed better. Chevrolet took advantage of this with what was called the Power-Pak which included dual exhausts and a four-barrel carburetor; the output went to 180 bhp.

Ford countered with the Thunderbird V-8, but as every kid in town knew the next day, stock for stock the Chevy would whip the Ford.

The subtle secret was in the valvetrain. The Ford, like the Cadillac, the Olds and the Lincoln, used a shaft parallel to the cam and crank, for the rocker arms. The rockers were cast, tiny walking beams that

Lee Petty was an early Chrysler fan, and made racing a family business. He also made friends with the corporation because he was willing to work with the factory, while Kiekhaefer thought the team was more important than the brand. The car here is a 300-B and looks absolutely stock. Daytona International Speedway

pivoted on the shaft. Thus, the valves had to be aligned with the shaft and the cam.

But the Chevy V-8, known within weeks as Mighty Mouse, had stamped steel rockers that pivoted on ball studs screwed into the heads. These rockers were lighter, so the engine could rev higher, quicker. And the ball mount meant the valves could be angled and the combustion chamber designed for efficiency and power, with the ports laid out to work with the chamber and the valves put where the porting was right.

All things said, this was a terrific engine. It was also a surprise to the public as nobody expected ol' Stovebolt Chevy (the name comes from the cheap square-head stovebolts used in the Chevrolet six) to have something fast and sporting.

The next surprise was that Chevrolet began to take Ford's customers, the youth market, before anybody had even defined such a thing as a youth market.

That in itself was a switch. Until 1955 big cars were more powerful and faster than small cars, and people with money had bigger cars than people with-out money. But the new Chevrolet Bel Air two-door hardtop with a Power-Pak engine was quicker and faster than the Buick Century or the Olds 88, and the Chryslers and Lincolns didn't even bother to show up.

The factories learned this last. For the most part the car companies were headed by smart, experienced, but conventional business executives. The engineers were chosen and organized along parallel lines; that is, they knew what to do from knowing what had been done and what was in the book. They hadn't been paying a lot of attention to stock car racing, especially the NASCAR-style racing in the South. Suddenly youths were a market and racing a form of marketing they couldn't ignore.

In the conventional sense, Chrysler got there first—although they did it at one remove.

The moving force here was an oddball industrialist named Carl Kiekhaefer. He owned Mercury outboards and he liked cars and racing. He also liked to win, and believed in careful preparation and iron discipline. He was good at taking care of Number One, as people a generation later would say when we all improved ourselves.

Fireball Roberts was a local hero, nicknamed for the speed of his fastball in high school. He got into racing and had help, as shown here, from Buddy Shuman, a mechanic and *tuner known for his skill in helping some chaps make their deliveries on time. Daytona International Speedway*

Kiekhaefer wasn't much for brands, or brand loyalty. In 1952, for instance, Chrysler and Lincoln had big solid cars with ohv V-8s, and he entered one of each in the Mexican Road Race. But he was keenly aware of engineering and the Chrysler hemi was the better engine, so he gravitated in that direction.

Chrysler Corporation meanwhile was moving in the same direction, as they investigated handling and chassis improvements, and beefed-up New Yorker sedans for the Mexican races. Their cars were fast, if not as fast as the Lincolns that dominated the stock car class in that event, and from that came a series of special New Yorkers for NASCAR.

In 1955 the export-kit-style racer was banned, but Chrysler had discovered styling. While their earlier sedans were big and square, the 1955 version was smaller and lower and slicker. There was a special version, with disc brakes, heavier suspension and a hemi with hot cam, high compression and two four-barrel carbs. The engine made 300 bhp so they called it the C-300, a regularly cataloged model and thus eligible for racing.

Then came the factories. Here's Fireball with a sharp new Ford, neater than two pins and fully sponsored as well. Ford's ohv V-8 probably put out at least as much power as was advertised and painted on the hood. Daytona International Speedway

Pure Oil Company was an early NASCAR backer and supplied more than fuel. This gas station (not the one owned by Bill France when he formed NASCAR) was used for office help and paperwork during the speed weeks at the nearby beach. This is the staff plus neighborhood kids. Daytona International Speedway

Kiekhaefer had been testing and developing his own parts while swapping info with the factory, so he acquired a fleet of C-300s, had them painted white and called them the Mercury Outboard Team. He hired drivers like Tim and Fonty Flock, Frank Mundy and Buck Baker, and he became the official Chrysler factory effort. If they didn't win, it wasn't the factory's fault.

Kiekhaefer was a smart man. If he had a flaw it was an inability to assign responsibility. He viewed his drivers as members of a high school team and himself as the gruff old coach—separate rooms for husbands and wives, bed checks, stuff like that. But the equipment was good and the pay was good so he got away with it.

Ford, meanwhile, had warehouses packed with cars and parts, personnel with racing experience, and outside suppliers and contracted help, all from the Mexican adventure. When that event was canceled, it was plain that the Lincoln was too big for closed circuit racing although the Ford had a new body and a V-8 for 1955. The company had all this expertise, so Ford switched to stock car racing.

They also did it at a partial remove. They'd learned from Stroppe and Smith that racing guys were better at racing than factory guys were, so Ralph Moody, the New England midget driver, and John Holman, the California truck driver, evolved into the Ford team. They campaigned cars for the factory and developed parts as well.

Chevrolet got into the whole thing backwards, almost by accident.

That the V-8 was great, everybody knew. But Chevrolet had gotten into the sports car movement with the Corvette. When they put the V-8 into the Corvette they had a real car, one that could compete with the Europeans. Further, the main force behind the Corvette was Zora Arkus-Duntov, who was a brilliantly unconventional engineer, a clever politician and a delightful man.

He was also a European. In Europe, the elite met to race and the masses got to stand alongside the road and cheer. So the official plan at Chevrolet was to emphasize the Corvette and if the glitter rubbed off, fine.

Bill France was aware of these currents. He and the powers in Daytona Beach were evolving that city's claim to fame right along with the cars and racing. There were the races on the beach (well, on the beach and the road); there were timed runs on the beach, open to the public and offering membership in the Century Club if your car did the magic 100 mph; and there were sports car races nearby, at New Smyrna Airport.

The privateers got there first. Ordinary owners ran on the beach and matched prepared cars from other factories. The Chevy sedan was light and cheap. When Hudson left racing, the best men from that effort, Herb Thomas and Smokey Yunick, shifted to Chevrolet, in large measure because Chevrolet could

The arrival of the factories and their performance options made inspection much more critical and difficult. Here's the genuine Cannonball Baker, first commissioner of racing for NASCAR, and two tech inspectors checking out a camshaft, cylinder head and intake manifold. Daytona International Speedway

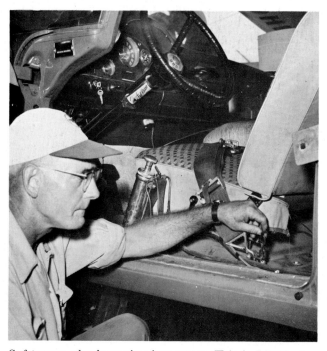

Safety was also becoming important. This is Bill Taylor, chief technical inspector in 1956, showing the camera the linkage and fastenings required for the newly required seatbelts. Daytona International Speedway

afford it. The Chevy didn't have the total muscle of the Chrysler, but it was made for short track.

A few savvy men at Chevrolet, and at Chevy's ad agency, noticed this, and realized that their brand was shifting the youth market away from Ford. They found listeners at the top and began developing racing parts, backing the best teams and advertising their success.

The Hot Ones, is how the ads put it, and it worked.

Not all at once, of course. The 1955 Daytona Beach race was won first by Fireball Roberts with a privately owned Buick Century. I say "won first" because when the Buick was torn down postrace, the pushrods were found to have been modified and the victory went to Tim Flock in a Mercury Outboard Chrysler C-300. There was some justice there, in that Flock was the man who crossed the line first in 1954 only to have his car declared illegal, but it also shows the other cars were in the hunt: how much difference can shortened pushrods make? And anyway, a C-300 was fastest on the beach, and the team cars used automatics, which helped in terms of long life but made the Chryslers slow out of the turns.

Convertibles were raced with the massive roll bar shown, and belts of course. Beyond that, racers could cover the rear compartment with a fabric panel, remove the window glass and add, as Turner did, an accessory tachometer. You'd have to add it because the rules required that racers keep the stock instruments.

Convertibles were the sporting machine in the fifties. They came with the same engines and drivetrains as sedans and the fans could watch the drivers at work in the open cars, so NASCAR created a convertible class. The rules were just like those for the sedans, except for things like roll bars.

This car is a replica, built by a fan who wanted a car like Curtis Turner raced but learned that none of Turner's convertibles had survived. He took a stock 1956 Ford convertible and, well, converted it.

During the 1955 season there was another non-technical development that was to have a major impact on stock car racing. At the Le Mans twenty-four-hour race that year a small car got in front of a team Mercedes-Benz and the collision sent flaming debris into the crowd. Scores of spectators died.

Here in the United States the disaster was greeted with shock and dismay and in one corner, perhaps, a glimmer of satisfaction.

The AAA began as an affiliation of motoring clubs, dedicated to the pioneer drivers, builders and tourists. As motoring changed, so did the AAA, which became mostly an insurance company with a smattering of other services. Racing was handled by the Contest Board, whom we met when they were not pleased by the appearance of stock car racing.

The AAA doesn't seem to have liked racing, period. They did certify record runs and the big cars, as Indy cars were called then, and they did get into stock car racing: AAA was sanctioning showroom stocks by 1950 in the Midwest.

But when Le Mans proved to be fatal, the directors of AAA declared that this proved racing was a bad thing. They dissolved the Contest Board and took AAA out of racing, period. Yes, this was sort of like

those small towns that declare war on other countries or adopt foreign affairs policies; even so, it stirred things up.

The AAA's board of directors could remove their organization from racing, and could cancel the various sanctions and dissolve the body known as the Contest Board, but the AAA couldn't ban racing itself. Nor could the directors make other people stop racing.

Some members of the Contest Board re-organized into the United States Auto Club, USAC for short. The rules stayed the same and so did sanctions for the Indy, sprint cars, midgets and even stock sedans.

The effect was to make NASCAR look bigger and more permanent, and that didn't hurt at all.

For love *and* money

More visible, more quickly, was the publicity that came mostly from Chevrolet's belated involvement. For some reason of his own, Kiekhaefer wasn't keen on advertising his victories in Chrysler C-300s, in the sense that it was a make of car instead of a car reworked by his team. Chrysler didn't make much fuss when their cars won either. Ford probably would

Kiekhaefer's Mercury Outboard team came prepared. While the others drove to the track and carried what they could, Kiekhaefer was ready with stacks of tires and rows of fuel cans, as seen at Darlington in 1956. Daytona International Speedway

Daytona Beach can be chilly and wet in the winter, so the racers used to take over the Coquina Garage, in Ormond Beach, where they and the inspectors did their work. They were warm and dry, but some of them did object to having to reassemble engines in public. Daytona International Speedway

have, except that Ford only won two Grand Nationals, neither a major event, in 1955.

Chevrolet, however, had the full complement of star-making machinery already in place. Herb Thomas won the first short track race of the year, and Chevrolet's ad agency, Campbell-Ewald, was ready with win ads for the newspapers the next day. Fonty Flock got another win and the drums banged just as loudly. Never mind that those were the only Grand National races Chevy won that season; what mattered in the long run was that the general public was told about Chevrolet's racing. Because the ads were big and appeared everywhere, obviously stock car racing was important, so let's go watch one. Chevrolet sales perked up, Ford got its racing program rolling and everybody won something.

The rules also began to shift. Although export and racing kits had been banned, there were enough component failures during this period to convince NASCAR's tech committee to allow things like heavier spindles, wheels and other chassis components. And because Hudson had been allowed to use the hot engine with twin carbs on the grounds that the public could buy such parts, it followed that because the public was offered four-barrel carburetors, dual exhaust and even optional cams with solid lifters as part of the Regular Production Option in Chevrolet's catalog, the racers could use the parts, too.

Chevrolet had a running start. The Corvette was supposed to be a racer, so the more speed equipment there, the better. The Corvette was based on Chevy parts, in the engine and drivetrain at least, and it made perfect economic sense to offer the speed stuff from the Corvette when it would fit the Chevrolet sedan.

Chrysler, meanwhile, collected most of the 1955 marbles. There were forty-five Grand National races that year, and Chryslers won twenty-seven of them. Tim Flock won eighteen by himself. (When you hear the modern television talk about Dale Earnhardt heading for Richard Petty's modern record of thirteen wins in a season, they say modern because Flock's 1955 record is out of reach.) The Oldsmobiles had only modest help from above, but they won ten Grand National races against the two apiece for Ford and Chevrolet.

These results for Ford and Chevy may have inspired the next step, the for-sale stock car racing machine. The two big guys had stumbled into full-scale war. They would collectively spend $6 million in stock car racing in 1956 but, first, they knew there was an advantage in numbers and they knew their showroom stock product needed help.

What they came out with was the old export kit magnified beyond anything imagined only five years or so earlier.

Somebody's not too terribly new or even clean Ford is getting valve lift checked with a dial indicator. Hot cams were favored when easy cheats were the rule and weren't really outmoded until the rules said racers could use any cam they wanted. Daytona International Speedway

Road & Track (of all places) tested a production stock car in its issue for February 1956. The test was done to respond to readers who wanted to know if, and how, they could improve their domestic sedans. *Road & Track* borrowed a racer, a 1956 Ford Mainline series Tudor business sedan, the one intended for salesmen and the lightest and cheapest Ford in the catalog. The car was owned by Scotty Caine, one of the leading West Coast stock car drivers. Thus the test vehicle was as good as the private buyer could begin with.

Caine's car was ordered and delivered with the 205 hp, 292 ci, high-output engine, also known as the Interceptor model when sold to police departments. The full parts list and description was contained in the Ford Division's Service Manager's information bulletin issued August 26, 1955. The equipment is available through normal channels, the bulletin says, and offers maximum performance "where it is desired by owners, as in stock car racing." There follows a list of wheels, springs, shocks, rear axle gearing, even special

The news stories first called him Bob, but that was his dad's name, so as the writing on the roof spells out, the name is

Junior Johnson. He was also described then as "a lanky six-footer" which was partially accurate.

cylinder block and heads, and a light flywheel, camshaft—all the way through a distributor with dual points.

Neatly included is the statement "Because sufficient stocks of these parts will not be available for some time, it is requested that orders be limited to established stock car racing drivers. In submitting orders, it is recommended that the name of the driver be shown."

Put bluntly, if you don't need the money, the bank will be happy to lend you some. And while the parts were for sale, not everybody could get them, at least not right away. This may have been the first time a factory got into this position and it surely wasn't the last.

Road & Track said Caine took this race-based car and reinforced the upper and lower arms of the front suspension. Lincoln spindles, hubs and brakes replaced the Ford parts and added fifty pounds.

"The net result" said *Road & Track* testers, "is not very satisfactory. . .the low speed boulevard ride was fairly good, a little jiggly perhaps but no worse than a Mark II MG-TD. But at high speeds the rebound action of the shock absorbers was very sudden and quite severe, powerful enough to flip the passenger up and off the seat cushions over even moderate road undulations.

"Cornering power was another matter. There is almost no roll and up to the limit of rear wheel adhesion the car goes around like the proverbial train.

"The combination of so much horsepower and an almost unbelievable weight distribution (58.5 percent on the front wheels) makes this machine a real handful when the rear end breaks loose, which happens easily and suddenly.

"We felt few if any owners would like the combination here. However, if standard shock absorbers were used this car would be a vast improvement for persons requiring an American car with some sports car characteristics."

The test didn't list the make or model of tires on the car, which was too bad because the test does say that the performance figures were hampered by wheelspin, off the line and through the gears. Even so, the racing stock car did 0-60 mph in 8.8 seconds, covered the quarter mile from a standing start in 16.4 seconds and was doing maybe 85 mph when it passed the finish line. With short track gearing of 4.27:1 the Ford did 111 mph and the magazine estimated top speed with normal gearing would have been at least 120.

These figures may not impress today. Performance, like everything else, is relative. Tests from back then showed the original Olds 88 doing 0-60 in 13 seconds, while the 1955 Power-Pak Chevy hit 60 mph in 9.7 seconds and had a true top speed of 104. So the Ford was fast. Quoting *Road & Track*'s last paragraph, the test "shows that a NASCAR approved 'stock' Ford can be a truly high performance auto-

Junior Johnson was also a fearless and fast driver. This shot comes from Junior's Wild Ride, on the beach course in 1956, when he rolled the car over and over and over and then clambered out, none the worse—the driver that is; the Pontiac was distinctly secondhand. Daytona International Speedway

mobile. It also suggests that no one has yet defined the term 'stock car' satisfactorily."

One might counter that it depends on who expects to be satisfied. Ford and Chevrolet began their 1956 spree at Daytona Beach with a duel on the sand: stock and modified Thunderbirds won the standing mile runs, while stock and modified Corvettes took the flying miles.

Daytona offered a race for a new class, stock convertibles. That race on the beach-road course was won by Turner in a Ford, with Roberts and his Ford second. Tim Flock won the Grand National race in a Chrysler 300-B, followed by a Mercury, a Ford, an Olds and then the first Chevy. Flock won the modified race, in a 1939 Chevrolet coupe with Olds V-8 power.

The ante had been raised in all aspects. Flock's winning average for the stock class was 90.836 mph, against 89.41 mph for his modified. Under some conditions, then, the specially prepared stock car, as they used to say, was faster than the lightweight, souped-up hot rod modified; the alternate guess here is that the modifieds had hundreds more horses than they could put on the sand.

The stock cars—truly stock as in showroom stock—were getting more power as well. The Chev-

Another hard charger on his way up, Rex White, Grand National champion in 1960, shown here in 1956. Notice the bolt and block keeping the door permanently shut. Daytona International Speedway

rolet benefited from the Corvette programs and offered a dual four-barrel carburetor option. Ford didn't do this for the Thunderbird, but made 100 dual four-barrel rigs during 1956 which were accepted by NASCAR as optional equipment and thus legal. The Chrysler hemi had more power and displacement, and Chrysler offered Dodge and DeSoto versions.

Backwoods engineer versus factory engineer

A new kind of conflict arose. As Leo Levine's Ford racing history mentions, the Detroit executives thought they knew Southern men, but the racers weren't like the desperate, displaced farmers who came north looking for work during the Depression. The racers ranked everybody on their own scale—how fast can you go and what can you build? The executives and engineers had their own ranking, based on education and title. Each group naturally thought it was in charge and the other chaps were there merely to help.

Most of the conflict turned up in the Ford camp, where the corporation had first found racers who could do the work, then sent businesspeople to see that they did it and engineers to see how. There was less of this from Chevrolet, in part because that division already had race-ready men on the staff, and in part because the Chevrolet executives sent to help were less inclined to think they knew it all.

Chrysler Corporation had Kiekhaefer, who usually managed to get into feuds with everybody, regardless of education, social status or even brand identification: Kiekhaefer had a Ford to race on tracks where the Chryslers were too big. The Ford won but Kiekhaefer refused Ford permission to advertise the victory. Kiekhaefer was more interested in letting people know about Mercury outboards than about the benefits of a Ford or Chrysler. The Ford camp got even the only way they knew how—by not letting Kiekhaefer buy one of the dual four-barrel manifolds. Kiekhaefer went roaring into NASCAR headquarters to protest, but Ford won because they could prove the public was allowed to buy the manifold; it was only Kiekhaefer who wasn't.

It's tough, keeping sportsmanship in sports.

In Paul Van Valkenburgh's excellent history of Chevrolet racing, he mentions the clash between racer and engineer, and wonders if this was because the self-taught racers were in awe of those engineering degrees. (Van Valkenburgh is himself a degreed engineer.)

Smokey Yunick is a self-taught mechanic and builder who developed those racing Hudsons and then worked on Chevrolets when that make became competitive. Asked about the Detroit engineers, but not told about Van Valkenburgh's theory, Yunick said, "The cars they [the Detroit engineers] built for the public were fine. They were simple, they were reliable, they were affordable and fairly safe. They did a better job then than they're doing today.

"When it came to racing, you got no help from the factories. They thought guys like Clay Smith and myself were crazy. If they had a couple of days they could prove that what we did was impossible. We could take their engines and use the same parts and double their power.

"All they knew about gasoline was, it burned and it smelled. They didn't know anything about gas. They didn't know about aerodynamics. They knew next to nothing about vehicle dynamics.

"They were the dumbest bunch of bastards I ever met."

So much for the intimidation theory.

Yunick concedes that the factory help did make racing easier. There was more part selection, more money for parts, and some of the racers got contracts or salaries and no longer had to worry, literally, about where their next meal was coming from.

Before that, Yunick and his peers picked their car on the basis of potential, and on whether or not they could talk the dealer into letting them go racing in his inventory.

Yunick: "We didn't have the loyalties that make people say 'I'd never run anything but a Ford, or a Chevy.' I'd run anything I could get my hands on if I thought it would be successful, if I could beat you with it. A lot of times we'd change in the middle of the year.

"Sometimes we'd buy the car but in those days it wasn't too hard to get a dealer to spring for it. If he gave you a car, he gave you seventeen or eighteen hundred dollars, big deal. Then you'd paint his name on the car.

"If you had a problem, the other guys would pitch in to get the engine fixed. Then we raced, then we fought and then we'd pitch in to get home.

"Sometimes we'd have no way to get home. Somebody would say 'How you fixed for money?' and hand you fifty bucks. Maybe next week it would be the other way around.

"We were motivated by survival. If I lost the car I wouldn't have anything to race the next week. Back then most of us worked five days a week so we could race.

"Carl Kiekhaefer was the first guy who had a major impact on our partying. He was the first to come in with cash money. . . .

"Carl Kiekhaefer and I hated each other until after he retired. I used to keep his picture right on the toilet, in the garage."

Head to head, you could say, factory versus factory. This is the convertible race on the beach in 1957, with Larry Frank in the Chevrolet going the right direction and Marvin Panch spinning the Ford. There's been some contact, judg- *ing from the Chevy's right side, and the roll bar rules have been upped since the previous year. Daytona International Speedway*

"After we both quit I got to know him quite well and we became friends . . . my problem with Kiekhaefer was that he was smarter than the rest of us. He realized that one fast driver and motor could be beaten by mass production.

"He didn't overwhelm us with any one car, he came with a team of cars, all of them equally fast and capable of winning, so if he didn't get us with one, he'd have a second shot, a third shot and a fourth shot.

"Back then we did our own engines, paint, body-work, suspension, everything. We were dead tired toward the end of the race and he had manpower that wore us out . . . He also had big engines and the most power.

"If it hadn't been for tires, he would have destroyed us. But tires were his downfall. The tires that were good enough for us, with our lighter cars and smaller engines, were way under his league. If he pushed things, really used the power, shortly he'd be in the pits for tires.

"In 1955 I whipped his ass with one Chevy. He'd get ahead but pretty soon that car was in the pits. He probably used a hundred tires. We were about 4 mph slower than them, but I had a set of tires nobody else had. I never changed a tire the whole time, and by the time the race was over, there wasn't any race."

So Kiekhaefer started it. The photos for the 1956 Daytona Beach Grand National race show an impressive spectacle. The Mercury Outboard Team had three new Chrysler 300-B coupes, with the hemi V-8 enlarged to 354 ci and rated at 355 bhp with the optional 10:1 compression ratio.

(Question: If the Chrysler engine carried this 354/355 designation in 1956, how did Chevrolet manage to make all the fuss about its 283/283, one horsepower per cubic inch, in 1957? Nobody knows, but they did, and nobody seems to have noticed, back then.)

The B Team, or Kiekhaefer's insurance, was a 1955 Chrysler C-300, presumably the 1955 winner; a 1956 Dodge D-500, a smaller version of the hemi V-8 in a smaller body; and a 1955 D-500, again presumably a first-string car to run interference. Drivers were Tim Flock, Frank Mundy and Charles Scott in the new big cars, Buck Baker, Fonty Flock and Speedy Thompson in the other cars.

(Another note: Charles Scott substituted in this race for Norm Nelson, a Midwestern driver. Scott, from Forest Park, Georgia, was black. Wendell Scott, made famous by the movie, *Fast As White Lightning*, was no relation but was the best-known and only full-time black NASCAR driver, then or now. The his-

The factories withdrew in 1957, under pressure from their public relations departments and their critics. Some of the teams, Holman and Moody for instance, had enough money to keep on running an effective operation. Daytona International Speedway

torical quirk here is that Wendell Scott wasn't the only black man who drove in NASCAR, and there wasn't any mention of this in the program or the results of that 1956 race. Charles Scott finished nineteenth in the Daytona Beach Grand National, and according to the NASCAR records that was the only Grand National race he ever drove. His ride may have been a tryout. In any event, there doesn't seem to have been a racial angle.)

When Kiekhaefer escalated stock car racing, he awakened two sleeping giants, as the Japanese admiral said on the way home from Pearl Harbor. Ford and Chevrolet entered the competition with a vengeance.

Ford had a direct outside link, with an engineering company headed by former Indy winner Peter De Paolo, with Bill Stroppe on the West Coast, and John Holman and Ralph Moody coming into the system and starting their operation at Charlotte, North Carolina.

Like Gilbert and Sullivan, Holman and Moody were not close, personal friends. Instead, they were complementary. Holman was a Californian, a former driver and a great man for organizing and getting things done. Moody, the classic taciturn New Englander, was then still an active driver—he was eighth in the national standings in 1956—but was even better as a builder and theoretician. They had Ford engineers and executives to help them, which is probably why it took so long to get going.

As mentioned, Chevrolet had Herb Thomas and Smokey Yunick. They also had a factory-racetrack liaison named Vince Piggins, who came from Hudson and thus knew how to work with racers and how to go

racing. It might also have been that he didn't see racing as a career move, unlike some of the Ford people. All in all, Piggins was a help, to the factory and to anybody who raced a Chevy, for the next twenty years.

Fair play requires admission here that not all the human frailty was on the side of the engineers and managers. Hollywood may have enhanced and improved on some of the things that went on, but none of the adventures or extremes of behavior seen in the movies and on television were pure fiction.

Darel Dieringer, who came from the Midwest and thus knew how the rest of the world worked, says yes, in those days "if you went to bed for three days before a race, you weren't considered a real race driver."

Leaders of that pack were Curtis Turner and Joe Weatherly, who were good pals (drinking buddies is the best term) off track and who had fun whacking into each other on track.

Turner, the timber cruiser turned pilot, was a natural talent at the wheel, but his real hope was to be as good in business, which he wasn't at all. Weatherly was a former motorcycle racer, another breed about which it's hard to imagine anything more spectacular than the truth.

There are literally too many stories to tell here, but one time Turner was invited to take part in a sports car event, and he was doing fine until they flagged him into the pits for a lecture.

In those days the overtaken driver was supposed to gesture at the overtaker, as in "Pass me on this

Nor did the excitement abate. This is the north turn at Daytona Beach, 1958, with two Fords, a Dodge, a Chevy and a Mercury in close quarters. Well, the Mercury has run *into trouble. And judging from the running spectators, more is about to happen. Daytona International Speedway*

The speeds and cars were outpacing the tracks. This isn't as bad as it looks, however. What seems to be a house at Bowman-Gray stadium, a dirt fairgrounds track, was actually the office, so when the modified here rolled up to the front door, nobody was home. Daytona International Speedway

side." Turner had been passing people left and right, and hadn't waited until they'd waved him past.

He had trouble believing this when it was explained, but he nodded, went back on the track and began bunting the other drivers into the weeds.

Back into the pits for another conference. Turner explained that of course it had been on purpose. Catching them was supposed to make them wave with one hand, so "I figured if I popped those fellows a good one, they'd raise *both* hands."

And then there was the day Turner pushed Fireball Roberts off the track while the two were dueling for the lead. After the finish Turner approached the announcer and said he'd give Roberts the money and the points, that he hadn't done the dirty trick merely for fortune or titles. Rather, "I just wanted to get there first."

He added that if it had been his father out there, he'd have done the same thing. And nobody in the pits or the stands doubted it.

Weatherly liked jokes. There was the time he noticed a row of old telephone poles sunk into the ground next to the hotel, to keep people from driving onto the beach. He painted the poles black. Then he waited until dusk and challenged Turner to a race, in reverse gear, from the parking lot to the beach.

And there was a wooden box Weatherly built, containing a fox tail on a string, which he could work so the tail darted back and forth while he, Weatherly that is, explained that the box held a deadly mongoose, whose bite would be fatal.

Just as he said that, Presto! the lid flew up and the tail popped out.

The other racers thought it was funny as hell when Joe did that to kids in gas stations.

They didn't laugh quite so hard when he did it to a group of Ford executives' wives.

One might reflect here that maybe Kiekhaefer was right. Stock car racing did contain a lot of children in large disguises.

Also, it explains in part why Turner, by all accounts the best driver of his day, never won the national title. He and Weatherly led many more races than they won, and they were assigned to the convertible class while Roberts, Moody and Marvin Panch, who were professional all the time, drove the Grand National races.

Kiekhaefer's team won the national title in 1956, with Ford close behind and gaining, and Chevrolet not doing well. There was a lot of acrimony late in the season as Kiekhaefer found that others could play his game, doubled or tripled. There were protests and counter-protests and the foolishness of the unobtainable intake manifold, and at the end of the year Kiekhaefer retired. Yunick says it was simply because Kiekhaefer realized he couldn't beat the factories at his/their game.

"Defensive cheating"

Continuing the escalation, Chevrolet went into the for-sale stock car business about as thoroughly as it was practical to go.

Early in 1957 Chevrolet Motor Division issued its Stock Car Competition Guide, which was just what it sounds like. Quoting from the first page, "This guide has been prepared for Chevrolet dealers, to assist individuals who plan to participate in this challenging American sport. It is advisory only, with material obtained from some of the top professional racing experts, performance engineers and independent mechanics whose skill and dedicated effort have made Chevrolet a leader in open competition. The Competition Guide is not intended to encourage, but rather to inform the newcomer of techniques that promote greater safety and higher entertainment value for all who enjoy stock car competition in the highest traditions of the sport."

That's a bit of a weasel toward the end, but anyway, the guide begins by suggesting that the "One-Fifty" utility sedan, a two-door sedan sold minus rear seat, most often seen as a fleet car for salesmen, was the lightest and cheapest model in the line-up and therefore the best place to begin. In certain events, though, the "Two-Ten" sport coupe was better streamlined, which could more than make up for the added weight if the car was to be raced on long tracks. And naturally you'd need a Bel Air convertible for convertible class events.

The guide then explains Regular Production Options, or RPOs, such as the brand new fuel injection for the 283 V-8, or RPO 410, the V-8 with a single four-barrel; the dual fours were listed as RPO 411. There were the wide- and close-ratio three-speed transmissions—the four-speed was still only listed for Corvettes—and special engine mounts, radiator, electric windshield wiper, fan drive with deeper pulleys, special axles and gears, wheels, steering linkage, Cerametallic brake linings. Suffice it to say here that

Driver turned builder Paul Goldsmith was a star who never became national champion. He had another distinction in that he was the only racer to win at Daytona Beach *on two wheels (1953) and four wheels (the last beach race, in 1958).* Daytona International Speedway

the guide contained a complete list of special parts, with parts numbers and with reasons for the racer and his helpful dealer to use them.

After that came the preparation section, with tips on careful engine measuring, balancing and assembly. The guide suggests that the body be removed from the frame, and tells the builder where and how to reinforce the suspension. There were pictures of bracing for the roll bar, and of the U-bolts used to secure the roll bar to the frame.

That calls for an interruption. At that time, the domestic passenger car was made the old-fashioned way, with a chassis-frame, usually two longitudinal rails, and front, center and rear cross-members. The steel body shell was dropped atop the frame and bolted down, with rubber-like mounting biscuits between body and frame to isolate the body, and thus the occupants, from road shock and noise.

A racing car built to the recommendations in the Chevrolet guide, or along the lines of the Ford tested by *Road & Track*, would have been a good local contender.

It would have been hopeless, barring some incredible genius driver, in a Grand National.

Banjo Matthews, the Florida circle track racer who came to North Carolina because he liked the people and the pace of life, was building and driving in the mid-fifties. He was making a good living with stocks and modifieds, and he says that even back then the smart guys were taking off the bodies and removing the biscuits—the mounting blocks, in his words—then putting body and frame back together. They braced each other, and the suspension was much the better for it. And where the guide shows the roll bar bolted to the frame through the floor, to protect the driver, the better builders were welding the whole thing together, again to make the car one solid unit.

This modification will be carried much further, as we'll see, but it was already underway in 1957. It's just as true that the car built to these rules and suggestions was, just as it was supposed to be, a production passenger car equipped and modified for racing.

Meanwhile Ford and Chevy had spent all that money and stock car racing as a business had escalated. Yunick says this was when racing got serious and people began to bend and break the rules for profit as well as fun. When it was a bunch of tough guys racing for ego and entertainment, he says, people cheated mostly to keep up: "If some guy started running a twenty-eight-gallon tank and you felt they weren't going to stop him, then you had to run a twenty-eight-gallon tank too. Call it defensive cheating.

"The only sacred thing was, you didn't violate the cubic inch rules. Any dumb SOB can stick fifty more cubic inches in an engine; I felt like if a guy cheated on engine size, that was an insult."

But when people were making big money, when racing was a daytime job to pay the rent and put shoes on the kids, and when the factories expected the team to win because the ad for Monday's paper was already

The convertible class began to fade when the teams began using the lighter sedan frame and body with the top cut off, and to bolt on hard tops later, for the sedan class. As the picture shows, making a bolt-on hard top wasn't tough.

How Billy Myers got his chop-top Merc into the rough wasn't explained. Nice to have friends, though. Daytona International Speedway

at the printing plant, it was a lot more serious. People began thinking more about advantages not in the book.

Bill France and company saw some of this coming. They knew how much money had been spent on the factory efforts. They liked that part, but they didn't want it to get out of hand.

For 1957 the rules were adjusted. In all seriousness, *Motor Trend*'s predictions for the season began with the headline "New NASCAR Regulations Help the Little Guy."

Well, they tried. As of January 1, 1957, all eligible late model Grand National race machines were supposed to have been announced and cataloged. The equipment and power ratings were listed. At least 100 of each unit had to be in dealer hands, and at least 1,500 were to have been scheduled for production. To be sure, the little guys, whoever they were, had a better shot, since there was to be a separate class for short track, with smaller engines and a limit of one four-barrel carburetor.

In part to counter these limits, Ford was mounting a major effort in USAC and other circuits, with Indy cars as well as stock cars. Ford had Stroppe on the West Coast, Holman and Moody in the South and Chuck Daigh in Milwaukee.

Lee Petty had switched from Mopar to the Oldsmobile team; Pontiac and Buick had builders as well. The options allowed the reappearance of the export kit or factory kit, albeit the term wasn't used. In fact the hot cams, triple two-barrel carburetors and such really were sold to the public, for use on public roads and at the drag strip, so it wasn't mere subterfuge.

The Chevrolet camp was just as deeply involved, in a different way. They were thinking Corvette, sports car and road racing, and were building real no-pretense road racing cars. This was the inspiration for fuel injection and the four-speed gearbox; the stock car and drag race camps inherited the parts.

At Daytona Beach in 1957 the feud resumed. The Grand National beach-road race went to Cotton Owens with a Pontiac. Matthews says the Pontiac engine was better than the Chevrolet in that they were the same except the Pontiac was bigger. Actually, Paul Goldsmith led most of the race in a Yunick-prepped Chevy but it blew just before the finish. Johnny Beauchamp was second in a Chevrolet, with Fonty Flock and a Mercury in third.

Rivals and friends. This is Ralph Earnhardt in the trunk, Richard Petty in the foreground, Ned Jarrett standing at right and a very young Bobby Isaac in the background.

Presumably Earnhardt has hurt his leg and needs the crutches. Daytona International Speedway

Curtis Turner, nicknamed Pops, and Joe Weatherly were close pals and fierce competitors on the track. They drove for Holman and Moody, who were careful to let people know whose antics they were watching. (One guesses the car says Pop, not Pops, because it's neater and fits the space.) Daytona International Speedway

This was an interesting speed week. At one extreme Yunick won a prize for fastest six, a Chevy clocked at 102.158 mph. (On another occasion he won a prize for fastest truck, but that's not important here.) The Chrysler people showed up with an experimental fuel-injected hemi rated at 405 bhp. Wally Parks of *Hot Rod* magazine drove a Plymouth equipped with this engine to a win in the special sedan class, 159.893 mph.

Speed week lasted two weeks, with the beach-road races, the clocked runs and the road races at the New Smyrna Airport, but there was rain and the wind blew the wrong way and activities were shifted around. There was more speed than people dreamed of, plus, as *Road & Track* said "The condition of the beach is too unpredictable to plan two full weeks of activities."

Chevrolet's fuel injection may have been meant for the Corvette and racing against imported sports cars, but it bolted right onto the Chevrolet engine and was adapted for stock car racing. That gave Chevy instant legs on the Ford. The Ford camp, with a massive investment and many careers riding on the outcome, went shopping and found an answer. They came up with a supercharger kit to mount on the Ford V-8, now known as the Thunderbird V-8, with 312 ci and an astonishing power rating of 300 bhp, which the engine had. At least.

Other factories entered the feud as well. Picking just one example, the DeSoto had an optional 345 ci hemi V-8 rated at 345 bhp, same as the Chevrolet—one bhp per cubic inch. A test of a production version gave 0-60 mph in 8.3 seconds, the sort of time you could only get with a racing stock car two years earlier.

And the ads? Ford and Chevrolet both were docked series points during the year for misleading advertising based on NASCAR wins, while the ad copy shouted about the "White Hot" 283 Corvette, and "Supercharged . . . and looks it!" Ford. There was a Plymouth ad with that car's driver relishing a trophy. In the background, shabby and neglected, sits a poorly disguised 1957 Ford. The ad copy urges "Get your kicks . . . tremendous power . . . direct fuel flow . . ." which sort of sounds as if they wouldn't mind if you thought direct fuel flow was some form of fuel injection. (The ad doesn't explain it but you could describe fuel being pumped into a carburetor and drawn out by vacuum as direct fuel flow, eh?)

The first factory ban

There were some social and political drawbacks to this emphasis on factory participation. The majors were spending money on racing that wasn't being returned in sales; if everybody wins, and they all did, then nobody proves a point, while if they don't win, they are disgraced.

So it came to pass that the Automobile Manufacturers Association agreed that they'd all get out of racing. Period.

Just how this came to pass is open to debate. Levine, in his Ford book, says the idea came from General Motors, and adds that Chevrolet was worried about Ford's improvements, which may have been so.

Going to the beach

For those who have a taste for history and for pilgrimage, here's a surprise and a secret: There are several race courses on Daytona's beach, and you can still find traces of the last one, if you know where and how to look.

Most of the city of Daytona Beach is on the Florida mainland. East of that is the St. John's River (which really isn't a river in the normal sense), then there's a long, thin island, then the beach itself and the Atlantic Ocean.

The very first races and speed trials were held on the beach at Ormond Beach, just north of Daytona's beach, in front of the Ormond Hotel (now gone, sorry to say). Ormond Beach got built up so the racers moved south, to Daytona Beach, for the measured mile. That was too crowded by 1936, the first beach-road race, so when they went to lay out that course they began at Wilbur Avenue, an obscure cross street now, went south to the nearest usable ramp to the beach, made the U-turn and came back. The first south turn was about 1.5 miles from the start and the actual course was 3.2 miles, down, turn, back and turn.

A major factor in the success of the races under France's control was . . . control. They put up fences and kept people in line—the ticket line.

After World War II the central beach area had become too crowded for racing. France arranged for a new course, at the south end of the island.

Accounts of details differ. The newspapers said the distance, down and back, was 4.1 miles for the motorcycle races in 1948, 4.3 miles for the cars in 1949, four miles even in 1952 and that the fifty laps of the 1958 race covered 198.4 miles, which works out to 3.968 miles per lap.

But those are mere facts and we are here for the romance. The last car race was held on the beach in 1958, the last motorcycle race was in 1960 and a lot has happened to the area since. That doesn't matter, either, as we can still visit and even drive the course, sort of.

Head down A1A, south from the commercial and residential sections of Daytona Beach. When the fast food and condos are behind, look to the left until you come to a tavern, closed now but still with the sign, Old Timers. The beach ramp next to the old bar used to be the north turn. South of the turn, between the dunes and the highway, are traces of the older, narrower road that was used by the racers.

Continue south on the present highway for approximately two miles. When the road swings right at Ponce's Inlet, we go left, onto another beach access ramp. The firm sections in the middle of the ramp are marl and yes, this is the old south turn.

Plow through the soft sand and when the beach firms, left again. If you can resist the urge to gas it just a bit and hang the tail out (Fireball Roberts Returns!) you probably shouldn't have bothered to come.

Cruise north on the beach, eyes peeled for the old bar, power left when you get to that ramp and you've driven the old course.

Not quite as it was in February of 1958, but worth the trouble just to know you've been where the heroes were.

Van Valkenburgh's Chevrolet history points out that the resolution to ban performance claims in ads, and to prohibit factories from having a direct involvement in competition, was passed unanimously and was voted on by Studebaker-Packard, White, Kaiser and Diamond T: what did they have to lose? he asked.

It is most likely that the ban was a natural development. Chevrolet's fuel injection was a big step. Ford's supercharging kit was even bigger, and was further from what the average buyer needed. NASCAR banned fuel injection and supercharging as soon as it became obvious that such devices would only make racing more expensive and would put the two biggest firms too far ahead of everybody else.

Nor were there screams of outrage. *Car Life* magazine commented in November 1957, months after the ban was announced, that "Horsepower has had it in Detroit," and that "the public's demand for power is just about satisfied."

Oh my, was this ever wrong! But nobody knew that, nor could they have predicted then what was to come.

What came first was what probably inspired the direction NASCAR racing would take in the future: the factories were out of racing and the top teams could once again compete with each other, head to head.

Both big guys got out of racing in the same way, by giving away the store. Ford's eastern branch of Holman and Moody became an outside firm, with a supply of racing parts to keep them in business. Rex White, Buck Baker and others kept their cars and equipment, with Chevrolet's permission. Neither company, nor the AMA board—never mind France and NASCAR—wanted racing to stop. They simply wanted to spend less money on it, and to appear less willing to indulge the public's taste for speed and power.

Baker was Grand National champion for 1957, with ten wins, all for Chevrolet. More indicative here was that during the season there were fifty-three Grand National races, twenty-one prior to the ban, thirty-two afterward. Fords won fifteen of the twenty-one pre-ban events, to five for Chevy, while post-ban the tally was twelve to Ford, fourteen to Chevrolet.

Hmmm. OK, we can be fair here and remember that racing luck, driver skill and circumstance all play a part. But it was also true that the Chevrolet V-8, in normal performance trim, one four-barrel, dual exhaust and a semi-hot camshaft, was quicker than the stock Ford in the same trim. The lightweight Mouse Motor with its high-revving valvetrain was the better engine, and it showed.

There was a balance with the factories gone. Performance parts could still be ordered for Ford products, GM products or even for Chrysler products. NASCAR's rules required a minimum of 1,500 examples, but that wasn't too much hardship, not as long as the factories were in the police business or had export kits again, as they did.

As the first factory era wound down, to the distress of those who wanted the factories involved, a sporting equality arose. The fair competition that had been pitched as the ideal when stock car racing began was again possible.

The 1958 season started with a thriller, closing out another era. This was the last race on the actual Daytona Beach.

First, a step backward.

Smokey Yunick had become disillusioned with Chevrolet. He says they were playing favorites toward the end and he wanted to help everybody running the bow tie brand, so he went with Ford briefly, then began building Pontiacs when the ban put Ford out of official business.

Yunick's Chevrolet with Paul Goldsmith at the wheel nearly won on the beach in 1957, but blew up. In 1958, Goldsmith and the Yunick Pontiac were nearly one mile ahead of Curtis Turner and Ford when the tide narrowed the beach section of the course. Goldsmith got into the salt spray, couldn't see and missed the north turn. Half a mile up the beach he realized what he'd done, so he pulled one of those J-turns that both Turner and Fireball Roberts were supposed to have invented and stormed back, hitting the lip of the turn just as Turner arrived. He put the chop on Turner and won by a car length.

Skipping around a bit here, the 1954 Oldsmobile was big and outsold the 1954 Plymouth for third place on the chart. Ford noticed, built the 1957 Ford as big as the 1954 Olds and outsold Chevrolet for the first time in generations. GM noticed, built the 1958 Chevy as big as the 1957 Ford and took the sales lead back. Note here for fun that the 1957 Chevrolet, now an all-time classic, was in second place when new: people are odd.

More to our point here, as production cars got larger, so did engines. But not at first. The original ohv V-8s followed the rest of the system; the Chrysler and Cadillac V-8s were larger inside and out than the V-8 Fords, Chevrolets and so on. And there was just one V-8 per brand, with the option being either the V-8 or the six.

As the small cars—Fords, Plymouths and Chevrolets—got larger, they had an initial handicap; the Mercury, Dodge and Oldsmobile V-8s were bigger to begin with.

And there was individual initiative. Lee Petty, the trucker, farmer and family man who'd wrecked the Buick he borrowed for that first stock car race, had always liked Plymouth. But he switched up, to Dodge, when Mopar gave the middleweight a V-8. He had factory help as well. Richard Petty has written about when he and his dad picked up a new Dodge body and converted it to a racing car while the horrified Dodge employees looked on.

Carl Kiekhaefer's effort left no room for another racing team at Mopar, so Petty became the Oldsmobile team, with backing, parts, advice and so on, from that division. Olds had a good engine, nearly as good as the little Chevy V-8, and a sound frame and body design. Petty knew how to build cars and had won the national title in 1954 with a Chrysler, so the Oldsmobile wasn't a struggle. (Even the random choices worked well: Richard Petty says his dad needed a racing number, glanced at the family car's license plate, which had 42, and decided that would be as good as any. When Richard followed Lee into the family business he picked the next number, 43, which would become the best known, most-winning racing number in history.)

At any rate, during the 1958 season Chevrolet got twenty-three Grand National wins, Ford got sixteen, Olds seven and Pontiac three. But the two former big team outfits had lots of drivers, and Lee Petty was always in the running and out of the way when other guys wrecked, so he was national champion again in 1958.

There were forty-nine Grand Nationals that year and, yes, on the face of that record Ford and Chevy were still very much in control of the races. But the equipment could be bought, building a winning car cost less and the important changes to come, would come on the track.

Better make that *in* the track.

Chapter 5

Speedway spectacular: 1959-1961

Not least among Bill France's talents has been his ability to make other people want what he wants. And close behind that virtue has been his ability to sense what other people will want and do, before they do it for themselves.

So it happened that in 1953, when NASCAR was just getting into business as a business and when most people in Daytona Beach probably were deciding that racing on the beach was here to stay—don't forget, the community leaders had written racing off and laid

the business on France—Bill France knew the beach was just about done. There were too many people in the way and too much progress had taken place.

So in 1953 the club newsletter and the local paper began mentioning the chances for somebody or some body to develop the next step, a real racing facility, to replace the old beach-road course.

Planning began early, with creation by the Florida Legislature of the Daytona Beach Racing and Recreational Facilities District. Then France formed a

Daytona International Speedway, 1959. Smack in the middle of this under-construction photo is the speedway itself, 2.5 miles around. It's called a tri-oval because the front straight, center left, has a gentle bend in the middle, so the shape is a flat, semi-triangle. The dark rectangle in the middle is the pit from where they got the dirt for the bankings. Then they filled the pit with water and proclaimed it a
lake. The white specks in the distance are buildings on the beach front, and between them and the track is the Daytona Beach airport. The small oval is a dog track and has nothing to do with the speedway. In the foreground is the major highway right at the track's front door, while at upper left is the other highway, direct from downtown.
Daytona International Speedway

One secret of the speedway's success is shown here, from the stands between the fourth turn and the finish line. The rolling thunder show comes at the crowd on a tri-oval, while an Indy-style square oval has the pack filing past. The garage area, greatly improved since this 1959 photo was taken, is at upper right. Daytona International Speedway

corporation to run the new track. Next came the state-backed Speedway Authority, all needed to enable somebody to buy land and build the new track.

The land turned out to be 377 acres then owned by the airport authority and adjacent to the Daytona Beach Airport, which at the time was way out in the sticks.

Then came an era of negotiation and maneuvers, while the concerned parties worked out who would pay for what, who'd pay rent and how the taxes would be levied. What this looks like now, and may have inspired, is the way major league football teams now arrange for their stadiums and franchises to be paid for and parceled out.

But that's a minor point. As it worked out, France and family took in some stockholders from the area, and Pure Oil Company (now Union Oil) held a share. The Frances and backers built the track on leased land, with delicate balances being struck as to who paid what.

More important, indeed vital here, was the design of the track. It was to be 2.5 miles around, the same distance as the Indianapolis oval. Beyond that, Daytona was different and improved.

The design was done in part by France himself, and in part by Charles Moneypenny, who went on to become the best known racetrack designer in the business, although back then there wasn't such a business.

Perhaps because he remembered the thrills of his youth, France made sure the four major turns were steeply banked, thirty-one degrees, as steep as the contractors could pave. Next, while Indy and most of the former horse tracks were ovals, Daytona was a variation on that shape, called a tri-oval. From the air it seems to have three sides, sort of a shallow triangle. The back straight is straight. The second and third turns are right angles, albeit wide and banked. But the fourth turn is less than a right angle and the track aims at the front grandstands. Then there's a bend in the middle of the gently banked front straight, so the first turn is wider than a right angle. The shortest distance between turns four and one, the straight line, is pit road.

What all this means is, first, the banking lets the cars go faster than they otherwise could. Obviously, being held on the pavement by gravity lets the driver go around corners faster. And it frees the engine's power to make the car go faster, instead of fighting the wind that in turn keeps the car on the road.

(Proof here will come years later, when *Road & Track* learns that a big, supposedly clumsy NASCAR sedan has a higher top speed than a smaller, lower, slicker, more powerful turbocharged Porsche 962. The Porsche road racer uses aerodynamics to keep on the ground and it uses its power to shove the air. Gravity keeps the NASCAR sedan on the ground, so it goes faster with less peak horsepower.)

Second, the shape of the track puts the action into view. When the snarling, thundering pack of jostling cars comes around the last turn and heads for the start-finish line, they are coming *right at* the grandstands. In the square oval, they merely file past the stands.

This sounds simplistic, but years later some financial wizards who didn't know anything about racing except that they meant to make it the sport of the seventies, built a copy of the Indy oval in Ontario, California. Flat turns, square oval. There were other factors, sure, but Ontario was a dull place to watch races, there was no tradition and the track went broke.

The third secret was that Daytona International Speedway was planned for huge crowds: 100,000 people and 40,000 cars. The track had literally

The other secret to the speedway's success was the steep bankings, as steep as the equipment could manage. Even then, as the crane shows, they were going beyond what had *been done before. But the banked turns let the cars use their power to go faster because gravity held them on the track.* Daytona International Speedway

The rivals

Philosopher Eric Hoffer was the first to point out that the winners of a war are much more willing to adopt the habits of the people they've just whipped than the losers are to take on the habits of the winners.

You'd think Hoffer had been writing about NASCAR versus AAA/USAC.

Before Bill France called NASCAR's first meeting, all he wanted was to promote races. He went to AAA, then the national body that controlled virtually all professional car racing in the United States, and asked for a sanction.

They turned him down. They scoffed at the very notion of stock car racing. They predicted the junk car races, as they said in those days, would be a miserable flop.

They were wrong, France was right, and the AAA old guard never forgot or forgave.

Instead AAA reversed course and began sanctioning its own stock car races, mostly in the Midwest. The AAA and NASCAR both were quick to suspend or fine any driver trying to belong to one club and race in the other. And France used to tell about the day he'd gone to Indianapolis and was in the track's high-roller area, as a guest of an AAA member, and simply at the race to enjoy the race. France began, as we all do, as a fan and he never missed a chance to see the races. But somebody learned he was there and in paranoid fashion decided he had to be up to something and had France escorted out.

He told the story with a grin, but as another philosopher said, there are no good sports, there are only good actors.

The height of this foolishness came with the opening of Daytona International Speedway.

This was a fabulous track. It promised speed beyond anything in the United States, matched perhaps by the banked track at Monza, Italy, but probably not even there. (As it happened Daytona quickly eclipsed Monza.)

France meanwhile didn't bear a grudge. He was capable of that, as are we all, but not when good manners meant good business.

For the inaugural orgy of speed at Daytona, France scheduled the 500 mile race for stock cars, a 100 mile race for Indy cars, a 100 mile race for Formula Libre sports cars and a 1000 kilometer marathon for sports cars meeting international rules.

First, there seemed to be agreement. Then USAC fired and re-hired some of its top people. Then the new man on top announced that the whole deal was in trouble, that the two clubs would have totally separate events and that the USAC drivers couldn't even practice at the speedway during NASCAR time; France (no fool he) had hometown heroes Marshall Teague and Chapman Root lined up to run for the record with their streamlined Indy car. The talk was of speeds of 170 mph, reasonable in that the qualifying speed record for Monza was 177.23.

Perhaps the prospect of Indianapolis losing the national record to Daytona was the key, as USAC reversed itself and banned any participation by their drivers on NASCAR time.

Then they switched again and let their guys run during speed week, provided that any and all times would be unofficial and wouldn't go into the books. (One can imagine France's glee on that one, as he knew how concerned the newspapers would be to distinguish between an honest 170 mph run and an honest 170 mph run that was accepted by some group out west—that is, no worry.)

In the event, Teague was killed. Fireball Roberts qualified for the stock car race at a higher speed than the Indy cars turned back home. Then during the April USAC event two drivers were killed.

For 1960, France posted a $10,000 prize for the first car to top 180 at the speedway. USAC replied with a firm ban, this time citing their good safety record at those speeds at Monza, and their belief that their cars as then raced, and the Daytona track as it then was, were not a safe combination. This time, the ban stuck.

As we all know now, the speeds will go up as the designers and tuners and drivers learn.

The obvious solution to the NASCAR/USAC problem arrived in 1961. Fittingly, it was a political answer for a political struggle.

There were cool heads in both groups. And there were new forms of racing. For instance, drag racing and sports cars, and the people in charge of those clubs had rights and concerns as well. At the same time the arrogance of the old AAA contest board and their dislike of everybody else in the business, was no longer a factor.

So in May of 1961 NASCAR, USAC, SCCA and friends formed the Automobile Competition Committee for the United States. The name was shortened into ACCUS, pronounced Ak-Us as U-Sack and Nas-car have become adapted and the SCCA never has.

ACCUS was simply a committee, a clearing house. It gave the United States a branch of the Federation Internationale de l'Automobile, so American drivers could race in other countries and foreign drivers could come to the United States. And it let the various US clubs agree to license interchange.

Lots of this was paperwork, in that not many sports car chaps ventured into stock car racing or vice versa. But it did let Danny Ongais move from the drags into Indy cars, and got Sam Posey into a NASCAR sedan. More useful for the fan, Dan Gurney, Mario Andretti and A. J. Foyt all had their days in racing sedans and happened to be very good at them. (Oddly, this didn't go the other way. Most sedan pilots have little interest in driving with wheels out in the open and not nearly the protection in case of a crash. And when they do try it—witness Cale Yarborough—they don't stand out. Just as dirt guys can move to pavement better than pavement guys take to the dirt, so do drivers of lightweights move into the big machines better than the big-car men adapt to the little 'uns.)

And the best and most useful over the long run, the part that let the rest happen, was agreement over the rules. In general, in the long run, NASCAR moved out of all racing except stocks in various forms, while USAC made its stock car rules just like NASCAR's and the two came to occupy the same level in different parts of the country.

If it took fifteen years for the rivals to do the obvious, at least they did it.

hundreds of acres for parking and by no coincidence at all, highways were built near the track's gates. A double tunnel led from the infield to the front gate. The highway and the speedway are even now the envy of Europeans who visit.

Talk started in 1953, the formal arrangements began the next year, but what with the juggling and arranging, the first race wasn't held until February 1959.

The beginnings were tragic.

A political battle raged. AAA had quit racing, USAC had been formed from the old AAA Contest Board, and USAC and NASCAR were rivals. USAC officials liked the idea of the new speedway. They didn't like the idea of a new (and successful) organization. This became so personal it was silly. USAC didn't want its drivers on a NASCAR-controlled track, NASCAR in turn had already fined its members who ran USAC races.

NASCAR had created a division for Indy-style cars and USAC had a stock division so the two *were* rivals. But negotiation prevailed and the two clubs came to an agreement that would allow all drivers to practice on the track, and would permit a USAC race on the track—a safe time after the inaugural NASCAR race.

France was keen to attract attention and stars to the speedway, into which he'd put all his money plus loans. One of the ways he hoped to get the public's attention was posting a $10,000 prize for the first man to lap the track at 160 mph.

The beneficiary, if that's the right word, of this battle seemed to be Marshall Teague, the Hudson driver, pioneer stock car tuner and Daytona Beach hometown boy. Teague had become an Indy driver and USAC member. His car owner was Chapman Root, a classic well-to-do sportsman. They had a streamlined single-seater, the *Sumar Special*. It had an oversized engine and the team reckoned to set the record on the banked track and collect the money.

Teague was doing an estimated 160 mph when the car went into a slide going into the west (second) turn. The car flipped into the air and Teague, still belted into his seat, was thrown out and killed. The exact cause can still be debated, although with hindsight it's likely that the streamlining, done before anybody really knew how it worked, didn't work.

Just to show how racing does work, on the very next day Fireball Roberts went out in a modified

So right after the race Beauchamp got to hold the trophy and kiss the girls. Then NASCAR's officials scooped up all the photos, and three days later . . .

The birth of a tradition. The number 73 car is a Thunderbird driven by Johnny Beauchamp. He's gaining on the number 42 car, an Olds driven by Lee Petty. They are both passing Joe Weatherly, who is a lap down. Petty and Beauchamp are on the last lap of the first Daytona 500. Problem is, the three cars will come virtually even just as they cross the finish line. They reversed this order when they were on the other side of the line. Daytona International Speedway

. . . Bill France presented Lee Petty, grinning as any of us would, with the official trophy, the money and the victory. A stop-action camera has been on duty ever since. Daytona International Speedway

69

sedan, complete with supercharger and 430 bhp, and set the track's first record, at 149.70 mph.

The premier Daytona 500

The first major race, the inaugural Daytona 500, was just as good.

Just like at NASCAR's first 500 mile race, the first strictly stock race and even the first beach-road strictly stock race, nobody knew what to expect. The difference here was that most of the teams knew how to build racing cars, and they all knew what the rules were and how they would be enforced.

Illustrating how the banking helped speed, Cotton Owens took the pole for Pontiac, at 143.198 mph. The previous qualifying record was 140.570, one-way down the beach and also in a Pontiac, so the new track was faster on average than the beach was on the straight.

In the inaugural race in 1959, there were countless lead changes until it came down to Lee Petty in an Olds 88 and Johnny Beauchamp in a Ford Thunderbird. They swapped back and forth until the very last lap, when they hit the finish line side by side.

Nobody had expected quite that close a finish. A photographer was present, so they had to get the film and have it developed. The shot wasn't quite straight on and was complicated by Little Joe Weatherly, one

lap down and lined up dead abreast with the other two at the line, so not until three days later did France announce that Lee Petty was the winner.

Even with the delay, the crowd had been on its feet most of the race, the stands had been full and everybody went home with their money's worth.

The best evidence of their satisfaction was that the next race, the Firecracker 250 on (when else?) July 4, drew another sell-out crowd. This time the winner was Fireball Roberts, the hometown boy who never won the biggest race, on the beach or at the speedway. He walked off with this one, however, and his average of 140.581 mph edged the beach's fastest one-way flying qualifier. The speedway had speed.

It also had a towering mortgage. This was pure Bill France and pure faith. France had spent all his money, all the money he raised from sale of stock and all the money he could borrow. The speedway was huge, so big they now had a lake created in the center when they dug a vast hole for the material to pile into the bankings for the turns. They had all those acres for parking. They had a road-racing course in the infield.

France quickly invited the Federation Internationale de l'Automobile (FIA) to use the track. They scheduled races for sports cars and motorcycles. They aimed for a balance between weekly shows, as

Petty's winning car. Just visible inside is a roll cage, while outside the lights have been replaced by flat panels and the body has been in contact with other cars. All normal. Daytona International Speedway

Flights that failed

NASCAR's founders weren't afraid to try new things or take chances or even to do what other people were doing—if it looked like something worth doing. And because the club in those early days was already practiced at putting the best face on every occurrence, one could assume that everything the organization touched was bound to succeed.

One would be wrong to so assume. In the background of NASCAR's biggest and best project, a national series of championship races for late model stock cars, there are a lot of different ventures, some of which worked and more of which didn't.

As noted, NASCAR came into being as a rival to AAA's contest board, not through any secret plan.But when the new club was underway, it struck its officials that they could do some of the other things the older AAA was doing.

In 1954 NASCAR's newsletter announced the club was going to begin rating and approving motels, hotels and restaurants, just the way AAA had been doing since the invention of the paved highway. And there would be insurance for passenger cars.

Neither got off the ground. When AAA started its program there were no maps or road signs or numbered routes. Places to eat or sleep were likely to be hovels. "Eat Here & Get Gas" wasn't always a joke. The AAA approval signs and traveling inspectors were needed.

But NASCAR's system arrived with the interstate highways. There were already chains of motels and restaurants with their own inspectors, and if you didn't like one place, a better one was twenty minutes down the pike. Insurance, meanwhile, was the captive of giant conglomerates working hand in glove with state legislatures. Not even Big Bill could whip that team, so the road service division was gone before it began.

Another odd suggestion at least included racing: a traveling show. The idea was to construct sort of an old-style hippodrome, the banked speedway one step less steep than the classic Wall of Death beloved by carnival motorcyclists.

This racetrack would be taken apart and hauled around the country, in company with subcompact cars. This idea first floated into view in 1950, when little cars were Crosley and Volkswagen and Austin sedans. They'd wow the folks over the weekend, pack up and move to the next county seat.

Once again, the timing was poor. Television was on its way to becoming the opiate of the masses, so folks in small towns had a choice of entertainment, never mind paved roads and reliable cars to get them out of town, or that at the same time two farmers in every county were building dirt tracks for the local heroes to race on.

The racing circus never happened, either. But other kinds of racing did.

Strictly stock's early rival, in other parts of the country as well as in the South, was midget racing. Sometimes these were classic midget racers, scaled-down sprint cars, single seaters with open wheels and scaled down Offenhauser 1500 cc engines. Or there were midgets with outboard engines adapted to dry land, or with power from Ford's little V-8 60 economy engine. The midgets were a big hit in California and New England before and after World War II, so NASCAR sanctioned midget races in its home territory.

Just as logically, sprint cars had been the top form of racing in America since the car guys moved to the fairgrounds tracks. At Daytona Beach in 1952 France unveiled a new class, the Speedway Division, for open wheel, single seaters to be powered by stock blocks.

This made sense. Such a car could be cheaper than the Offy-powered sprint cars that ran in AAA and at Indianapolis. They'd be as fast, they could run the same tracks as the sedans did, and the sedans drivers and tuners already knew how to use and improve the engines.

But as movie magnate Samuel Goldwyn is supposed to have said, if people don't want to go to the show, you can't stop them.

And people, the people in NASCAR's home territory at least, weren't interested in midgets or sprints. This came at the same time as crowds elsewhere lost their enthusiasm for midgets, and the sprints moved from dirt to pavement. Also, the sprint cars were more expensive to build than sedans were: this came when the racer could buy a stock car and prepare it with more time and skill than cash. But the sprinter needed a racing frame and body and wheels and tires and the rest. It was harder to persuade Jones Motor Co. that they'd benefit from sponsoring a racer that didn't look like what the fans drove. Without crowds there was no prize money; the sprints and midgets faded fast.

Another logical experiment was a class for racing convertibles.

Ragtops were big in the fifties and early sixties and they were what the fans drove. With the top down the driver could be seen at work and besides, the domestic convertible usually had the same chassis, drivetrain and engine as the sedan. So there was a convertible class, running on the same program as the sedans, one after the other, under the same basic rules.

This was a good show. Joe Weatherly and Curtis Turner, showmen to the core, were especially energetic and thrilled many a crowd by running each other into the fence or off the track. (For reasons never explained the Ford convertibles were much more competitive during the late fifties than the sedans were, and the two Ford drivers were the best in the class.)

The same basic rules meant that the sedans and convertibles were so similar that somebody discovered how to make a zip-top, an open car with a roof that could be bolted into position, and which could be raced in either class. At first this meant a convertible with a metal top, but because the sedan was a lighter body, everybody switched to cutting off the top of a sedan, keeping the panels intact and racing in both classes with the same car.

And that took care of that. The same cars weren't much of a show and they lost favor until they faded from the scene, like the sprints and midgets before them.

A quirk in the record book came from the early days due to an occasional lack of entries. When that happened the race would be held under sweepstake rules, meaning whatever anybody had at the track could be used. This was during the convertible era and NASCAR was experimenting with road races for imports and compacts, and there were races held for all the groups.

It also happened that some of these sweepstake races also were counted as Grand National events.

If you want to win a trivia contest, see if anybody else knows which make of import won a Grand National race, the class where only domestic products are eligible.

The answer is Jaguar. And Charlotte's Humpy Wheeler has the photos to prove it.

All this sounds like a recital of failure. As the full record shows, this wasn't so. The attempts to expand were more like experiments, and just as one learns when the lab project doesn't work, so did the organizers learn when the public didn't respond. Just as they learned when the public went wild.

While they were toying with the traveling track and with sprint cars, they were also expanding, signing tracks as far away as California as early as 1954. And they set up a West Coast championship and regional championships because the new teams and the unsponsored teams stood a better chance of getting backing if they had a title to win.

At the same time the modified and sportsman rules were revised so there could be cheaper racing on the smaller tracks, a homemade farm team system. You can't have a top unless you raise it with a bottom layer, a pyramid of talent and hunger.

By losing some battles and risking some positions, NASCAR won the war.

seen at small tracks like Ascot in California, and the annual race such as Indianapolis or Le Mans. Nor was it an accident that Speed Week and Cycle Week came at the height of the tourist season, when northerners head south and when Daytona Beach needed something to distinguish itself from all the other beach towns.

In short, France had overbuilt and overbooked for the present because he knew in his heart that the future would pay him back. As of course it did.

All-new stars

Daytona began to attract new people. Some of the drivers in that first speedway race had come up from the beach, or the dirt bullrings of the small towns. They were good at getting the maximum from a car at 100 mph, which didn't mean they were comfortable, ready or even willing to head flat out into the banked turns to swap paint at 150 mph.

Richard Petty

Richard Petty drove his first Grand National race in that first speedway event, and recalls seeing the drafting phenomenon and deciding not to tell anybody, not even his dad, Lee. He also had the realization that even if the other racers knew more than he did about dirt tracks and mile tracks, when it came to the bankings and long straights of the superspeedway, they all were starting equal. It might even be that he had an advantage because he didn't have habits to unlearn.

Petty himself was a new phenomenon. His dad was *the* family man, and Richard and brother Maurice were literally raised at the track or in the shop behind the family home. Richard considered himself crew chief from the age of twelve or so and was working on his dad's car even when NASCAR officials were trying to throw the kid out because he wasn't old enough to be in the pits.

Lee Petty was not an indulgent father. He allowed his sons to drive if they did their chores, you could say. Maurice was better at the wrenches than behind the wheel, but Richard had an aptitude for driving and went on the family payroll when Lee offered the security of a salary versus living on his own winnings.

Junior Johnson

Another new driver became a different kind of classic. When he first appeared, he was called Bob. The press described him as a "lanky six-footer" but everyone called the Johnson boy Junior and like everyone else, he gained weight as he grew older.

Junior Johnson was cut from the old cloth. When *Road & Track*'s elegant English gentleman Rob Walker went to his first NASCAR race, he and Johnson hit it off right quick, in part because the Walker family fortune, as in Johnnie Walker Red, comes from the same place as the Johnson family income once did: whiskey.

Johnson was a big, strong, aggressive young man from the hollers. He drove whiskey and graduated to driving in races with more orthodox rewards. Then, when he was there just to help out, a raid caught Johnson at the family still and he went to jail. His career was interrupted, although he'd go on to win fifty Grand National races anyway.

By chance Johnson was the Chevy man in 1964 when Ford was spending all the money and Tom Wolfe, the chronicler of culture and heroism (and the best writer of our day), went to the races for *Esquire* magazine. Wolfe's "The Last American Hero" made Junior more of a public figure than he liked, but it did a lot for stock car racing. It may have made racing acceptable in circles where they'd never heard of such activities, so Johnson came to terms with the idea.

Fred Lorenzen

A third newcomer was a carpenter by trade, a hard case motorhead from Illinois. Fred Lorenzen built his first racer, powered by a lawn mower engine,

The first draft

When the superspeedways arrived the fans were delighted and fascinated to see what looked like an entirely new racing technique. One car would tuck in close behind the other, and the two cars could go faster together than either one could manage solo. In effect, they had divided air resistance in half.

This technique gained an extra dimension when it was learned that the car in the draft, the one tucked in, could run on part throttle and could have some power in reserve, so that as the pair came out of the last turn and headed for the finish line, the car in back could swerve out of the air pocket and power past the leader. "Slingshot" was the word used.

Richard Petty wrote in his autobiography that he found out about this for himself, at the new Daytona International Speedway, in 1959. It was, he said, one of those things you don't even tell your daddy about.

He noticed his dad and another driver running tucked together, however, and by the end of the 1959 Daytona speed week, the new idea was in all the newspapers, and it's been a known factor ever since.

Richard Petty is too smart and too experienced ever to claim that he discovered or invented anything in racing. Instead, he writes that nobody told him about this, that he stumbled across the technique for himself. But the press has sort of assumed ever since that drafting was something the racers learned about when they first hit the high banks of the speedways.

Not so.

Speed Age for March 1953 contains a letter from Pat Kirkwood, Fort Worth, Texas. Kirkwood was a sportsman, a good driver and a Chrysler enthusiast. He raced carefully prepared but private Chrysler sedans in 1951 and 1952, at Daytona and in the Mexican Road Race. He was a good driver, taking third place in the beach race in 1951.

The *Speed Age* letter was generated by the controversy of which car was fastest in stock form versus which car had the best factory kit, or the best preparation. Kirkwood naturally claimed that the Chrysler was the fastest, and paid tribute to the Hudsons and Lincolns only in that they had factory help and parts.

But our purpose here is another kind of research. Kirkwood writes that in the 1952 Mexican Road Race he was clocked at 113 mph, "but look what the Lincolns did to me . . . Walt Faulkner cruised by. I dropped in about six feet behind him and tried to let him draft me . . ."

The letter goes on to say the Chrysler couldn't keep up, but the point here is that in 1953, six years before drafting made the newspapers, at least one racer not only used and knew about the technique, he had the name of the game, too.

This is the first known reference to drafting. Because Kirkwood simply mentions drafting in passing, and doesn't need to explain what he did and why it worked, we must assume that racers knew about it, and used it, long before the speedway era.

Junior Johnson, eating a little better now, with builder Ray Fox on the occasion of their winning the 1960 Daytona 500. Johnson averaged 124.74 mph, in a 1959 Chevy. Road & Track

when he was eleven. Then he went through jalopies, motorcycles and borrowed junkers, racing in Illinois and venturing out of the state when he had the cash and a car.

That wasn't often. Lorenzen dropped out of racing and worked in construction until he could get enough of a stake to go racing again, then he'd have to recover. Not at all by chance, Lorenzen attracted the attention of Holman and Moody, who were always looking for such talent. Many years later Lorenzen would say that he'd only gotten into racing for the money. Leo Levine comments that to anybody who knew Lorenzen in those early days, such a notion was "laughable."

Bigger and better and faster

The giant Daytona track joined the paved and banked 1⅜ mile Darlington, and was followed by Charlotte and Atlanta, both banked, paved 1.5 mile speedways. This gave NASCAR four tracks on which the cars would average better than 100 mph, and it gave television a convenient way to get into the game and the sport. (Trivia fans take note: ABC's broadcast of the 1961 Firecracker 250 was the first Grand National race on network television.)

Then came mechanical changes.

The first big change was the disappearance of the modified class, the old whiskey-runner replicas that were faster and more thrilling back on the beach course. As the stock class was allowed more power, so was the modified class until the latter machines were simply old light cars crammed with new heavy engines topped by rows of carburetors or even superchargers. They made a grand show on the dirt tracks and hurtling down the beach, but they were overpowered and underequipped for the speedway.

This became clear when scores of the little monsters piled up in the first turn. To keep this from happening, and to give the new guys and the poor guys something to do, the modifieds became learner cars and sportsman cars, and were moved back to short tracks and local racing.

The Grand National class didn't change its rules for the speedways, but the cars themselves did.

Most of the change came from the new car market. Big cars were more popular than ever. As the cars grew, so did their engines. Back in 1949, Cadillac's 330 ci V-8 was considered big. By 1959 you could get a Chevy with a 348, a Ford with a 352 or a Pontiac with a 389. And the optional big V-8s also came with performance parts.

The ban on factory participation in racing? Still in effect, from 1957 through to the middle of 1962, but this wasn't the handicap it was supposed to be.

By this time racers and builders with deep wells of resources in parts and experience were working in NASCAR. They had become professionals and the rent money depended on doing well, so whatever it took to do well, got done.

Item: Harry Hyde began testing his engines on the dyno while they were tipped on their sides. That's the way they'd be run on the banked ovals, so that's how they would be examined.

Item: Smokey Yunick showed up at a road race with an engine that ran in the reverse direction from stock. He reasoned that when the stock cars turned left, there was a benefit to having the engine running in the direction that countered the car's roll. Thus, road racing was more turns to the right, and running the engine the other direction would stick the car better on right turns.

In theory he was right. In practice, a tech inspector noticed the fan pushing air where it should be pulling, so we'll never know. Anyway, Yunick's cars won even when he didn't do things like that. But the thinking and sophistication were well established.

Pontiac was the hot brand in the late sixties, as the engine was like a Chevy but larger. Top guys, Yunick and Matthews to name two, were building them and getting sub rosa support. This is a 1960 model, in the 1961 Daytona 500, pulling out of the pit lane. In the background is a 1960 Ford, driven by Herman Beam, one of the first drivers who raced for years and never won. Beam was famous for this feat and was even nicknamed "Herman the Turtle." But he built well and drove carefully, and nobody minded his lack of speed. Road & Track

So were the lines of supply. The 1959 NASCAR programs carry ads for Holman & Moody equipment. Countless firms carried camshafts and such for Chevy and Pontiac engines and, it turned out later, GM engineers had designed the parts that went on sale. So there was no shortage of speed equipment.

The racers swapped just as they did when they went to a dealer and talked him out of whatever model they reckoned would win. Ford had just signed Yunick and Paul Goldsmith away from Chevrolet in time for the racing ban, so Yunick built Fords until the parts ran out, then went back to GM, in the form of Pontiac.

Lee Petty went back to Mopar, in a Plymouth, when Olds dropped out, but Richard's first Grand National races were in the Olds because they wanted to use it up. On one occasion Lee protested his son's win, won the protest and got the victory for himself. He said later that he did it because NASCAR was paying an extra $500 when a new car won; the Plymouth was new, the Olds wasn't and the family business needed the money.

Petty and Sons wasn't a democracy. While Richard and Maurice never complained in public, Richard did lose half his stomach on the way to racking up 200 Grand National wins. Or 201 without his father to help him.

Anyway, the record books here show some surprises. They list Roberts in a Ford, Petty in an Olds and Goldsmith in a Pontiac one week; the next week they'd all traded places.

Assuming the degree of factory help to be equal, the Pontiac seemed to have the edge. It was better than the Chevy because it was bigger, as Banjo Matthews said, and the brand did get some support from a division management team that liked competition.

There were different ways to do the same thing. At Pontiac they relied on outside suppliers, such as camshaft grinder Iskenderian, to make parts the division engineers had had a hand in. Ford had Yunick, then Holman and Moody and Bill Stroppe.

Chevrolet either cheated better or had a built-in advantage with the Corvette program. Many people high within GM had emotional or professional involvement with the Corvette, sports cars and racing. Favorite son status, as it were, conferred a degree of exemption for sub rosa help to the 'vette.

And because a major share of the Corvette's drivetrain came direct from the Chevrolet cars, most of the racing Corvette program also applied to stock and drag racing. If that didn't help, the new truck engine—a 348 ci V-8, listed as optional for the car as well—did.

Ford spent too much time with neither hand knowing what the other was doing. One group conducted an investigation of the other camps and was shocked to learn that Chevrolet dealer Jim Rathmann, who was also an Indy car champ, was able to buy unfinished body parts from GM. And they got hold of a Pontiac engine block and solemnly reported that they'd found fourteen illegal features on it.

Meanwhile the Thunderbird that gave Lee Petty such a run on the speedway was using a 430 ci engine that didn't meet the NASCAR requirements. Except one—that it gave the fans something to root for.

In the foreground is Jack Smith, in a 1961 Pontiac and leading him by two feet is Fred Lorenzen, soon to become the Golden Boy, in a Holman and Moody Ford. Road & Track

Higher speed meant more attention to safety. This 1960 Chevy, dropping out of the 1961 Daytona 500, shows the larger and more elaborate roll cage and the extra hood tie- *downs (and the ever-growing decal collection) that came with the speedway's popularity and the added stress. Road & Track*

Beauchamp's 'bird was one of six racing Thunderbirds built by Holman and Moody, and by golly it turned out that the former Ford team was able to buy parts direct from the plant, just like the Chevy dealer could.

In so many words, all the factories were run by people who at the very top probably meant what they said—the factories were out of racing. But as they got further from the boardroom and closer to the outside world, the anti-racing party got smaller and smaller, and everybody did what they could get away with.

Above that, the Chevrolet engine had a running start. It was a better engine off the drawing board, so the hot car guys went with Chevy. There was a market for performance parts so the division could sell them to truly private teams and owners, and make a profit for the parts department while keeping the make's reputation. Neat.

While this made the bow tie boys happy, it made Lee Iacocca, then an ambitious engineer turned marketing manager at the Ford Division, angry. He'd tried to sell safety when Chevrolet sold power and he knew what worked and what didn't. Iacocca wanted to get Ford back into racing, but he didn't (yet) have the power.

He kept his and the other Ford guys' eyes open. In 1959 there were still runs on the beach and really stock Fords were 10 mph down on really stock Chevys. Junior Johnson, of all people, who had been the only driver who could win in a Ford in late 1958, had switched to Chevy. The 430 Ford truck engine had less power than the 348 Chevy truck engine, so Ford left Holman and Moody to do their best with that project and began building prototype racers on their own, in disguise.

Lee Petty won the national title in 1959, for the second straight year, followed by Cotton Owens, who drove a 'bird in public and was testing Fords during the week.

Total Performance

Technically this was the beginning of the small-block and big-block era, as the original passenger car engines were used most of the time with truck-born V-8s coming into the picture. The little Chevy was 265 ci in the beginning, grew easily to 283, then 327 and later 350, but beyond 350 meant too long a stroke for reliability at racing speeds. The Ford V-8, which wasn't that small when it appeared in 1954, went to 352 ci, and a 360 bhp rating with optional racing parts.

Although there were twenty-eight Fords in the 1960 Daytona 500, none of them came close to the lead and Junior Johnson won in a Pontiac. The 421 Pontiac was king of the superspeedways, assuming it held together, which it didn't always do. Which is why Rex White won the 1960 title with a Chevy, followed by Richard Petty.

Late in 1960 Iacocca got the promotion he needed, and the competition program got some recognition and a few bucks. This came just in time, as during Daytona's speed week one of the Ford guys got into a car supposedly prepared for the press, spun out, got his picture in the papers and was ordered to keep away from the place.

The 1961 Ford stock car engine was 390 ci and rated at 410 bhp. That looked good in the brochure but it wasn't enough, as both Pontiac and Chevrolet had more power at the track and on the ground, plus a deeper supply of talent.

There were some hints, though. Lorenzen was talked into giving it another try—he'd run out of money again—and won his first NASCAR race, on the half mile at Martinsville, Virginia.

Then came a more important event. This wasn't for the title, but back then there were separate short track and convertible classes, and the Fords always did well with the open cars. Lorenzen and Turner got into a shoving match while fighting for the lead and Lorenzen did the better job. He went on to win the race and right after that, the shouting match.

During the race Lorenzen had run harder than he'd needed to, and worn out tires, forcing pit stops that then had to be made up. While this was going on, Ralph Moody stood at track side, pointing at his head.

Finally, the light bulb went on—use your head. Lorenzen did, and he beat the legendary Turner at Turner's own game of intimidation. Fearless Freddy finally had the confidence he needed. After that, painted on the dashboard of Lorenzen's car, was a cryptic "Think! W.H.M.?" standing for What the Hell's the Matter?

Turner, sadly, was going in the other direction. He wanted to be a businessman, a wheeler-dealer, and he and Bruton Smith were partners in Charlotte Motor Speedway, one of the four speedways. But where France had come up with just enough money in the nick of time, Turner and Smith had almost enough money, almost in time.

Charlotte's first race began on the heels of the last paving truck. They covered the cars with rubber flaps and steel mesh to keep the asphalt out of the radiators. The winner of the first race, just as way back when on the beach, was the car that survived when the faster ones fell out.

Then the track ran out of operating capital.

The happy ending here is that Bruton Smith handed over the keys, left town, made a comeback, honored his commitments and bought up stock until,

Another experiment. In 1959 Detroit reintroduced smaller cars, so NASCAR and others provided classes for them. This is Ford's Falcon, powered by a 144 ci ohv six with a rating of 105 bhp, driven at the speedway in 1961 by none other *than Joe Weatherly. The compacts raced on the infield road course and this car came to grief when Joe flipped it. Stuck throttle, he said. Right. Daytona International Speedway*

once again, he was the owner of the track, which he runs well and at a profit today. Meanwhile he and Humpy Wheeler drove the France family nuts with such innovations as The Winston race. The other tracks have to try and match them, and it costs money.

The sad part is that Turner went looking for loans and was promised money by the Teamsters' Union, in exchange for help organizing NASCAR. The Teamsters could see that this was going to be a big and profitable venture.

France made another of his effective speeches to a packed crowd of drivers, mechanics and car owners. Then he said he'd shut the whole thing down rather than allow union influence, never mind control. He vowed to shoot the man who tried to stop him. With the crowd on his side, France banned Turner from NASCAR. For life, he said at the time, although he relented later.

On the tracks, the 421 Pontiacs were flying. Yunick built one for Roberts, and Fireball took the Daytona 500 pole for 1961 at 155.7 mph. The engine blew while Roberts was well in the lead, letting through Marvin Panch, also Pontiac. Panch won the race at an average of 149.6 mph, faster for the first time than the Indy 500.

The Pontiacs weren't the only fliers. Lee and Richard Petty were running the Plymouth team—better make that a team of Plymouths—but Richard tangled with another car in the first qualifying race at Daytona and went over the wall. His worst injury came when he undid his harness and dropped to the ground. Richard was walking around during the second qualifying race when the excited announcer got his attention and he looked up to see his dad's car go over the wall, also after a tangle.

This wasn't a joke. Lee Petty and Johnny Beauchamp, by luck the two who'd so nearly tied for the 1959 win at Daytona, locked together and went over the side. Both were badly hurt. Petty recovered in a few months and drove until the middle of 1964. Beauchamp never raced again.

Here's a quote.

"I've heard people say after a spin-out that this driver or that driver did a good job of bringing the car under control. When a car starts spinning at today's speeds you don't control the car on the speedway. Only Fate does that. The driver behind the wheel of a speeding race car that spins out has no more control over it than a fan sitting in the stands."

That was Lee Petty from his hospital bed in 1961, when "today's speeds" were 150 and 160, the same speed that put Marshall Teague over the wall when the speedway opened. The same remarks will be made again and again, and are still going on today: today's speed is always as much or more than the cars and drivers can handle. The thought's the same, only the numbers change.

Another kind of change was to come early in 1962, when Ford came up with the slogan "Total Performance," and division managers got the power to live up to the slogan—only to learn that they weren't the only ones who'd been working behind the ban on racing.

Chapter 6

Factory feuds: 1962-1970

One of life's shared conceits is that things are much more complicated now than they were in some earlier, supposedly more placid and natural, age. We see today as a jumble of contradictions while the confusions and questions of yesterday would have been easy for us to handle. Or so it seems.

Even allowing for that common mistake, it does look now as if things were simpler in stock car racing when they began, and that they got a lot more complicated in the early sixties.

The best teams were inventing strategy, and becoming racetrack lawyers as well.

There was the Rebel 300 in which Joe Weatherly had a precarious lead and stopped for gas with the green flag out. He came back in last place, not much worried . . . except that it began to rain.

The race was stopped. France announced that the finish would be delayed for a week, the cars would be kept under guard and the restart would be under a yellow flag for five laps, to allow refueling.

Weatherly naturally didn't think that was fair. He went public and threatened to go to court.

There had been 30,000 people in the stands when the race was stopped. There were 37,000 there for the restart. Fireball Roberts, who'd gotten the lead when Little Joe pulled off, was booed. Weatherly was cheered. France had stood firm the whole time, per-

State of the builder's art, 1962. This is John Holman, and in the background is a 1962 Ford Galaxie with 406 V-8. Between them is the professional's best for 1962, a Ford frame with body removed and roll cage permanently installed, along with all the heavy-duty components, such as the wider wheels and high-lift camshaft Holman is holding. No longer did you have to buy a passenger car and strip it; Holman and Moody would sell you a race-ready machine. Don Hunter

The Grand National cars still looked stock, though. This is Ernie Gahan in a 1961 Ford being passed by Richard Petty in a 1962 Plymouth on his way to second in the 1962 Daytona 500. Road & Track

haps knowing that his obduracy would create a hero and a villain, essential to every heroic saga.

What the crowd didn't know was that Roberts' Chevrolet was slower than Weatherly's Ford and Roberts' team figured (planned and hoped is more like it) to make Weatherly angry. Which he was. He was angry enough to storm through the field with such force and abandon that he literally drove one wheel, the right front, off the car. Roberts won and Richard Petty was second, having sat through the whole show grinning from ear to ear. Everybody went home knowing that the evolving rules would help or hurt and could build the gate at the same time.

There were mechanical changes, too. Detroit was coming out with smaller cars, called compacts. The middle-range cars were called intermediates. They were smaller, shorter and lighter, but still large enough to accommodate a V-8 engine if needed, and several divisions thought they were.

There was also a major change of design. Formerly, cars came with a frame, big iron or steel rails and cross-members, and had the body plopped down on that, insulated by mounting blocks. One of the ways to make suspension work is to give it a firm platform to brace against. The less flex in the body and frame, the more controlled and predictable the motions of the suspension.

When stock meant strictly stock, the innovators began removing the mounting blocks. The separate body and frame could then brace each other. When roll bars were required, the smarter builders tied the roll bar hoops and braces to the frame, again making it stiffer.

Now the car factories began to eliminate the frame. They made the body shell also serve as the mounting platform for the front and rear suspension, often with a subframe in front, but with most of the strength coming from what was called a unit, or one-piece, body.

First, the body got modified. Dan Gurney drove the first stock car race at Riverside, a USAC rather than NASCAR race (but we'll ignore that), in a Chevrolet built by Bill Thomas, special effects expert for Chevrolet advertising, and Don Edmunds, one of the West Coast's better sprint car constructors.

Gurney qualified fifth fastest with no practice. It was his home track and hometown, of course, and he won the first heat and was second in the second heat.

Then, at technical inspection, the car was found to have illegally enlarged wheelwells and unallowably strengthened body panels, and was disqualified. The lesson was that the new design would lend itself to new ways to modify stock cars, and that there were some helpful people high in the various factories: Thomas and Edmunds weren't in it as a hobby.

There was also an engine trend. As noted earlier, the original V-8s were being stretched to their limits. The later engines were larger to begin with and had provision to grow without penalty. Chevy's 348 became the 409 of the song, the Ford 312 was the 352 and then the 390 and so on. (The actual terms big-block and small-block didn't become common until the 1965 Corvette was offered with either of the division's two V-8s.)

Then came politics. Ford had a limited and secret racing budget in early 1962, with experiments and drivers on hire. John Holman played lowball for Ford, citing the new body for the big Galaxie as not as slick as the 1961 body. He hoped the 406 V-8, rated at 390 bhp, would make up for that.

Chevrolet had outside contractors doing investigations and getting parts, and a strong program of selling performance equipment and even some race-style show cars, in the Corvette mode, with spin-offs from that.

Chrysler hadn't been as active, but they did have Buck Baker for Chrysler, Lee Petty for Plymouth and Bob Osiecki, a drag race engineer and NASCAR charter member, for Dodge. And they had a 413 V-8, and new, smaller, unit bodies.

Pontiac had Yunick, whose work with the 389 let it grow into the 421. And Yunick had Roberts, who collected records at three of the four speedways in 1961.

Stock options

By the 1962 season the rules had taken a few more steps. The struggle over what option makes for stock had resulted in free choice for camshafts; the engines could be blueprinted, that is, taken apart and brought to perfect tolerances and balance, while using stock parts. The limit was one four-barrel; the chassis could have just about anything done that could be claimed as a move for safety. And everything could be. There was no limit on engine size, what with

all the top makes being in the same group, and the car had to weigh what it weighed. Lee Petty was happy to predict that the new Dodge, lighter than its rivals, would gain something there.

The first impression for the season was teamwork. "A reciprocal trade agreement" is how *Car Life* described the 1962 Daytona 500. Roberts and Junior Johnson, both in Pontiacs, had decided to draft each other and run as a team early in the going. Roberts' qualifying runs were a record 158.744 mph, so the speed was there anyway.

Johnson's engine threw a rod, Roberts' held up, and Richard Petty in a Plymouth had already learned several lessons. He ran high on the banking to make up for a relative lack of power, then latched on to Roberts' back bumper and drafted into second place until late in the going, when he had to stop for gas and wound up twenty-seven seconds, or nearly a thirty-second lap at 150 mph around the 2.5 mile oval, behind. Weatherly in a Pontiac was third, Jack Smith in a Pontiac was fourth. Roberts and Weatherly won the qualifying races for Pontiac and a new guy named Lee Roy Yarbrough took the modified event in a Ford ... with a Pontiac V-8. It was an impressive testimony to Pontiac, Yunick and Banjo Matthews, who'd also done work in the cars (and it was to be nearly a swan song).

Speed week in 1962 was two months of races for cars and motorcycles on the oval and around the infield road course. The promoters had economy runs, western music, everything they could do. It was quite a show and nobody missed the point that this was "the world's fastest 500 mile race," quoting *Car Life* again, even if nobody mentioned where the fastest 500 mile race used to be held.

And then a bombshell hit. In the middle of 1962 Henry Ford II, the president of the AMA, calmly and

The hot car, and the Daytona winner in 1962, was the Pontiac, as driven here by Fireball Roberts and prepared by Smokey Yunick. Road & Track

Ford officially returned to racing in 1962 and by Daytona 1963, they were completely public. This is the Holman and Moody display, with the prepared stock chassis, roll cage and bracing, put next to a real race car. The CP insignia, by the way, stood for Competition Proven and was a Holman and Moody trademark. Road & Track

firmly announced that he and his company no longer believed in the thinking behind the withdrawal from racing. Ford was getting back into the game, on as many fronts and as hard and fast as they could do it.

There was the slogan Total Performance. There were the ambitions of Henry Ford II and Lee Iacocca to make their marks on the world. And there may have simply been the infuriating sight of all those non-factory-backed Pontiacs cleaning the clocks of the racing world.

There may have been a confidence factor as well. Henry Ford the original hadn't liked his peers in the auto business, and Ford didn't join the AMA until just before the factory ban was voted in. So Henry Ford II hadn't been a member long and it could have taken him the five years to wonder just why he'd let truck makers and non-racing car companies tell him what his company could do.

Car Life commented, "We consider it most unlikely that any manufacturer will commit to a full-scale racing program," which was to be proven wildly in error. NASCAR announced an upper limit to engine displacement, 427.2 ci, which came just before some of the makers could present whopping 480s and up. The limit made sense, while it was a major switch; until then, the displacement of the engine used for racing was free, provided that it was the engine used in mass production.

Ford's return was more than a return; it was an involvement beyond anything envisioned in racing.

Dan Gurney used to all but own the Riverside road course, and here he is in a Holman and Moody Ford, winning the Grand National race there in 1963. Road & Track

Ford leaped back into stock car racing, helped Carroll Shelby with the Cobra, and went to Indianapolis and the drags. They financed the construction and development of the Cosworth-Ford Grand Prix engine, the most successful motor in that field ever, raced the fabulous GT40, and on and on for the next twenty years.

Suffice it to say that the limited program carried out in 1961 and early 1962 had put the Ford teams just where they wanted to be. They were ready. In fact, they were competing with each other. Holman and Moody worked for one branch and the Wood brothers, led by a canny family from Virginia and the best pit teamwork in the business, also worked for Ford. Bill Stroppe, the Californian who did so well in the Mexican Road Race, was to run a Mercury team in NASCAR.

The results of the factory's return illustrate the contrast of what you get when a car is truly stock, versus what happens when one team commits with no limit on time or money.

While the ban was theoretically in effect early in the 1962 season, *Car Life* tested the Ford Galaxie 406, the Pontiac Grand Prix 421, the Chevrolet Impala SS 409, the Chrysler 300-H and the Dodge Dart 413—the performance cars of the year. In stock form, allowing for differences in gearing and transmissions, they compared as follows:

	0-60 mph	¼ mile time	Top speed (est)	Gross weight
Ford	7.0 sec.	15.3 sec.	130 mph	3,880 lb.
Pontiac	6.0	14.3	135	3,990
Chevrolet	7.3	14.9	125	3,730
Chrysler	7.7	16.0	133	4,220
Dodge	7.4	15.1	107	3,540

These figures hid some valuable lessons. The most obvious is that the super cars of that year were fairly evenly matched. The market had seen to that. They were all big cars with big, conventional engines. Beyond that, the Pontiac was clearly faster than the others; back then the press said to one another (but not often in print) that Pontiacs seemed mighty quick to be stock. Oh heck, why hedge? The Pontiacs given to magazines to test had frequently been prepped beforehand to better-than-showroom condition.

Next, the light Dodge wasn't as quick as its figures should have made it. That was about to change. In 1962, when Ford made a large, public announcement, some of the upper middle guys in the Dodge division had also decided to get into racing.

But even if the competing cars were or weren't stock, or were or weren't better than they should have been, their limits had been set by the factories and the public. The starting points were what people bought. The engines, if large and converted into full race powerplants, nonetheless were normal cast-iron V-8s

These cars weren't as stock as they looked. This is a Fred Lorenzen car, restored and photographed in 1987, but just as it was raced in the sixties. The huge drum brakes were used for years after disc brakes had been adopted elsewhere, as the giant drums worked better than the small discs of the time. And note the dual shock absorbers; one wasn't enough for the job.

Holman and Moody made their own dashboard panels to house all the instruments they needed, and to bolt right into the stock bodywork. This car was a frame and body car but the roll cage is much more elaborate, with extra fore-and-aft bracing and bars across the left doorwell. "Think" explains itself, but "WHM" is short for "What the Hell's the Matter?" a question Lorenzen was supposed to ask himself when things weren't going well.

with overhead valves, two per cylinder aligned in a row parallel to the crankshaft and cam. With the valves in line and the combustion chamber tapering toward one side, these cylinder heads would come to be called "wedge" heads. They were the norm, as Chrysler had stopped making hemis in 1959 because the extra cost wasn't returned in sales appeal.

One semi-exception was the W series Chevy V-8, made first in 1958 for trucks and as a car option. This engine had the stamped rocker arms from the little V-8 that allowed the valves to be staggered, placed to take advantage of Chevrolet's odd way of putting the heads on the block at an angle. The cylinder heads were flat, the bores angled at twenty-nine degrees and the pistons gabled so the combustion chamber, a true wedge, was in the cylinder itself. Different, but not demonstrably better in terms of power and thus not demonstrably better in competition.

In that sense all the V-8s were normal; their power came from displacement and tuning and matching the engine to the car in which it was installed. What made the difference on the track was who was working on the car, and how much they'd invested in time and money.

The 1962 season was the crossing of some curves, as Ford made public plans, Chrysler got its equipment ready and GM made something of a retreat. General Motors had gambled on keeping quiet, which meant no support, above or below the table.

So Pontiac stomped on the others at Daytona's first race of the season, with Roberts and the Yunick Pontiac taking the pole, one of the qualifying races and the race itself, the first grand slam there. Banjo Matthews took the pole for the Firecracker 400 and Roberts won the race, with Junior Johnson and his Pontiac second.

But those were the high points. Lorenzen began to demonstrate an uncanny ability to be in front when it mattered most, and won for Ford at Atlanta. Pontiacs placed second, third and fourth. It was Fords

And some guys worked full time. The man inside the fence is Wendell Scott, the first black to earn a living racing Grand National. He did it the hard way, as his battered Ford shows. Scott used to buy the Ford team's used cars and rebody them to keep them legal for the class. Scott never won a major race, but he did earn a living, put his sons through college and won the respect of some people who weren't happy when he first went racing. Daytona International Speedway

1-2-3 at Darlington. Richard Petty, with his light, underpowered and factory-assisted Plymouth, took the short tracks like Martinsville, Virginia and North Wilkesboro, North Carolina. This was an apprenticeship, as Petty learned to make the most of the least, to run his own race and to plan—lessons which would pay off very soon.

The season ended in Riverside, California, where Ford hired world class road racer Dan Gurney to win, which he did. Riverside marked the last appearance of the factory-backed Pontiac, which came in second in the hands of A. J. Foyt, who'd begun visiting NASCAR when he had time. Grand National champion for the year was Joe Weatherly, who'd driven a Bud Moore-built Pontiac to top finishes, if no headlines, at all of the year's fifty-three Grand National races. Pontiacs won twenty-two of the Grand Nationals, compared with fourteen for Chevy, eleven for Plymouth and six for Ford.

Small-block, big-block

The 1963 Grand National rules were announced in August 1962, and contained few surprises. Detroit factories were beginning to make different sizes of cars, so there was a minimum wheelbase of 116 in., and a minimum ground clearance of 4 in. Full-floating rear axles, with wheels supported by the hub instead of the axle so the wheel wouldn't fall off if the axle broke, were made mandatory.

Then came some routine announcements. Bill Stroppe would field a team of Mercurys. The Dodge Dealers Association had hired Cotton Owens, a top driver turned builder, and David Pearson, a sensational newcomer from the modified and sportsman ranks. Rex White and Junior Johnson had been seen testing a 1963 Chevy at GM's Phoenix, Arizona, proving ground.

Then came the big news and it arrived backward. Chevrolet had the Corvette, and the division had some top men who weren't willing to concede the sports department to Ford. They'd been working on competitive Corvettes, but the little Chevy engine wasn't better enough than the new Ford lightweight V-8 to keep the heavy Chevy in front of the new Cobra—not when the Cobra weighed 1,000 pounds less.

So the engineers took the W series engine, enlarged it and fitted it with an entirely new and different set of cylinder heads. They took full advantage of their freedom to locate the valves and ports where they would work the best. The valve stems protruded at some odd angles, which led to the engine being named Porcupine or stagger valve, along with the official tag of Mark II and later, Mystery Engine.

The mystery was how the thing existed at all. GM policy limited the displacement to 396 for the Corvette, at least until it was proven that the engine needed all the displacement it could get.

What buyers couldn't do in early 1963 was get the engine in a Chevrolet sedan, not with those heads or that displacement. Instead, Chevrolet officials told NASCAR in time for the engine to be declared eligible, they had submitted samples for testing and it looked as if they would have a competitive engine and not

Chrysler returned to racing in 1962 but really got serious in 1964, with the arrival of a new hemi V-8, built on the modern big-block wedge engine but using the principles proven back with the first hemi in 1951. This is the drag race version, with two four-barrel carbs and tuned exhaust, stock. The NASCAR engine was limited to one four-barrel when the rival Ford had two. Chrysler Corporation

Ford replied to the hemi with a 427 that used two camshafts, one in each cylinder head. When it was first shown, to the public's and even NASCAR's surprise, it also had two carbs. Ford Motor Company

surprisingly, it was bored to the full allowance of 427 ci.

The competition was still in the running as well. Ford's 406 was enlarged to 427 and the Mopar 413 was now 426.

Ford's sohc 427 was a toolroom engine, made virtually by hand, and with lots of extra parts. The first timing chain runs an idler gear, in effect, and the second chain takes the drive to the cams, with roller tappets and rocker arms to the valves, which are set at a near-hemi angle. This was an expensive engine, and while Ford announced its availability at bargain rates, few if any were ever sold to the genuine public. Ford Motor Company

Chevy's entry was the 427 Porcupine, or stagger-valve or even Mark IV Mystery Engine. It was first raced in 1963, then withdrawn because it wasn't production and got whipped. But it came back in 1965, as shown here, and outlasted the others. The Chevrolet 427 was a production engine that raced, the hemi was a racing engine that was produced, and the Ford was an exotic engine that never was. Road & Track

The field for the 1963 Daytona 500 was one of the best and most varied ever, then or now, with full teams from Ford and Mercury, Plymouth and Dodge, a fleet of stagger-valve Chevys and even a good supply of Pontiacs driven by the likes of Roberts, Weatherly, Foyt, Paul Goldsmith and Bobby Johns.

There were two incredible epics in 1963. First, the Chevrolet Impalas (big cars) were easily the best in the field. Johnny Rutherford put his Chevy on the pole with 165.183 mph, up 7 mph from the previous year. He and Johnson won the preliminary races, again at record speeds.

Then Hollywood took over.

Tiny Lund was a good driver but never a great driver. He was huge, an amiable giant, and he'd had some good rides in between running his fishing camp, but he wasn't in the top twenty.

He was also brave. Marvin Panch was driving a monster sports car, a Maserati type 151 coupe fitted with a 427 Ford V-8, when it got away from him, crashed and caught fire. Lund led a group of five men who dove into the flames and pulled Panch out to safety and eventual recovery.

Yes, just as the script would have it, from his hospital bed Panch suggested that the Wood brothers let Lund drive his Ford in the big race.

Could the Fates argue with a setup like that?

Junior led the first 175 miles, until his engine let go. The same thing happened to Goldsmith and Foyt in Pontiacs, then to Rex White in his Chevy. Meanwhile, back in the pack, Rutherford was nursing his mount and waiting for Yunick to signal, Go! While in the pack, Rutherford spun and whacked the fender. He lost time getting it hammered out, so his 166 mph laps didn't do him that much good, except perhaps that his was the only strong Chevy when the flag waved.

That checkered flag waved first at Lund, however, followed by Lorenzen, Jarrett, Nelson Stacy and Gurney—Fords 1-2-3-4-5, then Petty in an underpowered, dodgy Plymouth.

The long term results of that race are with us still.

Lund was a fairy-tale hero; he got on television and into the mass magazines. Because he was a good guy, shy and huge and all that, and because he could drive, he made friends for racing and that didn't hurt. He went on to win several Grand American championships and even raced in Europe and Japan.

Behind the scenes, Ford's team knew they had the glory but not the power. They knew their slick body wasn't as good as it could have been, not at those speeds.

Chevrolet headquarters was angered and disgraced. Not only had they gone racing against the rules, they'd been whipped in public, which may have been worse. All the engines they could find were taken back. Yunick managed not to be home when the collectors called, so he and Johnson ran the rest of the year on their spare parts, earning the title of "Last American Hero" for Johnson and the affection of Chevy fans for him and Yunick.

Stroppe and the Mercury team had been eclipsed. They'd had six cars and all the parts on earth, yet their best qualifying run was fifteenth fastest and they finished out of the top ten. The Mercurys weighed in at 3,875 lb. while the Fords weighed only 3,600 lb. with the same engine, but that shouldn't have mattered on the banked oval. What did matter was the shape of the Mercs, which had such wild underhood turbulence that the air cleaner elements were ripped to shreds. Stroppe had been away from stock car racing six years, and things had changed.

The Mopar camp was in equal disarray. They had used proven builders and drivers, and even run three sizes of car: a big Dodge with 122 in. wheelbase, a smaller Dodge with 119 and a Plymouth with 116. They were all slow.

The Pontiacs, meanwhile, were used up. Roberts and Weatherly moved, as soon as invited, into the Ford camp. No complaint there; they were in business to race and so was Ford.

The rest of the year was spelled F–O–R–D. Weatherly won the national title again, consistent and strong and determined as ever, while Fords won twenty-three Grand Nationals, compared with six the year before. Pontiac plummeted from twenty-two wins to four, Chevy dropped from fourteen to eight. The only semblance of a threat came from Plymouth, up from eleven wins to nineteen. The wins were mostly on the short tracks, from Petty's apprenticeship training, but they put Petty into second place in the drivers' series, followed by Lorenzen for Ford.

Now the fun begins. This is one of NASCAR's legends, the Smokey Yunick Chevelle of 1966. Check the location of the front tire versus the front bumper, the rear tire with the rear side window, and the radius of the rear fenders. Compare them with the profile of the stock Malibu. Don Hunter and Road & Track

Nobody was satisfied with their year, win or lose, and they were all busy planning ahead. So was NASCAR. As early as May of 1963 the newsletter said there would probably be a limit of 6.5 liters—396 ci—imposed for the 1964 season.

Or maybe not. During 1963 Ford, Chrysler and Chevrolet revised and improved their big-block engines, each billed (in *Car Life*) as that make's Mark II. All three also developed new cylinder head kits, with the material trimmed back from around the valves and valve seats, currently called "open chamber" heads. And they had high-rise aluminum intake manifolds and the new Holley four-barrel carburetors, with throttle bores of 1.6875 in. and a rating of 780 cu. ft. per minute (cfm) of airflow, enough, calculated *Car Life*'s Roger Huntington, for an easy 500 bhp.

This increased bhp surely was why NASCAR was thinking about decreasing engine size, as the cars were already having trouble keeping their tires on the track with 450 or so bhp.

There was much more to come.

The hemi returns

When Mopar eased back into racing, it was low key. Plymouth gave some technical help and parts to Petty Engineering. Dodge's interest came from its public relations department—actually two men, Moon Mullins on the East Coast and Jack MacFarland on the West Coast. They enlisted the dealers association to sign up Owens and Pearson and ferried parts to

Here's Smokey, obviously very worried about how the technical crew will react to his car. Don Hunter

and from drag racer Don Garlits when parts were needed.

But the debacle of Daytona in 1963 got Chrysler management's attention. They weren't so publicly opposed to racing, so when Chevrolet pulled back, Chrysler went forward.

They did so at two levels. First, for right then, they hired a former driver, ex-midget racing professional Ronnie Householder, to run the racing program. Second, a team of engineers was assigned to develop a new racing engine. The design team drew on two excellent sources, the original hemispherical combustion chamber as seen on the first Chrysler V-8s in 1951, and the strong lower end of the 426 wedge engine.

Everything was revised, naturally, but the overall design of the new hemi, with opposed valves and ports, centered spark plug and domed piston, and two rocker arm shafts per head, was like the first one. And because the 426 hemi would have more power than the 426 wedge, the block had a deep recess for the main bearing caps. The caps were held in place by four bolts, two vertical, just like all engines have, and two horizontal, giving strength in that direction (Ford did the same thing in their 427, by the way).

The first new hemi was fired up December 6, 1963, and it was just in time.

Joe Weatherly and Bud Moore had run out of Pontiac parts, driven borrowed Plymouths and Dodges until that got old, and signed with Mercury. Ray Fox and Junior Johnson switched to Mercury at about the same time. Fords had won seven straight 500 mile races and the publications were asking if there would be anybody in Ford's way for 1964.

The answer was yes. Mopar had told NASCAR the new engine was on the way. They described it and made samples available, in plenty of time.

NASCAR meanwhile announced the final 1964 Grand National rules. If the car had a wheelbase of at least 114 in., it was limited to 396 ci. If the car had a wheelbase of 116 or more, it could run at 428. And there was a list of eligible models for 1964. (As a hint of what NASCAR officials had in mind even then, the Studebaker Hawk was an eligible model, never mind that the rules required passenger sedans and the Hawk was a coupe. NASCAR wanted to be sure any factory that wanted in could get in.)

An added clause in the 1964 rulebook required all specifications to be on file by December 10, 1963, imposed a forty-five-day wait after the parts were announced before they could be used on the track, and stated that NASCAR must be convinced said parts were or would be in production and offered for public sale.

Sadly, there was another change to come. In the last race of the 1963 season, at Riverside, Joe Weatherly's car slammed into the outside wall at turn six. He was held in place by his harness but his head was

Ford was more serious about building cars to match what the other guys had. (All the builders said what you would expect, that they were hitting the other guys back.) This is the Yellow Banana, *so called because it was painted yellow and had some funny curves and droops in profile. Lorenzen hit the wall in it once, and when questioned, he asked if they thought it was easy, driving a piece of fruit 145 mph.* Don Hunter

catapulted out the window and into the wall and he was killed. In virtually a running change, Grand National rules were changed to require a catch panel, first of metal mesh, later of fabric, to prevent such an event from happening again.

When Daytona time came, Mopar was more than ready. Goldsmith and his Plymouth took the pole with a qualifying lap of 174.910 mph. Johnson, "cool as the other side of a pillow," showed up with a Dodge. He had signed with Mercury, true, but when he heard about the new Mopar engine he reckoned that was the way to go, and Mercury graciously released him from his contract. He won one qualifier, a new guy named Bobby Isaac won the other.

Richard Petty—still not famous and so shy he'd not yet told the press that "my mother named me Richard" so he got billed as "Dick" Petty by *Car and Driver*—won the race.

More than that. He had a lap on the field and was followed by Jim Pardue and Goldsmith. The race was 1-2-3 Plymouth. Jim Paschal and his Dodge were fifth. Johnson was ninth, by the way, and soon moved to the Holman and Moody team, with Banjo Matthews on the wrenches, a move that caused Lorenzen, his new teammate, to bark, "When we go racing, it's every man for himself."

At Charlotte's World 600 that year, Fireball Roberts' car tangled with two others on the back stretch. His car caught fire. Other drivers pulled him out, but Roberts died several weeks later. Shortly after that Jim Pardue was killed during tire tests.

The good news was that Mopar was cleaning up and Ford wasn't giving up. Lorenzen especially kept his foot down and the Fords, which handled better, at least could put up a fight against the more powerful hemis.

Racetrack lawyers

Off track, there was a struggle. Hemis were a production engine in that Chrysler was making them, and making them in three versions—two for the drag strip and one for stock car tracks—and they were for sale. But they didn't come in passenger cars and the engines weren't intended for highway use. So they were sort of stock, but not exactly what the original rules had in mind. Ford didn't like that and began making plans.

Another oddity in the rules was that money and points didn't follow the same format. Petty had the driving title wrapped up by the end of September, while Lorenzen in a Ford wasn't even in the top ten. But he fought Petty to a standstill at Charlotte, for example, and won the race when Petty's tire blew. While Petty started sixty-one Grand National races in 1964 and won $98,810, Lorenzen only started sixteen races and collected $72,385.

Next, another bombshell. Ford announced they, too, would have a production-block, racing-only engine, but with a single camshaft in each head, sohc as the designed is called, for the 427.

That was too much. The hemi was rated at 415 bhp, but inside information ranked it at 450, against

425 for the Ford 427 and 440 for the Chevy 427. A special version of the Chevy 427 lapped a GM test track at 180 in a full-size sedan and that one was putting out better than 500 bhp!

The return bombshell came late in 1964, with the announcement that the 1965 engine limit would still be 427. "However, engines must be of production design only, thus eliminating overhead cams, high risers and hemispherical heads."

NASCAR installed two wheelbase classes, 119 in. for the speedways and 116 for the shorter tracks, and for the first time, a minimum weight. The weight would be the average weight of a Ford, a Chevy and a Plymouth.

For safety, a new fuel tank design was under study which would limit spillage in a crash. Roberts' death was a blow to the sport and nobody wanted a similar occurrence.

The 1964 season was closer than it looked. There were sixty-two championship races, with Ford winning thirty, Dodge fourteen, Plymouth twelve, Mercury five and Chevy one. So it may have been just as Bill France said it was, that the rules change was to make engines more "normal," and perhaps less powerful and thus safer and more sporting.

In keeping with the spirit of the times, Ford and Chrysler both filed protests against the ban of their engines real and imagined. France disallowed the protests.

Chrysler withdrew, and moved all their stock car support to USAC, where they were happy to have the money and the stars and let the hemis run. (One exception was Richard Petty, who stayed close to home, built a Barracuda with a hemi for drag racing, won a national title in that field and kept the Mopar-Petty Blue flag flying.)

Ford simply put the sohc heads on hold and went back to the improved 427 wedge engine. They began in 1965 to mop up the field, just as they had expected to in 1964.

They had better luck this time, except that luck didn't have much to do with it.

Nor did good racing.

Gossip from the past says that the original reduction to 396 ci was a pitch to General Motors, a way of persuading the biggest maker that the rules would allow them to take apart, without making actual racing engines. GM showed not a peep of interest and the reduction was withdrawn, and so was France's threat to field his own team of GM cars, just to give the fans something to watch.

That the fans wanted something to watch—real racing—was easily proven in 1965. The year began as an all-Ford show. There were only forty-three entries for the fifty-car Daytona 500 field, and twenty-six of these were Fords, with a smattering of Mercurys, Pontiacs, Plymouths and Chevys.

The only competition was internal as teammate Johnson raced ahead of Lorenzen and held the lead until a tire blew. Then Marvin Panch had a shot, but was slowed down by drizzle. Darel Dieringer in a one-year-old Mercury pushed Lorenzen until the rain got serious. The race was stopped after 332.4 miles, with a

Up close, the Yellow Banana *looks even less like a stock car. The chassis has obviously been lowered and the body panels attached at angles that turn the car into a wedge. This was a*

1966 car, when the flagrant body revision was at its best . . . or worst. Don Hunter

caution-slowed average of 141.539 mph, way off the 154.344 turned by Petty in 1964.

The year was lopsided—the worst yet and still the champ in that department. Ned Jarrett was driving champion, with Dick Hutcherson, a Ford driver, second and Dieringer third.

Fords won forty-eight of the fifty-five Grand National races, against four for Plymouth, two for Dodge and one for Mercury. Less obvious was the bias toward money for major events. Jarrett won thirteen races in fifty-four starts and collected $77,966. Lorenzen made seventeen starts, the major races, got four wins and took home $77,965, one buck less than the champion. Lorenzen was thirteenth for the year. Wendell Scott was eleventh, with fifty-two starts, no wins, four times in the top five and year-end winnings of $16,230.

While Ford took out win ads and Lorenzen sang on the way to the bank, other things were happening.

The technical news was safety. Goodyear and Firestone were both working on better, safer tires. They were spending vast amounts of money and running tests both for speed, and for durability and control. Dieringer was champion at this work and reckoned to have destroyed some 500 tires at speed by wearing them out and blowing them up. This was dangerous work: Billy Wade, an upcoming young driver, was killed during tire testing early in 1965. It was also vital work. Goodyear announced the development of a tire with an inner liner, a tube that could be inflated separately from the normal tire and which would keep the car in control if the outer tire blew. Two months later NASCAR made such tires mandatory on the right side, then for all four wheels, as Firestone joined Goodyear in building the devices.

As a demonstration of power and progress, recall that in 1961 a supercharged, airfoiled single seater built for such an attempt lapped Daytona at 180 mph.

Madder than hops, Curtis Turner heads for the garage with shattered hopes and windshield. The Fords were plagued by this problem at the 1966 Daytona 500. It wasn't until *later that pople began to wonder if the light body panels might be flexing a bit too much.* Road & Track

In February, 1965, Lee Roy Yarbrough was clocked around the oval at 181.818 in a full-size Dodge, albeit with a supercharged 1,000 bhp hemi V-8 built by Ray Fox. The right front tire picked up a bolt on the run, the tire blew and the car stayed in control.

During that same month of February Bill France had another bomb to drop. He announced the 1966 Grand National rules.

Major news: the hemi would be allowed back in.

Next, there would be a class for standard cars, with 119 in. wheelbase, 430 ci and 4,000 lb. minimum weight. There would be a class for intermediates, with 115 in. wheelbase, and a 430 engine with 4,000 lb. or a 405 engine carrying 3,500 lb. plus twenty pounds for each cubic inch. There would be a class for compacts, with 115 in. minimum wheelbase, 335 ci engines and 2,500 lb. minimum. Further, there would be a claiming rule, allowing any licensed entrant to claim, for $2,000, any other entrant's engine minus carburetor and camshaft.

This last idea is an old one, based on the hope and belief that if you make a man give away his engine, he won't invest in it. The idea has never worked in any form of racing; it has always generated bitter disputes and hard feelings, and in this case it faded away, thank goodness.

Shortly after announcing the 1966 rules, France revealed that by 1967 NASCAR and USAC would have the same rules. That is, no factory could play one racing organization against the other.

And in June 1965, at the peak of Ford's dominance, and the pit of public attention, the hemi was readmitted to Grand National racing—with some provisions. The first requirement was that such engines carry 9.36 lb. per cubic inch, which meant 3,985 lb. wet. The average minimum weight for the others worked out to about 3,700 lb., so the requirement was a definite handicap. And second, Mopar was made to run the larger Fury and Polara on the superspeedways, while the smaller 1964 models had to run the older wedge 426 engine.

In the same breath, one could say, Chevrolet's new 427, a Corvette engine with all the stagger valve and open chamber tricks learned in 1963, was readmitted to the Grand National, just in case anybody at Chevrolet was watching. (They were.)

That's a lot of news, a lot of detail and a lot of regulation. It was so much that France had to explain the whole thing again several months later: racers were expected to run the big car on the speedways, where overall size and shape was the major thing, and use the intermediates, Category II in NASCAR's book, on road courses and shorter tracks, where the winner was determined by power-to-weight ratio. Oh, and there was to be a ninety-day waiting period for any new engines or equipment; the minimum for production was 5,000 units. Period.

The hemi *really* returns

Chrysler Corporation's contribution to this escalation was to make the hemi engine a real production engine, offered as an option in the mid-size coupes from Dodge and Plymouth. This made sense in several ways. Mopar was active at the drags and the National Hot Rod Association also had production rules for stock class racing. There was a circuit hemi, a drag race hemi and a street hemi; the latter was, as you'd expect, the hottest, baddest production street engine

The 1967 Fords were a lot closer to stock than they had been for several years. This is Lorenzen's Holman and Moody car, a lot tidier than the Banana ever was. Lorenzen was second in the Daytona 500 in 1967, behind Andretti in a similar Ford. Daytona International Speedway

ever sold. They'd even beat the, uh, *prepared* Pontiacs in the magazine tests.

Ford reannounced their sohc engine option and this time NASCAR approved it, with a waiting period and some details: overhead cam engines would have to haul 10.36 lb. for every cubic inch; the engines would only be allowed in Category I, the big cars; and sohc and hemi engines would be limited to one four-barrel carburetor while wedge engines got two.

This announcement was the tip of a serious iceberg. The battle began in 1963 as the rules were bent to allow a nonproduction engine. This encouraged the factories to build special racing engines and by now, NASCAR was beginning to see that they'd unleashed more power, so to speak, than they'd expected.

Meanwhile again, NASCAR and USAC officials expressed concern because they hadn't been able to buy or borrow the Ford powerplants. If the weight was too high in the rules, one official said, too bad; we had to guess because we had not been able to get an engine to try. Nor had anybody else, a lack that would go on for years.

The actual racing was doing just fine. Petty showed up for Daytona in 1966 with a 405 hemi in the mid-sized Plymouth Belvedere. Goldsmith and Indy star Jim Hurtubise had 1965 Plymouths; Yarbrough, Pearson and new guy Sam McQuagg had Dodge Chargers, a fastback version of the mid-size Dodge.

Curtis Turner had finally been reinstated and had a Ford, while wily Smokey Yunick had recruited a sprint car pilot, a kid named Mario Andretti, for Yunick's sharp Chevelle.

Oh, the hints here! Richard took the pole at 175.165 mph. Goldsmith won the first qualifier, at 167; Earl Balmer took the second in a Dodge.

In the race Petty waltzed away to a 160.627 mph win. Some of the Mopars blew up, many of the Fords had their windshields crack and disintegrate—they blamed chunks of rubber—and there went Turner, while Andretti tangled with another car and retired.

The year balanced out in the end. Pearson won the national title, with fifteen wins and thirty-three times in the top ten from forty-two starts. James Hylton, also a Dodge man, was second. Petty was third, with eight wins and twenty-two times in the top ten from thirty-nine starts—Petty was fast but pushed the car beyond its limits. In the manufacturer's series, there were 713 Fords entered in the forty-nine Grand Nationals, of which thirty-four were on pavement and fifteen on dirt. Fords got ten wins and 216 points, while the 196 Dodge entries had eighteen wins but only ninety-eight points. The 195 Plymouths had sixteen wins and ninety-two points. All finishing positions were tallied, so the more entries, the more points—except that the 294 Chevys only won three, for fifty-two points, and Mercs were forty-seven entries, two wins, eleven points.

Fireball Roberts' legacy arrived September 1, 1966, with the mandatory fitting of fuel cells, tanks that were filled with material to keep the fuel from sloshing and being hurled out in a crash. There would still be fires in racing but never again as bad as they'd been.

The rules face the facts

In August 1966 the 1967 rules arrived and another major revision in stock car racing was underway.

First, engines must be the street version of an engine that had been sold and titled, minimum number 500, to the public as of January 1 or April 15. If the engine hadn't met the requirement by the second date, it couldn't be used all that year.

Second, Categories I and II would continue. (Category III, the compacts, would be revised into a separate series, Grand Touring.) There would be no weight or displacement handicap for any car, except for a minimum weight of 3,500 lb. and a limit of 9.36 lb. per cubic inch.

Third, hemi engines could use one four-barrel; wedge engines could have two fours or three two-barrels. All would use a production intake manifold. Frames could be altered and reinforced for 8.5 in. wheels. The wheelbase rules would remain, except that the wheelbase would be referenced from the door jams and the front wheel centerline.

Unit construction cars had to retain configurations and dimensions from stock; bodies had to keep their original contours. The type of differential was optional, but no quick-changes were permitted, nor were any remote controls for altering weight distribution.

Then came some elaboration. Hemis could use 1.69 in. carburetor bores on box manifolds and 1.75 in. bores on log manifolds. The sohc engines were limited to 1.69 in. bores, period, and the wedges could run the same size on any manifold they could fit under the hood.

Further, disc brakes could be used, and further still, anybody caught with sheet metal modified beyond the limits would be allowed to use that body with the addition of a nonadjustable rear lip, estimated to take 5 to 7 mph off the top speed of a car.

When all this was announced NASCAR made a big point of having it all come from ACCUS (Automobile Competition Committee of the US), the club formed by NASCAR, USAC and SCCA.

Then France himself commented that "most of the cars that competed in 1966 can be corrected to be eligible for the [1967] year."

The next month, he warned that the tech crew had templates ready to check against the cars for 1967, and that even if the windshield was flush it must still carry the stock-looking chrome trim.

What was going on? Why all this?

Templates: The shape of things to go

When the factories and teams first began reshaping cars to gain speed, some of the examples were so obvious as to be a joke, like the Ford *Banana,* and others were much more subtle, for instance the Petty Plymouths or Yunick's legendary Chevelle.

NASCAR determined to correct these abuses but the changes were so clever they couldn't always be spotted by the naked eye. The answer was sets of templates, full-sized profiles of the tops and sides of all the models accepted for Grand National racing. The rules specify precisely how high the car's hood must be at an exact point behind the front edge of the front bumper, and the templates go over the car from there. They must meet or brush against the hood, windshield, top, rear window and trunk lid. And there are patterns to check cross-sections, to be sure the car is the proper width and profile there as well.

The technical inspectors travel with full sets of templates for all eligible cars in Winston Cup and the current Grand National, and the cars are checked at the beginning of each race meet and every time they go on the track: the officials don't expect any changes between practice and qualifying, but if they check every time, they won't be surprised.

When the templates appeared for the 1967 season, the rules required each racing car to have the profile and wheelbase and fender flare and so on that it had when it came from the factory. The templates were made from cars as they came from the factory.

But by 1988, with the Winston Cup cars all built to a specified wheelbase, and made with bodies that never saw an assembly line, and with various changes allowed to accommodate an engine not designed to go under the hood of the model in question, the templates are profiles that have been negotiated at the beginning of the season.

At the start of Daytona's Speed Week in 1988, just about all the new Pontiacs arrived with rear decks a useful inch or so longer than the plan had called for. Gosh, grinned Bobby Allison, the car must have stretched on the way down here.

The cars were reworked to meet the rules, but even so, the smart guys are still at work and Smokey Yunick has the last laugh.

The template was standard equipment by 1968, and outwardly the cars had returned to normal. This is Glen Wood, of the Wood brothers team. It looks as if close is good enough in Grand National as well as in horseshoes and hand grenades. Road & Track

What was going on had been going on for years.

And if you didn't know how to make it work for you, you'd probably have said it was illegal.

Cheating versus creativity

The new rules and procedures were another milestone in our history. We have to back up a few years to see how and why.

Smokey Yunick spoke for the majority when he said he has always figured that if they didn't say you couldn't do it, you could do it. Rules define their own violation. If you stick in a racing camshaft when the rules say strictly stock, it is illegal. But if cams are free choice, the racing version is fine.

By 1966 the racers and builders were doing incredible things, within and without the rules. And the rules had become much less restrictive; in a sense they had followed along behind the top tuners and made legal whatever they had just invented.

There were some good reasons these modifications were allowed to happen. First and foremost, the changes were improvements and they were needed.

By 1966 the racers were talking about 180 versus 160 mph speeds. They said 160 was as safe and comfy as old shoes, forgetting that within their memories, Marshall Teague, as good a driver as there was in his day, had been killed when he dared 160 in a special Indy-style car. Now the stockers cruised at 160, while flirting with 180. (Twenty years later, of course, the drivers will be saying 180 is easy and 200 is right on the edge, but that's racing.)

The stock car racers were safe at 160 and were still on the ground at 180 because the cars . . . weren't stock.

Amazing things were being done. The rules spelled out a ride height, for instance, so the guys used to pack the coil springs with blocks of wood, bars of soap or both. They would roll through tech inspection at the required height, but when they hit the first turn and loaded the suspension, pop! and down the car went. Chrysler products used torsion bars adjusted with lever arms that bottomed on the frame. If a piece of brittle plastic were greased and wedged between arm and frame, the same thing happened, except that the Dodge boys used to say shucks, them torsion bars sure are tough to keep adjusted. Yunick had a hydraulic system running off the power steering pump to raise and lower the car from the driver's seat. Johnson, who by this time had retired to become a car builder and owner, had a system with a cable, by which the nose could be dropped after the car went onto the track. There were people who said this should have been allowed because it was so difficult to find, and there were those who said the trick was camouflage, that it was there for the inspectors to find so they would miss the other stuff.

And there were stories about iron bars mounted inside the bumper only at weigh-in, and concealed tanks of water in the fender panels, known only because the guilty cars trailed water vapor down the back stretch.

The only rule not stretched to the snap was that of engine size; Yunick and the other bright guys had only contempt for such a simple way to get ahead.

Along about here the engineers got even with the backyard crowd. The main factor was that Detroit was shifting from the separate body and frame to unit construction, with central body and frame in one piece but with a front subframe, perhaps an extra perimeter frame. These were good designs but they knocked the edges off the rule book. And the better they made the roll cage, the more it lent stiffness to

Some of the cars had become more subtle. This one came from Dodge's race shop, for Buddy Baker, and had the virtually stock body relocated on its wheelbase; the Mopars *had gone to unit body/frame construction, so the relocation could be done more easily.* Road & Track

the body and the less they needed the frame rails anyhow.

Add to that the engineers' knowledge of aerodynamics. The real, if secret, reason the cars were going so fast, so safely, was that they were literally being reshaped. This is where the factory engineers had to come in. The speeds and loadings from the banked tracks had taken the cars beyond pragmatism.

Lary Rathgeb, one of the Chrysler Corporation engineers who worked on the racing program, recalls that when racing director Ronnie Householder first went to work, he wanted heavy-duty parts so he got Pontiac suspension pieces and instructed the engineers to use them on the Dodges. Told the geometry would be wrong, he said he had asked for parts, not advice.

And he learned a hard lesson. The hemi-powered racers were fast but didn't handle with the Fords, so the engineers got permission to revise the suspension.

They went beyond that. When the minimum weight rules arrived, the factory guys were able to get, or make, thinner body panels, which moved the weight lower, where it was useful.

The body panels themselves became subject to change. In mid-1963, the Ford Galaxie was offered with a fastback roof. It looked good. More important, it was slicker and less liable to create lift in the rear at speed.

The next step was replacement. Fred Lorenzen prepared and raced a 1964 Ford. In 1967, the car was sold to Wendell Scott. The rules required Grand National cars to be no more than two years old so Scott repanelled the car as a 1967 and raced it for three more years.

Some of these changes and more happened at the factory level. In 1964 Dodge engineers built what was known in-house as the one-one-one-and-one-half car.

Profiles aren't everything. At the top we have the stock 1967 Plymouth Satellite, as it came from the factory. Below, the Plymouth Satellite as raced by Petty Engineering in 1967. Looks just right, until one checks the distance between the top of the front fenderwell and the top of the fender, or the distance from the end of the front bumper to the beginning of the wheelwell. The profile is the same, but the body itself has lost a few inches. *Road & Track*

It was a Dodge coupe, except that the body was cut loose from the pan, one inch trimmed from the bottom of the body, and then rewelded. The engine and mounts were moved back 1½ inches in the pan, and the front and rear suspension mounting points, and thus the wheels, were relocated one inch farther back in the pan. The rules said the frame had to be stock, and the wheelbase had to be left alone, and both requirements had been met. Sort of.

Fair is foul and foul is fair

Then there was the *Yellow Banana*, a Ford built by Johnson. And there was the Yunick Chevelle, arguably the most famous illegal car ever seen.

Johnson's car was simply, obviously, wildly revised. Yunick's had more going for it.

First, Yunick's car actually began as a Chevrolet engineering exercise, back when the Chevy people were only allowed to experiment and not race. When time got short and the executives got edgy, the car was shipped to Yunick's Daytona Beach garage and finished, then shown, entered and occasionally raced.

Legend says the technical inspectors at Daytona fell upon the Chevelle with cries of rage, removed the fuel tank, measured, calculated and then rolled the car out of the shed, with the comment that they had found thirteen illegal modifications, at which Yunick snapped, "Make that fourteen," climbed into the car and drove home, without a visible fuel tank.

Sorry, Yunick said twenty years later, but in point of fact he had to add gas before driving the Chevelle to his shop.

The Chevelle legend grew until it was larger (or smaller) than life. Ever since the car disappeared—which happened because Yunick was playing pranks and having fun; he knew he'd never get the car onto the track again—folklore has said the car was built to ⅞ scale, or maybe it was ¹⁵/₁₆ths.

It wasn't. The proportions had been rearranged; the engine and the wheelbase had been moved within the body's overall length and most of the curves weren't as acute as they'd been and there were some aerodynamic aids built in. The proportions were changed but length and wheelbase were just as the book said they should be. Sorry, but in this one case, the fable improves on the facts.

And then there was the time Lee Petty blushed because somebody looked in the trunk of his street car and found aerodynamic textbooks.

The stories go on and on. The critical change, however, came when Ralph Moody figured out that he could take a floor pan and use it to build a completely racing machine, with the pan, the heavy-duty front and rear suspension, and a roll cage that actually was a space frame. Then he could weld body panels to the tubing. The result was known as the surface plate frame because all the dimensions and alignments were checked on a flat and true surface plate.

It was obvious to everybody that, first, if they had a structurally sound car before they put the body panels on it, why, that meant they could redo the body panels to help slip the car through the air, and keep on the ground at the same time. Everybody began building their cars that way, with factory help, advice and approval.

By late in 1966 the rule stretching had gone as far as it could go, with Fords and Chevys both arriving at tracks in flagrant violation of the rules, but allowed to run because they were all like that.

And they worked. Petty's 405 powered Plymouth was faster than it had been with 426 ci in part because the rule had been a hood height of 31 in. The new rule

The work goes on. Plymouth's factory team was Nichels and Goldsmith. Here's Paul Goldsmith in the 1968 Plymouth at Daytona. Road & Track

allowed the hoods to be only 27 in. off the ground and presto, Richard was running 185, in control.

This meant better, faster and safer racing. To NASCAR's credit, they rewrote the rule book for 1967, allowing some improvements; the clause requiring a stock frame simply disappeared. The rules recognized the platform frame, while expecting a return to stock body contours and giving everybody the same weight minimum.

The engine dispute would go on, however. The sohc Ford 427 was officially claimed as a production option, replacing the 289 V-8 in the Galaxie for only $1,963, but that was in the books. Nobody ever saw one sold and the ban held.

The production rule for 1967 became 500 units sold. Ford announced they had run the Fairlane, with two square feet less frontal area than the Galaxie, and that sohc 427s were available in crates, for $2,200. Again, nobody ever saw one.

Pay any price, bear any burden

The 1967 rules were supposed to bring production units, engines disputes and that sort of thing under control.

Instead, the rules channeled the racers' energies into new and more clever gambits. And they raised stock car racing to a new plateau of skill and popularity.

The main force here was Petty Engineering. The Pettys had something of the right team at the right time, but they also had some luck and circumstance. When Chrysler Corporation set up its racing program

Secrets revealed: The builder's blueprints

When Chrysler got serious about getting back into stock car racing, they unleashed a group of engineers who had both degrees and empirical knowledge. And they liked racing, and they built some interesting cars.

These drawings (courtesy of Larry Rathgeb) show a progression, from the car of 1968, through 1970, when other concerns shut off the funds. As the notes on the drawings show, the cars were built with relocated wheelbases, new frame parts, the body shells dropped on the pans, and with allowances for engines, like the Westlake-head V-8, never seen in stock car racing.

The cars built before the rules got tough were raced. Officially the later ones were used for practice only, or so we are told by men who are keeping their faces straight. They built some fine cars, in any event.

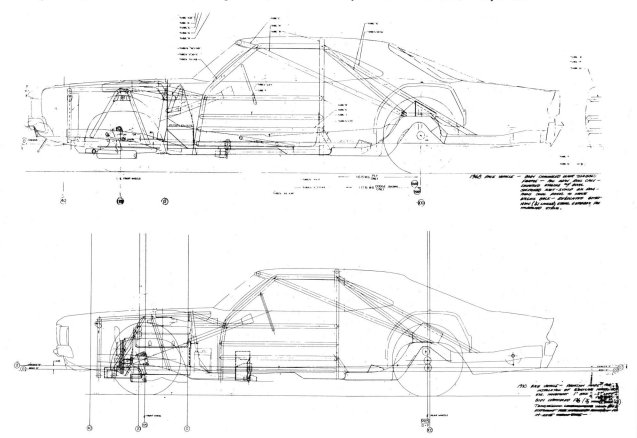

it had three main teams, with Ray Nichels and Paul Goldsmith as the prime connection with the factory. They did the experiments and passed along what they learned. The Pettys were next in line for Plymouth; Cotton Owens did the same for Dodge. (One of the reasons Johnson left Dodge was just that—he didn't get the new stuff as soon as Nichels did.)

This structure allowed for freedom of expression. If one team found something, they were supposed to tell the others, but they didn't always do so, and the managers at Mopar knew better than to get mad if the teams kept their tricks to themselves.

As of course they did. The 1967 season started fairly fair, with the legendary Turner in the legendary Yunick's new Chevelle on the pole for the Daytona 500 at 180.831 mph. Next to him was Richard Petty in a new Plymouth at 179.068. In short, the cars hadn't been slowed down much by the rules and the templates.

But Turner's car blew up on the 142nd lap and Petty's did the same on the 193rd lap, so the winner was (pause) Mario Andretti, the sprint car star and future world champion, in a Ford Fairlane. Freddy Lorenzen's Ford was right behind him and James Hylton, in a 1965 Dodge (pre-template, wink, nudge), came in third. The new cars were fast and they were pretty close.

Except that the Pettys then waltzed away, or so it seemed. Richard got his fifty-fourth Grand National win, tying his dad, then won the Rebel 500 at Darlington for his fifty-fifth win. He won ten straight and took three of the four national events on NASCAR's north-ern tour, a careful and successful attempt to go national.

By what can't have been coincidence here is that, just as Richard tied Lee for most wins, Fred Lorenzen retired and went back to the Chicago area to work in real estate. He'd done it for the money, Fred said, and he had enough at the age of thirty-two, so he was hanging up his helmet.

One wonders if it was that simple.

Meanwhile Petty worked as hard as Wendell Scott, drove as hard as Lorenzen, and won more money and more races than anybody in the sport's history. And of course he got the driver's title.

Nor was that all. Richard was devastatingly handsome, with a photogenic grin, while he was the perfect gentleman. Men could admire him and so could women. And kids. Petty has always been willing to stand and talk and sign autographs for as long as there were fans to be appreciated. He took business courses in college and did some extra homework in the form of creating and perfecting an autograph that's a work of art. No scribbles for King Richard.

By the evidence, Petty made an early decision that if he wanted to be a champion driver, he would have to make some sacrifices and live a public life, always on stage, no flaws allowed. He has done just that. Petty has been the sport's main hero for twenty years at this writing. His popularity is worldwide . . . and aspirin and tension have eaten away half his stomach. Take what you want from life, the Spanish proverb says, but prepare to pay for it.

The Pettys did their own cars. Mighty close here, but the 1968 Petty car had a vinyl roof cover and the metal beneath was so thin it began to come loose, thus the tape. Compare the profile of the left front fender creases. Petty's has been sculpted for less lift at speed. What also doesn't show here, and nobody knew for years, was that the Petty speedway cars had been built with a side-to-side weight bias, heavy on the left, while all the other teams and the inspectors were only looking at total weight. Road & Track

Back on the track there were forty-nine national races in 1967. Plymouth got thirty-one wins, to ten for Ford, five for Dodge, three for Chevy and none for anybody else (specifically Mercury, as they were the eligible make left out). Petty won twenty-seven races in forty-eight starts. Bear in mind here, when comparing old and new, that nearly twice as many races were held in those days, which is why the newer guys will never run up records to top Petty or his peers.

At the end of the season Bill France had a few words. He mentioned that the results hadn't been as one-sided as the headlines, that because there were more Fords entered they finished high. Ford was the manufacturing champion, 199 points to 101 for Plymouth, ninety-nine for Dodge and seventy-five for Chevy. Ford had twenty-three poles to twenty-one for Plymouth. Ford won Daytona, Riverside and Atlanta; the cars were close in speed and talent.

In 1968, said France, there would be a 430 ci limit and hemis would have one four-barrel to two for wedge engines and the coming Chevrolet stagger-valve would be treated like a hemi: one carburetor. Builders could juggle weight and displacement if they wished, 9.36 lb. per cubic inch. But builders who wanted to run a new GM product, with 115 in. wheelbase, had to add one inch. And the minimum weight was now 3,650 instead of 3,500 lb. The template rules and restrictions were still in effect, of course, and smaller cars in the Mustang/Camaro class had a new division, called Grand Touring. (The SCCA was doing well with a road race series, the Trans-Am, for such cars and France could see opportunity there. The drag racing division was also going strong.)

Car Life did a complete analysis of Petty's Plymouth late in 1967, which appeared in the March 1968 issue. The car was, the magazine said, the best, fastest and winningest stocker ever. They explained the attention to detail and figured the hemi cranked out 600 bhp under Maurice Petty's care, compared with the 500-plus available direct from Chrysler and with the 600 bhp the best of the Ford guys could wring from the 427 wedge. The overhead cam engine had disappeared by this time but the wedge engine had new heads (tunnel port by name) and a new manifold, and NASCAR said customers couldn't buy them, either.

Going with the wind

The real work was being done elsewhere. When the gates opened by Daytona the Ford teams, which by then were major operations, with 120 guys on the Holman and Moody payroll, were ready and the Mercury teams were back in force.

Their secret was bodywork. Their engineers knew what they could get from their engines and had decided—they were not alone, as we'll see—that they could get greater speed more efficiently with aerodynamics. And the cars handled, as can be seen by the results of the Motor Trend 500 at Riverside, the real season opener. Dan Gurney won in a Ford, followed by David Pearson and Parnelli Jones, also in Fords. (Pearson had been hired away from Dodge to replace Lorenzen. That will also be important again.) And Lorenzen came to the races as a coach, helping a tough new guy named Bobby Allison.

But the big news was new metal. Ford and Mercury had new versions of the mid-size sedans, Torino and Cyclone. They came with fastbacks, tapering rooflines with nearly horizontal rear windows, and roofs virtually dead level when the cars were dropped in front, as the racers were allowed to do. The body sides were flat and the fenders were contoured so the tires, which create air drag, were tucked away out of the airstream. The mechanicals were the same in 1966 and 1967, but in 1968 Cale Yarborough took the pole with his Mercury, the brand that was shut out in the previous year, with 189.233 mph.

Yarborough was a type: the bravest kid in town. He had played football up to the semipro ranks, and had planned on a pro career except that for all his speed and strength, he wasn't tall enough for the big leagues. After sky diving and rodeo riding got boring or too risky, he campaigned the dirt car he'd built when he was fifteen. Yarborough lied about his age and raced the outlaw circuit, then the NASCAR sportsman division. He was too young for a Grand National license by four years, but he bluffed his way through until his football fame caught up with him.

By 1968 David Pearson, shown here with Miss Darlington, had had lots of practice showing trophy girls what they were supposed to do with winners. Road & Track

Ford's 1968 Torino had a clean shape, especially when the rules allowed enough rake to put the roof and trunk panel nearly horizontal. Shown is Foyt's car, which lost to the slicker number 21 Mercury. Road & Track

They threw him out of the pits; he snuck back and drove until he wrecked the car.

But he had impressed John Holman and got a ride in Banjo Matthews' Ford and later with the Wood brothers. He was on his way.

So was Ford-Mercury. During practice, setup for qualifying, Pearson was clocked at 193.2 in his Ford Torino. The Mopars were running 183 and 184: only Petty could come close to the Fords, running some 5 mph up on the others from Mopar. Yarborough won the race after a duel with Lee Roy Yarbrough (tricky names here but both are spelled correctly) in an identical Cyclone.

What had happened was streamlining. First, the Mercury had a pointed grille and the Ford had a flat one, recessed into the car's nose. The Cyclone was 1.5 mph faster around the track than the Torino, and the Fords were 5 mph faster than Petty and 10 mph faster than the other Mopars. Jon McKibben, technical editor for *Car Life*, calculated that it took 20 bhp to gain 1 mph at Daytona, so the quick answer was that the Fords had 30 bhp less than the Mercs and the wedge 427 was some 150 bhp stronger than the hemi; obviously this wasn't so, proving that the advantage was in the bodywork. Further, McKibben bit a sizable bullet as he pointed out the subtle changes made in the Petty Plymouth, the car he had analyzed the previous month, while not noticing that the front was sculptured where the new templates didn't go.

The difference here was that Mercury had a better shape and Merc and Ford had raceworthy bodies from the factory while the Mopars had to make theirs at home. Ford Motor Company began to sweep the boards, to the extent that at midseason the rules were revised to let the hemi and the Chevy stagger-valve have two four-barrels like the formerly inferior wedge.

There were a lot of people taking notes and a lot of parallel stuff happening. On the track, Cale Yarbo-rough won the Firecracker 400 with Lee Roy Yarbrough second again, trailed by Pearson in a Torino. Charlie Glotzbach and his two-carburetor Dodge Charger had the pole and Petty was next to him, but the Fords had been sandbagging—they knew France didn't like no contests—and walked away in the race.

Ford got twenty wins in 1968, trailed by Plymouth with sixteen, Mercury with seven, Dodge with five and Chevrolet with one on a $^1/_5$ mile track on Long Island, part of the northern tour and not a true NASCAR Grand National-style place. The money and points system were different so Cale collected $130,000 but was eighteenth in the driver standings while Pearson, with more starts and a better average, won the title but less money. Petty got sixteen more wins, on tracks where speed wasn't the answer, and was third for the year.

Who's running this show?

The 1969 rules, announced midway through the 1968 season, raised the minimum weight to 3,900 lb., kept the limit at 430 ci and the formula of 9.35:1 for the short track cars with less weight and smaller engines. Wheel rims were allowed to widen to nine inches. Dry sump oil systems, with a separate remote tank and thus an engine placed lower within the car as there was no deep pan below the block, were permitted on the belief that a remote tank would allow less oil to spill if the engine blew. The rules displayed new, more detailed templates and the warning that in future there would be a list of eligible engines. As sort of a subclause, it was announced that all engines would be limited to one four-barrel, and that cars must start the race on the tires they used for qualifying.

Below the surface, NASCAR was worried, primarily about speed, especially since the France family was deeply involved in building and financing a new track.

They were planning an even faster version of Daytona to be constructed near an Alabama town within reach of lots of people, but with the awkward Indian name of Talladega (the magazines tried to tell readers it was pronounced tal-a-dee-ga but nobody ever has).

Back on the drawing boards, pens were flying. Ford was at work on revised and improved versions of their fastbacks, and Dodge was going to take a big by-God step.

Ford Motor Company stretched things just a little. The basic shape of the mid-size two-door coupes was right, so they began with an extra six inches in the front fenders and hood, a lower nose and flush-mount grille, and a rear bumper in front, canted into a small air dam. Ford's was the Talladega and Mercury's was the Cyclone Spoiler, a tip to the track for one and to the little lip on the rear deck for the other.

Over at Dodge they were ready to get even. In 1966 the division had an exclusive model, a Dodge coupe with a sloping fastback roof, a personal car in intent. It was largely a fad at the time, but the sloping roof did give some speed, although it also created lift and made the car not quite right for racing. But the idea was there.

The next version of the Charger was a better-looking car, with a rear window recessed between two panels, flying buttresses in architecture, from the edge of the roof back along the rear fenders. This lovely rear end caused turbulence and lift, however, so it was a handful on the track.

The Dodge Special Vehicles Group had a cure. They borrowed the flush grille from the Dodge Coronet and kept the flowing lines by filling the space between the buttresses with the rear window. They created a fastback, and a good-looking car. To meet the rules,

they made 500 of them; they called the model the Charger 500.

The Dodge group still had problems. One was natural, in that they arrived with their new body only to learn that Ford and Mercury had been going the same direction, but a few steps further.

Also, this was a Dodge project, not a Chrysler Corporation project. Because Dodge had done the work and Plymouth hadn't, this car was only for Dodge. Petty, having been outrun all year and eager to get back in the hunt, saw the new car and asked to drive for Dodge instead of Plymouth. Chrysler Corporation said no, and after deep thought, Petty switched to Ford. His first race for the new boss was at Riverside, opening the season, and he won it. (There were no hard feelings, by the way, or if there were, they've been forgotten. But the guys who were there then said that letting Petty go was a mistake.)

Keeping track here, Ford and Chrysler were locked into a duel, each ready to do whatever it took to win. NASCAR was not happy, since the cars were less and less stock. Chevrolet and the other GM divisions were lying low; they had performance parts all right and they helped some racers most of the time, but they didn't have permission to build the equipment that would be needed to keep up with Ford and Chrysler. Instead, they ran sports car and road races, where more restrictive rules let them match blow for blow.

The 1969 season was marked—perhaps one should say marred—by another form of controversy.

Talladega, 1969. Richard Petty has become a spokesman for the drivers and crews, who want a professional association and more money and are not happy with the pavement at the new, fastest-in-the-world track. Petty and the other stars didn't drive in that first major race, but they did get a fairer share of the proceeds, the track was improved and Petty's stand was understood by the fans. Chrysler Corporation

Behind the scenes, Richard Petty had immeasurable help from his brother Maurice, left, and cousin Dale Inman, who built his engines and ran the pits. Road & Track

There was no direct link here, but when Dodge announced its streamliner and Plymouth didn't have one, Petty asked to drive for Dodge and Plymouth said no, so Petty went with . . . Ford. This is the Talladega version, the stretched and smoothed Torino, and Richard is in the process of winning Riverside, 1969, his first race for Ford. Road & Track

The Talladega track was a 2.6 mile tri-oval, with thirty-three-degree bankings. It was supposed to be faster, the new king of superspeedways, as indeed it became.

But when Dodge tested there before the first race, drivers Charlie Glotzbach and Buddy Baker, son of pioneer Buck Baker, reported blurred vision at speeds above 183 mph. The suspensions and tires were in balance but the track was found to have bumps. The Dodge team talked with aerospace experts from NASA at nearby Huntsville. They were told that the effect came from the brain getting confused by lateral acceleration such as that from a rocket lift-off, or from hitting sharp bumps at high speed. It was called the Pogo Effect.

The Dodge cars used to discover this unpleasant problem were themselves a new project. Dodge had learned of the Ford and Mercury work and decided to do the same thing but more of it. They took the standard Charger 500 hemi and put on a new nose—a long, low tapering cone with tiny intake—while the rear deck got a big wing. The car looked odd. On the street, it was vulnerable when parked or driven into driveways. It was called the Daytona 500 for the race and because that's how many Dodge had to build to make the model eligible for competition.

The car was supposed to be a 1970 model but it went so well—Glotzbach lapped the five-mile oval at Chrysler's proving ground at 204 mph in July, 1969—that Dodge decided to use the car for the Talladega race.

If there was a race. The drivers had all heard about the Pogo Effect. The tire companies were wor-ried as well about who would be blamed if the chassis loadings and speeds created problems, which seemed likely.

Another factor, approaching on a collision course, threatened to halt the race. The drivers weren't convinced that they were getting their share of NASCAR's prosperity. The drivers—joined by mechanics and crew members—formed the Professional Driver's Association (PDA). It was as much a union as an association; the PDA was supposed to be a way for the rivals on track to join ranks for economic reasons.

Talladega was France's new dream. He had all his and the family's—and some of Union Oil Company's—money tied up in the track and now the track had a legitimate safety issue. The drivers lined up behind Richard Petty and said that if the track wasn't fixed and their other wishes granted, they wouldn't race.

France met the challenge head on. He borrowed a car and turned a few 176 mph laps himself, not racing speed but faster than the average old codger would go and fast enough, he said, to prove it could be done. And he offered a raincheck, a ticket to the next race at Talladega or Daytona. What he didn't do was agree to recognize the PDA, who in turn agreed not to race.

The 1969 Grand National had the most varied and least equal field in memory. All the factory-backed drivers, except Dodge's Bobby Isaac, stayed home. Ford went home with its drivers. Dodge, with a huge investment at stake in its Charger Daytona 500, let the contracted drivers sit but offered their cars to qualified guys who didn't have rides. The tire companies in turn refused to mount tires unless the drivers promised not to exceed 190 mph.

Ford's 427 wedge (shown here in a 1969 Mercury Cyclone but the same engine in either brand of car) was more compact than the sohc version and was sold to the public, albeit in limited quantities. The air cleaner here is ducted to an intake grille at the base of the windshield, where at speed a high pressure area rams cool air into the engine for some free horsepower. Road & Track

France's contractors meanwhile were fixing the track, so it was smooth enough to handle the speeds, provided the tires were stronger. They were, but until the race was over both sides were so politically polarized, they didn't want to listen to each other. In any event, the Pogo Effect was never heard of again.

The race began with only thirteen Grand National sedans, followed (the right word here) by twenty-four GT cars, racing compacts that had run their 400 mile race the previous day.

One of the entrants was Richard Brickhouse, making his second Grand National start, but this time in the Dodge Daytona built for Glotzbach. When Brickhouse promised to stay under 190, he must have had his fingers crossed, for in the later stages he ran the Daytona up to 195, and he won, the first Grand National victory for him and the first that year for Dodge, but nonetheless a hollow triumph.

It could be said that there were no winners. France was talked out of banning the drivers who walked out, while the drivers never did get what they asked for; not quite in the way they wanted it, anyway. Later there would be a rearrangement of the finances, meaning more money. The war wasn't exactly won, but the issue became moot.

There was a lot going on. Racing had adopted the slogan Sport of the Seventies. Michigan had a new speedway, a two-mile tri-oval with eighteen-degree

banking, as did Texas, also two miles around but with the turns banked at twenty-two degrees. There was talk of merging the several Southern track-owning groups into one, and while it didn't happen, it did reveal that all the tracks were in the black and paying dividends. There were ongoing talks with the television people. The superspeedways were going to be important and therefore so were the superstreamliners.

The rules get rougher

Despite the Daytona for Dodge, 1969 was another Ford year. Petty won ten races for the make, including his 100th Grand National. He said he would go home and begin work on the next 100. (Son Kyle, who on the occasion of his dad taking the all-time win record from his granddad had said he himself wanted to be a cowboy, not a driver. This time he said he wanted to be an astronaut, not a driver.) Fords won twenty-six of the fifty-four series races, to twenty-two for Dodge, four for Mercury and two for Plymouth. David Pearson took the driver's title again, the second man (after Lee Petty) to win it three times.

Before this, however, NASCAR officials announced that in 1970 they would have tougher rules. They were going to clamp down on the streamliners, by requiring that there be 1,000 examples or half the number of the make's dealerships, whichever was the larger. Chevrolet had 6,000 dealers, so any racing Chevys would be made in lots of 3,000. The engine rule, 500 examples, would remain as it was, as would the displacement limit, the weight rules and the displacement to weight scale.

In 1971, there would be an engine limit of 366 ci.

NASCAR wasn't happy with the way things had gone; the racing executives liked close races versus runaway winners. The Dodge Daytona 500 was the freak, made all the moreso because it won races. Plymouth was inspired to see the light, hire back Petty and begin work on the Superbird, the same car in general as the Daytona except that some of the panels were refined, some of the Plymouth pieces were actually Dodge, and the front had a larger and more attractive intake. The size of the intake for cooling air is critical, and the Dodge engineers chose to spend their time getting it right for the speedway and the devil with style or traffic. The Daytona overheated in road use, so the Superbird got a radiator intake that was larger, and worked better on the road, while being as aerodynamic and thus as useful, at racing speeds.

Ford began laying out the King Cobra, and Mercury the Spoiler II. Both were respective versions of the Talladega and the Cyclone Spoiler; that is, they were racing versions of the mid-size two-door, but with drooped and pointed nose and a rear wing.

The new rules contained an interesting escape clause: there didn't have to be as many engines as there were bodies. Dodge was building the hemi 426, which was in principle the big-block 413 grown into the 426 and topped by new heads. For less money and equal power there was the Dodge 440, an enlarged 426 but with wedge heads and less bulk.

Ford somehow managed to have three big-block V-8s, the 427, the 428 and later the 429, all in the same class but otherwise completely different. The 427 was strictly for racing and near as the records show, none were sold for street use in a passenger sedan. The closest the 427 ever got to the public was in the later Cobra roadster, which even in road trim was pretty much a racing car. There was a canted-valve head conversion for the 429, also not sold to the public.

The 428 (the enlarged 390) went into the Talladega, Spoiler and even the Mustang road cars on occasion. You could buy the racing body with a standard engine, in other words, which meant the factory could qualify the racing body and not have to sell the racing engine. (As a further muddle, Ford was required to build at least 500 Talladegas. Their records list 754 produced, but at least two more, Research and Development mules, were constructed from stock Torinos by the engineering staff. One of the two was painted Petty Blue for one day, to appear in a Ford ad when Petty won a race. It was later reverted back to white, and is now the proud possession of Banjo Matthews, a gift from Ford.)

The dam was in peril of breaking, while the tables were being turned on a daily basis.

Item: Ford began 1970 with ads listing all their NASCAR victories. When they offered the Torino with 351 V-8, an enlargement of the thinwall small-block and nothing to do with the big-blocks, they said the car included "A piece of Daytona, The Atlanta 500, Donnie Allison and a wide-open induction system... Many better ideas now found in the 351-4V were being tested during 1969's grueling races."

And they probably were. But the engine itself wasn't.

Item: Ford went testing and learned that the 1970 Torino with the same engine was down 10 mph on the 1969 Talladega. And, making their ads a bit closer to fact, Ford was trying both a de-stroked version of the 429 and a bored-out version of the 351 in preparation for the coming limit and had decided on the small-block as the way to go.

Crusher item: Henry Ford said as the season opened that Ford's racing effort would be cut back, by a full seventy-five percent. There would be backing,

The Talladega Torino had the hood and front fenders extended several inches; the longer body had less drag. It didn't weaken the car any, as Tiny Lund is shown here sliding into the wall at Daytona in 1970 at better than 200 mph. He ground away the right side of the car, and cracked three ribs, but walked away. Road & Track

however, for Pearson, Yarborough, Yarbrough and Donnie Allison.

Why the cuts, Mr. Ford didn't say. There was mention in the news accounts that the sainted Ralph Nader had a blue nose in on the deal; Nader used Ford's ads showing kids at work in the garage to claim that Ford encouraged reckless youth. (Talking out of the other face, when Nader attacked VW engineering he said all Beetle accidents were the fault of the car because hot rod types—that is, reckless, speed-crazed youth—didn't drive Beetles. And if you think that's hard to believe, consider that people made this man into a hero.)

The 1970 season started on a sour note, at Riverside. Ford had A. J. Foyt and Parnelli Jones, driving a Torino and a Cyclone respectively, against Petty and Dan Gurney in Superbirds. The Ford entries had the new 429 and they were faster.

Jones took the pole, after an argument. He was a substitute, filling in for Yarborough while the latter recovered from a crash. Jones was (and is) a Firestone tire dealer and couldn't run on Goodyears, even though Firestone had dropped out of NASCAR. And the 1970 rules allowed wider rims, up to 9 in. from 8.5 in. So Jones used the tires he had run in USAC, where they already had wider rims. He went through tech inspection and nobody worried. He got the new 429 going good and suddenly the tires were declared illegal because somebody said a tire could only be used if there were enough for the full field, 600 tires; Firestone could only promise 400. So the tires couldn't be used and Jones got to run only by switching brands and moving from the pole to thirty-eighth on the grid. There were those who said NASCAR had given in because Goodyear was unhappy and Firestone had left. They were probably right.

It took the enraged and inspired Jones twenty laps to get the lead. He was leading late in the race when the clutch let go, Foyt took the win and the streamliners were left out.

Then came Daytona. Ford's pointed answers to the Dodge and Plymouth answers to the slicked Fords and Mercs were victims of the cutback in the end. Ford ran its 1969 cars early in 1970, because they were smoother and faster and never mind sales for the moment.

Petty had a Superbird for himself and one for Pete Hamilton, the team's junior driver. Hamilton was from New England, son of a college professor, and had worked his way up through the Grand Touring ranks and won Rookie of the Year in 1968.

Unflappable Cale Yarborough and his old Cyclone Spoiler got the pole at 194.015 mph, edging the winged wonders. But in the race, with everybody's engine running with the blow-off valve welded shut, you might say, nearly everybody's engine blew up and what with all the yellow flags, Hamilton won at a nonrecord 149.601 mph.

The Dodge streamliner at least used some production parts. Here the Daytonas of Buddy Baker (6) and Bobby Allison (22) are passing the Plymouth of Frank Warren. The roof- *lines are the same, while the front panels are completely different. Bill Warner*

Later in the year, at the Firecracker 400, Donnie Allison won in a Banjo Matthews Torino. But that win was nearly all the Fords could manage on the big tracks.

We pause now for drama and entertainment.

Fun first. Herb Nab, tuner for Lee Roy Yarbrough, showed up for the Firecracker 400 with exhaust pipes sited high and pointed straight back. So everybody who tried the by-now-traditional draft got a radiator full of hot air and in a few minutes, a face full of steam.

Before a driver could even think about getting even, NASCAR rules required that the exhaust pipes exit the car to the side, in front of the rear wheel. Later, as a convenience and public relations gesture, the cars would all come with exhaust and fuel filler on the left for ovals, which are raced to the left, and with pipes and fuel filler on the right for road courses, which traditionally have more right-hand turns. The neighbors of the tracks have less noise to complain about and the crews can more easily fill the tanks. It makes sense, even if the rule did begin with a prank.

The other new rule was more serious, perhaps even infamous.

It began with speed. In March 1970, after Daytona, Buddy Baker and his Charger Daytona lapped Talladega at 200.447 mph, a record for a racetrack (if not a closed circuit; remember Chrysler's larger and faster oval). Later that year Bobby Isaac, who won eleven Grand National races in 1970 and the driving title as well, raised the record to 201.104 in another Charger Daytona.

This made NASCAR ver-r-ry nervous. The sheer speed added to the concern about the incredible power of the neo-stock engines and the bizarre but efficient bodies of the Mopar entires.

So in August NASCAR's rules committee announced that for the rest of the season all Grand National cars would be required to run with a NASCAR-furnished restrictor plate. The plate was to be fitted between the carburetor and the intake manifold, with a maximum opening of 1.25 in. for each of the carburetor bores.

With that ruling came permission to race with side glass. Side glass had been removed for safety reasons some seasons earlier but the cars were now so fast that the air being rammed into the cars from the sides was putting as much as 800 lb. of downforce on the chassis, and the tires. Or so the tire companies said, and this extra loading made them nervous.

The last skullduggery

The restrictor plate was restrictive engineering at its most basic. The internal combustion engine burns fuel and air to convert heat into power. If you limit the amount of fuel and air the engine can take in, presto, you limit the power that can come out. Simple.

There were modifications to the blank rule, mostly because it was more difficult installing one

plate for all engines, bodies and manifolds than had been expected. So the builders talked the inspectors into allowing a passage instead of just a hole, knowing (as the inspectors didn't seem to) that if they shaped the passage right, it would flow as much as a larger hole would. And there was sly substitution of plates made from certain plastics that—yes, the stories are true, or so say the men who were there—melted away when subjected to high-speed streams of gasoline vapor.

The restrictor plate, which became a long-running series as we'll see, was exactly the sort of rule clever men could turn to their advantage. Which they did. Speeds didn't go down.

Instead, tempers flared up. Ford's trimming of its racing effort literally clipped the wings (and beaks) from its racing sedans. The 429 canted-valve, tunnel-port, hemi-head, never-seen-in-street-trim engine could, if wound and stressed to the max, keep up with the older sold-in-stores Chrysler hemi in the slicker Dodge and Plymouth bodies. But the more powerful Ford engine lost more than the Mopar engine did with plate installed, so Ford suffered. And Ford's racing was run by executives from the home office, men whose careers were involved and who believed they should make the rules because they supported the sport. They had spent their money on the new engine and saved NASCAR a headache by not building the winged cars they had designed. Now, this.

The streamline era arrived quickly. This is Pete Hamilton and his Plymouth Superbird, winners of the 1970 Daytona 500. The Plymouth had a neater, slicker nose and higher, more effective wing. Those odd bumps in the front fenders were put there because the tires rubbed when the body was otherwise low enough for maximum speed and it was easier to make the holes than reshape the rest of the car. Bill Warner

There were personnel troubles as well. Curtis Turner's comeback never quite worked. But he didn't quit trying and he never lost his nerve. That may have been why Turner's plane crashed, killing him and another man, in rural Pennsylvania October 4, 1970.

Investigators couldn't find anything wrong with the plane. His friends said Turner used to have this trick, where he'd put the plane on automatic pilot, then hand the controls over to whoever was in the other seat at the time, and climb into the back for a nap. The only thing they could guess was that he'd done it, the plane didn't respond and the passenger hadn't been able to get him back at the stick in time.

Nothing was ever proved or disproved about this, but it does line up with how Turner lived his life. And he's still a legend. It's hard to believe when you look in the book that Turner never won the national championship and in fact won only seventeen Grand Nationals in his career.

Another comeback ended more happily, but still it wasn't happy.

Fred Lorenzen got bored with playing with his money and selling real estate; one wonders if the former all-time top money-winning driver didn't wish for some of the larger purses that arrived after he left. So he tried a comeback. Lorenzen got some fair rides and turned in some fair drives, but not in the speed or style he'd had earlier.

Then, practicing for the Southern 500 at Darlington, in a Wood brothers Mercury, he wrecked the car. He was injured enough to go to the hospital. Glenn Wood didn't visit him there. He had tried to wave Lorenzen in, his times were good enough, but Fearless

Even the supposedly production bodies worked with the air. Here a Holman and Moody Talladega and a Harry Hyde Charger 500, at speed, are both lower and flatter than they were when they left the assembly line. Chrysler Corporation

Freddie had kept on and tried too hard. Car owners seldom forget or forgive a car destroyed against orders. Lorenzen got no more top rides and he went home to Illinois, got married and settled down again, this time for good.

Also in 1970, Richard Petty set a record by winning the last Grand National race held on dirt, at the Raleigh, North Carolina, half-mile.

But the driver of the year, the new champ, was Bobby Isaac. He was a driver in the Turner and Roberts mold, the guy whose skill and daring make you ask, "Who the hell is that?" before you're close enough to read the number.

Isaac came from a mill town. He didn't just come from a poor family—he didn't even have a family, just an older brother who drank a lot. When he and the other modified racers first went out of town to race, they stopped at a hamburger joint. Isaac said he wasn't hungry. When they got to the track, he said the same thing, and even on the way home, he wasn't hungry. Later on, his friends realized the problem was that Bobby had never been in a restaurant before and literally didn't know what to do.

He did know how to drive. And he was flamboyant and a natural—and hungry to race.

This star quality is hard to define, but some people have it and some, who may go just as fast and win as many races, don't.

Instead of adjectives, the thing to do here is to say that parked in the maintenance garage at Charlotte Motor Speedway is a replica Bobby Isaac dirt car, a modified from the early days, a 1934 Ford with flathead V-8. It was built by the man who built Isaac's dirt cars and is a dead ringer for those cars, painted and numbered the same, done by the guys who run the track simply as a memorial from the fans, kids and aspiring racers. Isaac was quiet, intense and intensely loyal, and he was shrewd and smart as well. He picked up stuff like multiple forks at the dinner table, and even got to playing golf.

He was also superstitious. His career as a team driver ended in 1973 when he pulled into the pits in the middle of a race and said only that he had been told, by unidentified voices, to get the heck out of there, so he did. Isaac kept on racing on the smaller tracks and died of a heart attack in the middle of a race. Maybe the voices knew of what they spoke.

Before then, in 1970, Isaac drove the factory-backed K&K Insurance Dodge Daytona Charger in forty-seven of the forty-eight series races, won eleven of them and was national champion. Dodges won seventeen races and swept the Southern 500, while Plymouth won twenty-one (compared with two in 1969!) and Petty and his Superbird took five of the Superbirds' eight superspeedway wins. Ford got six wins, Mercury four. It was the first year in ten years that Ford didn't win the manufacturer's title.

The new rules

As usual, NASCAR issued the next year's rules well before the end of the season. As promised, the basic change was a downsize, but there was much more to it than that.

NASCAR was in the position of a political party in a country with only one party: just because you can get away with stuff doesn't mean you don't need to follow the proper forms. The teams had considerable investment in their equipment, and the rules had always provided for continuity and had promised that change would be gradual. For example, a two-year-old car could still run in NASCAR races.

And so the 1971 rules allowed a 366 or a 430 ci engine. Both could begin with one four-barrel carburetor but the big engine had to run with the 1.25 in. plate and the little engine didn't.

There were the two categories, full-size and midsize, and either size could use either engine, same as before . . . but (this is section 2, paragraph d) "special cars including the Mercury Cyclone Spoiler, Ford Talladega, Dodge Daytona, Dodge Charger 500 and Plymouth Superbird shall be limited to a maximum engine size of 305 cubic inches . . ."

The rule goes on to allow the smallest engine the bigger carburetor bores. It spells out the various ride heights, defines where the engine must be located in relation to the front spindle and so on. The big engine cars had to weight 3,900 lb. and the smaller engine cars 3,800 lb. There was allowance for an approved front spoiler. The template rules were enforced, improved.

The major points were clear. First, the big engine was going to be forced out and second, so would the special bodies.

If this wasn't war, it was at least a contest of wills.

Ford and Chrysler had been in combat with each other since Ford (officially) and Chrysler (quietly) renounced the AMA racing ban. And they had been in a contest with NASCAR to see who was going to run

Ford was caught off-balance in 1970, when their new cars were much slower than their old ones. This is Lee Roy Yarbrough posing at the 1970 Daytona 500, first race of the *new season, with his 1969 Talladega. Even with the old car he was out of contention. Bill Warner*

stock car racing. (NASCAR people said in their publications that there was some Ford support for the drivers' union, and from the track owners that weren't NASCAR officials, but that's not verified.)

NASCAR wanted production engines and required them to be sold to the public, but nobody in the club expected Chrysler not only to build the hemi but have street versions as well. More than 10,000 street hemis were eventually sold.

NASCAR raised the limits on special bodies, a clear try at keeping them out by making it impractical to build them, but Plymouth went right ahead and produced the 2,000 Superbirds needed to qualify the car. Not only did the dang thing win, but Plymouth also sold all of the freaks they made.

For reasons discussed earlier, the racing stock car by 1970 was really a special frame-floor pan built with a full roll cage that was also the frame. A modified version of the production car body was mounted on this special frame and reshaped to make the car faster and keep it on the ground while looking like the stock car it was supposed to be.

There were good reasons for letting this happen. But once they happened, what won on the track didn't directly relate to what the buyer used on the street.

Ford quits

About the time everybody had had a chance to read and digest the new rules, Ford quit cold. There would be some help, in that Holman and Moody could go on selling parts and building cars for customers with an assured supply from Ford, but there would no longer be a factory team or direct racing involvement.

There's some truth in the partisan view that Chrysler's method of using the engineering department as the racing arm had provided more and better results than Ford's involvement with racing as a marketing tool. Ford had the titles, but Chrysler had the reputation.

There were other factors behind Ford's retirement.

Pollution of the air, water, earth and so forth had become a political issue. Not really an issue, in that nobody was in favor of pollution, but the car companies were on the defensive because their products burned fuel and produced exhaust that didn't smell good.

Next, the performance car had peaked. All the companies were turning out cars that could cover the standing quarter mile in less than fifteen seconds, which was the marker for supercar versus ordinary car. When all the showrooms had them, all the buyers could get them. The incentive to compete, to rub the other guy's face in the asphalt, or be cooler than the man next door, was done for. Right along with this came the insurance company execs, who decreed that high-powered cars were dangerous and so were young men, and they jacked up the rate—when they'd sell a policy on a hemi Charger or Torino at all.

There couldn't have been a better time for Ford to quit, in other words.

Chrysler neatly followed with a practical reduction. There was, after all, no need to drop bombs when rifle fire would do, so Chrysler cut back to Petty Engineering as its one team, and as a supplier for the other teams they hoped would run the brand names.

This was a watershed.

As we'll see, the big blocks and special bodies weren't completely gone yet, and Ford and Chrysler were still out there on the track. But in the sense of the monstrous engine and factory-made racing bodywork presented as stock equipment, an era had ended.

They were good times, a peak in its own way. When Ford quit, Chrysler cut back, Firestone quit and Goodyear eased off, which all happened at the same time, lots of other things were bound to change as well. Just as logically, the loss of money from the factories had to have an effect, or even threaten, NASCAR.

It's the end of an era as Richard Petty wins the Grand National race at Greenville-Pickens Speedway, a short track. This is Petty's short track Plymouth, but compare *this profile with that of Goldsmith's 1968 Daytona car.* Road & Track

Chapter 7

Television and tobacco to the rescue: 1971-1980

Hypocrisy is always entertaining but seldom do those who don't practice it get to profit from it.

NASCAR is one of the few.

The hypocrisy came first. In 1964 the Surgeon General declared cigarette smoking bad for people. This put the official stamp of approval on the already rolling social problems smoking had picked up since the thirties, when smoking showed that one was hip, cool and with it.

But Congress was—as usual—happy to meddle while not doing what Congress is supposed to do. After they decided to design the nation's cars, they made it illegal to advertise tobacco on television.

This is the sort of thing that makes Martians and Venusians land in the desert, read the local papers, watch the six o'clock news and cancel their search for intelligent life on this planet.

Our founding fathers had the brains and experience to keep the press out of the clutches of the government, as best they could arrange it. Politicians can't control the press, and they fear and resent anything they can't control. Broadcasting arrived after the Constitution, which meant the government gave itself the power over the airwaves it was (rightly) denied over the press.

Again because they can't control it, politicians tremble at what they imagine are the powers of advertising. Congress decided to reduce, limit or at least discourage smoking by forbidding the tobacco companies to advertise their products over the air.

How one gets the power to ban the advertising of a legal product is hard to imagine. We're not speaking here of false claims, misleading images or outright lies. The law says you can't ask the public to buy your cigarettes, cigars or pipe tobacco over the air, period, and never mind that the courts and the tax-free foundations chartered to protect us from such abuse have been totally silent on this issue.

The big, the fast and the slick: A. J. Foyt in a new Mercury leads Buddy Baker in a new standard Dodge while behind them are Pete Hamilton in a new Plymouth, Bobby Allison in an older, smaller Dodge and Richard Brooks in the streamliner, handicapped with a destroked 305 hemi. The little engine and slick car will lead this race, the 1971 Daytona 500, but won't win. Although the old combination was competitive, it was never raced again. Bill Warner

The tobacco companies had huge advertising budgets. They had guys with leather office furniture and corner offices with views and staffs of assistants, all in peril when advertising was taken off radio and television. They may have known that ads don't in fact make people smoke, that at best they switch the buyer from brand A to brand B; but never mind that, their jobs were at stake. One solution was to switch to print media, enriching that sales force beyond their wildest dreams. (None of it went to the editorial staffs, by the way. The author speaks from experience.)

The Congressional bludgeon had two sides to it. Television was hit just as hard as the tobacco companies' advertising staffs and agencies were. The money handed to the print media was of course taken from the broadcasters. As if that wasn't enough, beyond the need and expectation for ad revenue, television is a hungry eye which needs a constant supply of material in front of the camera, something for viewers to watch.

Even in 1970 there were more channels and hours than there were brilliant scriptwriters or actors.

The public likes sport and likes sitting at home, beer in hand, couch potatohood intact, so sport and television are natural partners. Throw in skill, speed, daring and amazing crashes in which everybody spins and flies through the air and most of the time nobody gets hurt, and it's all the better.

In January 1970, NASCAR and ABC TV signed a contract in which ABC agreed to broadcast nine races, and to pay NASCAR $1.365 million for the privilege.

In December 1970, just as Ford and Firestone were pulling out and Chrysler and Goodyear were pulling back, NASCAR signed a contract with RJR, also known as R. J. Reynolds and best known in terms of Winston cigarettes. RJR would contribute to a points fund and the winner, the driver with the most points, would be awarded the Winston Cup.

This timing was no accident. If it hadn't been for ABC agreeing to broadcast the races, NASCAR probably wouldn't have received any tobacco money.

More important, NASCAR had proved that the club could get along without General Motors, and

Bobby Isaac, on his way to winning the 1971 Firecracker 400, makes a pit stop. This is the big new body but note first the air dam/scoop under what used to be the radiator intake, and the shaped sheet metal at the rear of the left-side window. There is no door there, nor has there ever been a window. It's all sheet metal shaped to the occasion. The jackman is behind the wall, by the way, because NASCAR has limits on how many crewmen are allowed on the other side. Bill Warner

The 1971 Dodge received a new body which coincidentally made it a good shape for racing. The rear spoiler on the trunk lid was optional—optional for NASCAR racing pur- poses, that is. And meanwhile, the old Torino Talladega was still in contention. Bill Warner

then without Chrysler (the hemi ban) and was prepared to get along without Ford.

Bill France, his family and friends had gone to the mat time and time again to show they were going to set the rules—not the drivers, not the tracks, not the car owners and certainly not the factories. NASCAR could get along without any of the above.

What NASCAR couldn't get along without was money.

No racing group can. Only at the most basic, in the hobby classes or the jalopy cars, on outlaw dirt bullrings, will the money paid by the fans pay for the track, the machines and the men. Everywhere else, some third party has to come forward and make up the difference between what it costs to race and what people will pay to see racing. Indy cars for years depended on largesse, sportsmen who liked being involved and would come through with the big bucks. Formula One gets even more base, with governments offering subsidies the way the Germans used to do, or with state-owned companies, Renault for example, using tax money to pay for the team that would—or was supposed to—enhance the country's prestige.

But America is a democracy. The people rule and they only get nicked for ballet and opera and lectures over tax-paid radio. Not one public dime goes for racing, one assumes because the public likes racing and doesn't like opera and will be punished for their lack of taste.

Anyway, end of lecture. The television and tobacco money came in the nick of time, at the perfect time.

Because this was a different kind of money, it changed stock car racing. When the factories had the money to spend, they handed it out early, to the teams on their payrolls or to the teams they expected to *do* well.

But the new money was paid to the teams that had *done* well. The difference here is more than words.

Just as important in the long run was exposure. When stock car racing was seen only by the hard core—the fans willing to hike from the parking lot, inhale the dust, fight the traffic and ignore the hooligans—sponsorship came only from firms with a direct link: dealerships, parts houses and such.

But with the races on television, the potential was multiplied. When a sponsor could reach all the folks who cared enough not to touch that dial, the field was instantly wider and deeper, all the brand names any car owner might see at the store.

Stock car racing was suddenly a business. Not just in the sense of making a living, the way the Pettys, Bakers and Allisons were already doing, but in the sense of getting a major backer: having the cash to build a good car or even cars; having parts, tires and expenses taken care of at the beginning of the year; and needing and getting business expertise and marketing savvy, even dealing with the public. (This will lead to an oligarchy, if not a monopoly, at first.)

The clincher here was social status.

Yes, status.

Money is how we keep score. People outside racing aren't going to appreciate the genius with which Maurice Petty constructs an engine, or the care and foresight displayed by Junior Johnson and his management of the team, never mind the raw talent of Cale Yarborough behind the wheel. But they will hear that Cale has won millions of dollars and they will tip

their mental hats; the man must be doing something well, to earn that kind of money, and if a sport hands out checks like that, it must be an important sport.

In racing, just as always in every other form of human endeavor, money talks.

Exit the hemi, in style

If the 1970 season was the end of the factory era, then the 1971 season was the autopsy, wake and rebirth all rolled into one.

There would be a transition, of course, as the teams worked to develop their smaller Ford and Chrysler engines and see how the new bodies would lend themselves to subtle improvements. They'd had a couple of years to see how the templates worked and didn't work, and to figure out what they could get away with. Further, all the good cars were purpose built, semi-stock body panels on pure racing frames, cages, platforms or a combination.

So the season began with a mixture of old and new, big and small. The Wood brothers built a new Mercury for the slower tracks and a 1969 Cyclone for the fast one, with restricted 429. Richard Petty was

Bobby Allison's Mercury has a reworked and blocked grille and the intake through the middle of the front bumper. It also has the sheet metal reworked where the rear left win-

dow would otherwise be. And look as how the sponsor has given the crew some nifty threads. Bill Warner

driving the sole factory-backed Plymouth, and went with orthodoxy: a 1971 body and a 366 or 426 wedge engine.

There was one daredevil, Richard Brooks. He worked with Keith Black, the drag racing builder who'd been developing aluminum hemis. They came up with a 305 hemi, ultra short stroke, and put it in Brooks' Daytona 500 for the 1971 Daytona 200.

Foyt had the pole in an old Merc, at 182.744 mph. The restrictions were working as they were supposed to, since that was nearly 12 mph down on Cale's pole-sitter the previous year.

Except that for five laps in the middle of the race Brooks and his streamliner and 305 hemi led the race. They led until a collision, a genuine accident by all accounts, slowed the car and after that he goofed up and passed a car under the yellow flag. Had it not been for that he would have finished fourth.

OK. All the teams knew that if they didn't make do, if they'd gone out and kept on winning with the little racing engine and the street-silly streamliners, even more drastic things would have been done. The stock-shape body and production-based small-block V-8 were a more sensible way to go, even if they lopped 12 mph off the speed. They all pretended therefore that Brooks' run was a fluke. Even Brooks seems to have seen this odd light. The car never ran again. Which might also have been because Chrysler had stopped making the hemi in 1970 when the restrictions were going into the book. So even if the little engine had won, it would have been awkward for everybody.

Other than that, the new rules and restrictions worked out fine. There were forty-eight lead changes in that 1971 Daytona 500, divided among eleven drivers, and only Petty led for more than fifteen laps at a time. Petty was leading the last lap and won, with Baker in a Dodge and Foyt in a Mercury tucked in behind. Bobby Isaac in a stock-bodied Dodge won the Firecracker 400 that year, after taking a huge lead

Pete Hamilton in the Plymouth, with outside help because the factory was cutting back and shifting to Dodge. The long pole is in front of the car as a guide, to keep the car in its assigned place on pit road. Bill Warner

and having the car begin to come apart, but it held long enough for Isaac to fend off Petty, who in the course of the season took the driving title for the third time, tying his dad.

Mopar had the edge, perhaps because they had factory help to a degree beyond anything in the Ford or GM camps, perhaps because they had honed their equipment in the drag race wars and thus could get more from machinery that was closer to stock that the rivals could. In the 1971 season, Plymouth got twenty-two wins and Dodge eight. The stock Mercury had a slicker shape, and of course Foyt and Bobby Allison behind the wheels didn't hurt. The Mercury team collected eleven wins, while the Ford guys only had four.

And one of them wasn't exactly a Ford.

This was a tough season and money was tight, so tight that not all the Grand National races attracted a full field of Grand National cars. When that happened, rather than see the track look empty race officials allowed other cars, mostly pony cars and compacts from the Grand American series, in the main event. As a rule this happened on the smaller tracks, where the smaller, lighter Mustangs and Camaros had a fair shot.

Some days it was better than fair. On one such occasion, at tight little Bowman-Gray Stadium at Winston-Salem, North Carolina, Bobby Allison took a gamble and won, in a Mustang.

So, first off, one of those four wins wasn't strictly a Ford victory.

Next we come to a really odd part: NASCAR has never resolved the question of how such races go into the record books.

Because his car wasn't a full Grand National machine, Allison isn't given credit for that Grand National win. The books say he had won eighty-four Grand Nationals as of early 1988, while statistician Greg Fieldon, who spent sixteen years researching the pioneer days of NASCAR, says if you count this race, which surely should count, Allison has won eighty-five.

Further, if Allison's Mustang doesn't get the win, how about the next guy across the finish? It was none other than Richard Petty, in a full-size Plymouth. But NASCAR doesn't give Petty the win, either. If Allison doesn't get his eighty-fifth victory, then Petty has won 201 Grand Nationals.

NASCAR's top folks refuse to discuss this, by the way, so for the rest of the recorded time, there will be more national races run than there will be a total of driver victories.

The return of Chevrolet

Between seasons, another lecture.

Chevrolet, and by extension General Motors, has been in racing for as long as there has been racing, in the trenches and on the front lines. The variation has been at headquarters, and in official policy.

This can be difficult for outsiders to fathom. It's true that people have been fired or had their careers blocked because they were involved with racing. It's also true that Vince Piggins was hired from Hudson by Chevrolet in 1955 and was deeply involved with racing from that day until he retired, full of honors and respect, some twenty years later. The difference between racing glory and racing horrors in corporate career terms seems to have depended on what one did and how one spoke about it.

Richard Petty and his 1972 Dodge. The car has a better shape than the earlier model and it's running much less spoiler in the rear. Those odd shapes, shadows and curves in the hood and roof could lead one to wonder how thick the sheet metal actually is. Bill Warner

A. J. Foyt, winning the Daytona 500 in 1972. The Mercury has a less useful front end this year, as the racing-designed cars are gone, but the low roof and semi-straight rear panels have allowed this car to run with hardly any rear spoiler at all. And the engine is nominally Ford's last big-block, the 429 V-8. Bill Warner

What Chevrolet did mostly during the years between the AMA ban and the official policy change twenty-five years later was engage in research and development, and in the sale of parts and equipment that naturally had to be developed by the engineering staff before it could go on sale. Chevy's R&D involved building single seaters, Can-Am cars like the Chaparrals and the full sub rosa program with Roger Penske and the Camaro road racers. The engineers did wind tunnel tests and farmed out engines to outfits like Traco to see how much power they could get from the stock block (just curious, of course). And if the test facility could come up with useful data, techniques and parts, they could use all that if they wanted to go racing or sell the material to racers. Chevrolet engines, big-block and small-block, were very popular.

Chevrolet had a vast stock of parts, skills and expertise. They didn't have enough money and staff to run head to head against the Ford and Chrysler teams in NASCAR, however. The production Chevrolet engines couldn't match the racing Fords or Plymouths either.

But then the hemi and semi-hemi engines were outlawed, or handicapped out of contention. And Ford withdrew from full team sponsorship at the end of 1970.

Chrysler did the same in 1971. Theirs had been an engineering effort and they never forgave NASCAR for changing the rules to take away any advantage they came up with. So when it was clear that engineering wasn't going to get to win races, racing lost its appeal. And one might as well add the insurance problems, the removal of lead from fuel, the loss of high compression and so forth.

Like Ford, Mopar provided for its people as best they could. Mopar had Petty Engineering as the factory outlet and provided help working on and servicing the wedge engines.

Petty meanwhile signed a six-figure contract with STP. Savvy man that he is, Petty passed up another $50,000 they offered if he would switch from Petty Blue to STP Red. Just as STP is the ideal trademark because it photographs perfectly in color and in black and white, Petty also knew that his special shade of blue—chosen by accident at first—was now his color and always would be. (By the same token, notice that Richard never has his name on the car. But be it Plymouth, Dodge, Oldsmobile, Chevrolet, Ford or Pontiac, it's always number 43 and it's always Petty Blue.)

And while that was going on Junior Johnson switched to Chevrolet. He signed some good sponsors and driver Charlie Glotzbach, and won three races.

For 1972, more changes. In format, Winston had gone from sponsoring a series within a series to having the full deal. By that time NASCAR's drag racing and pony car series had disappeared, so there was the Winston Cup Grand National and the full nationwide top championship, and the Grand Nationals East and West were the junior varsities. The rules were a little looser and the cars could be a year older, the better to keep the farm teams solvent.

But the Winston Cup was the prize. Television expanded while the national series was made bigger by being less frequent; that is, there were forty-eight Grand National races in 1971, and thirty-one in 1972. They all had to be 250 miles or more, and they were all on pavement. The crews had more time to prepare, and the drivers to rest, while NASCAR followed the Indianapolis technique of increasing demand for the race by restricting supply.

The small-block gains

Backyard scientist Smokey Yunick was on retainer from GM, doing research in his garage near the river. Early in 1972 he told *Motor Trend* what he'd been up to.

Basically, he'd been up to 490 bhp with the Chevy small-block V-8 with normal 4 in. bore and stroke of 3.625 in., for a displacement of 366 ci. He'd done another small-block with larger bore and shorter stroke that gave 482 bhp, and he'd seen 486 bhp from a big-block with long stroke and 472 bhp from another big-block with a big bore and short stroke.

Sounds contrary to common sense, eh? Smokey said the big-block lost power because there was more friction and more pumping loss; he couldn't get the best combustion chamber shape with high enough—12.5:1—compression ratio if he went with the larger bore.

Odd though it sounds, when Yunick was on the Ford payroll, back during that brief interval when Ford was the only sponsor in town, he did some nifty work on the Ford cylinder heads and raised the exhaust ports for a straighter exit. Work done by Yunick and others gave Ford a good small-block, too.

Um, make that a good engine; they didn't have a good block. In fact, that was the weak point. But Ford came through with a racing block, stiffer than the passenger car version but otherwise similar. The new block cost $2,500 but Ford did sell it to the public and it did hold up.

The rulemaking in this interim period was so creative it approached art.

The rules allowed the two sizes of car, the full-size and the intermediate, and permitted the 366 or 430 engines, minimum weights of 3,800 or 3,900 lb., and wheelbases of 119 or 115 in. But the body style had to be recognized and approved, as did the engine type, and the engine had to come in that model car, which forced the maker's hand because the oil crisis was looming and the engines were going to get smaller no matter what.

The salvation here was the SCCA's earlier series, the Trans-Am, in which pony cars raced with full-race, stock de-stroked small-block V-8s, very much like the engines NASCAR was now encouraging.

The 1972 restrictor rules allowed the 366 wedge engines the full 1.6875 in. throttle bores, while the 430 wedge was restricted to 1.3187 in., the small hemi and big tunnel-port Ford got 1.1875 in. and the bad old 426 hemi, 1.125 in. A neat sliding scale. If, as it happened, the small-block Mopar wasn't strong enough yet, the teams could use the older, larger engines and do fine.

Chevrolet wasn't the only revival. American Motors, nominal descendant of the AMC brand with Hudson and Nash heritage, had lost interest in the Trans-Am series when they won it against nobody at all, so Roger Penske and Mark Donohue were assigned to race NASCAR with an AMC Matador.

The Matador was the car of the future. It began life with a Holman and Moody chassis, and was built by Dick Hutcherson and Ed Pagan, two former drivers and students of Ralph Moody. The car had a standard NASCAR roll cage with frame stubs front and rear, topped by Matador panels, powered with a Traco-built 366 based on the winning Trans-Am engines, and used relatively new things like a Watt link to locate the rear axle and huge disc brakes. Disc brakes had been

Chevrolet began a comeback in 1973, with the qualification of two sizes of car, and the introduction of some new, low-drag bodies. This is Cale Yarborough, who obviously has *attracted some outside sponsorship, and who will do very well in the short tracks with a short car. Bill Warner*

An odd one. This Ford was built to run road races in 1973, to some degree because there was the hope that American sedans might race as part of international events, and in non-NASCAR races. The car ran IMSA events, and was ready for all-nighters, hence the driving lights. Different sets of rules dictated the flares for the front fenders.

legal for several years but until the serious Trans-Am road races, nobody had used them in NASCAR because they hadn't been big enough to outbrake the old drums.

The plan was to have Mark Donohue, arguably the best American road racer at the time, in the car for some events and use substitutes in other events. The team didn't win that first season and only won a few races during its time, but just having been there proves NASCAR was an important marketing tool.

Junior's Chevy did much better. He began the 1972 season by hiring Bobby Allison, who'd been looking for work because Holman and Moody decided to split up now that the factories weren't paying the bills. The Chevrolet was nominally a Monte Carlo, meaning that's where the body came from, but the front subframe and the roll cage were . . . Holman and Moody, just like the (wink) Matador. But the rear suspension had longer and stronger trailing arms, from the Chevrolet pickup truck, held away from the body by coil springs with Ford Galaxie parts numbers on them. Junior chose the big-block Chev engine and had some help from Chevrolet in advice and technical help, but not in cash or even parts. But Junior and Chevrolet were heroes; they got upfront support from the then-president of Charlotte Motor Speedway and collected appearance money from the other tracks.

Inside, the road-race Ford was normal NASCAR, with an elaborate roll cage braced by having all the bars join each other in the middle of the cockpit. The tank at left is the oil tank, for the dry sump engine, and the electrical switches are at the driver's left.

119

The other hero, one of the best among a group, was Richard Petty. He won the 1972 title, the first driver to win it four times and (so far) the only driver to win the title more than three times. He did it with eight wins and he did it on skill and preparation in

Look closely at the center of the photo and you'll see what seems to be a giant Allen head bolt. That bolt is the control for the static ride height of the right front wheel, and thus for the tune of the front suspension. The engine is a Ford 429.

All but lost in the engine bay, the small-block Chevy V-8 was (in 1973) the powerplant of the future. This is the car Banjo Matthews built for Cale Yarborough, with the front subframe of tubing on the Ford pan, and Chevy engine and body panels. Bill Warner

that he won the Riverside road race, six events on half-mile tracks, and only one superspeedway, the two-mile Texas track.

At Daytona Petty and Foyt, in a Wood brothers Mercury, ran off from the field with only Baker, in the other Petty car, in contention. Baker collided with another car and was out. Then late in the race Petty's engine failed and Foyt cruised home one lap up on Charlie Glotzbach's Dodge.

In the second Daytona, the Firecracker 400, one of the best and most entertaining professional feuds in racing began: Petty versus Pearson.

It was a natural contest in that the two drivers were so much alike: handsome and outgoing (Petty more than Pearson in full public, Pearson more than Petty at party time). They were also both aggressive racers. Both are Southerners in background and temperament. A century ago they would have been cavalry officers whose men would have followed them anywhere.

But in 1972 they were rivals, and during the Firecracker 400 they swapped the lead fifty times in forty-eight laps, with Allison in the Chevy tucked in close and getting into a turn first every so often. (If Bill France, who was to retire that year, ever had any doubts about his rules in 1972, the sight of the Plymouth, the Mercury and the Chevrolet side by side at 200 mph on one side of the fence, while tens of thousands of cheering fans leaped up and down on the other side of the fence, would have convinced him again. He'd done it right.)

Coming out of the last turn on the last lap, Pearson had half a length on Petty, and he kept it, saying later that he didn't know why Petty hadn't pulled out and passed, while Petty said Pearson had so much power that he, Petty, was barely able to keep second place. With the carburetor rules subject to change in a twinkling, reverse brag was the order of the day.

The order of the year was unusual, in that Petty's seven wins for Plymouth were that make's only wins, against nine wins for Mercury, shared among drivers, and ten, yes ten, victories for Chevrolet. But there were more guys driving Ford and Chevy, so Allison was second in points and Pearson, who didn't run the full schedule, wasn't in the top ten. Oh, and France juggled the points fund payout to encourage all the drivers to run as many races as they could. Petty, who of course ran every race he could find, had by the end of the year won a career total of 150 Grand National races, and collected $1.4 million in purses and Winston Cup funds.

The 1973 rules allowed only one model of carburetor with some minor—or so they seemed to everybody except the engine men—adjustments to the bore size rules, giving another nudge in the direction of the small-blocks.

There were the usual internal changes to teams and personnel. Petty switched from Plymouth to Dodge, a formality in a way because the two brands were much the same, except that Dodge was supposed to be the performance name (what performance was still legal on the street, that is) so the car decked out in Petty Blue with STP Red got a new nameplate.

Junior Johnson signed up Cale Yarborough, who'd had good rides with the Wood brothers and had gone exploring in USAC, at Indy and other single-seat venues but hadn't been comfortable, nor had he found a top team to drive for.

There was still some imbalance in the points system, in that the 1973 driving championship went to Benny Parsons, who was a solid technician but not—no offense intended—a star in the Petty and Pearson style. Parsons drove a good Chevrolet, won at Bristol and backed that up with a season full of seconds, thirds, fourths and fifths. He deserved the title.

Pearson meanwhile entered eighteen races, won eleven of them and became the second NASCAR driver to top one million dollars in career earnings. He was named Martini & Rossi driver of the year, in contention with the stars from all the other clubs and series.

The hemi really exits

The 1974 rules put a larger and sharper stake through the hemi's heart.

There were two basic changes in the rules. First, all engines displacing more than 366 ci were restricted to one carburetor with a flow rating of 340 cfm. Second, all engines, regardless of size or type, were required to use a circular air cleaner of a given size, breathing air from the engine compartment rather than from ducts in the body.

These were genuine limiters. Power depends on fuel and air, so when you limit the air that can flow into the engine, you limit the power. And the outside air was cooler and denser, thus it would produce more power than air already heated by passage through the radiator; the ducts were taken from places like the base of the windshield, where there was positive pressure as air packed against the car. (The place where an air scoop looks good, the center of the hood above the engine, has negative pressure unless the intake is raised several inches, by the way. In the performance car era some companies offered scoops where they looked good but Chevrolet and later Mopar had them at the rear of the hood, where they worked.)

The team that was the most detailed in their anguish was Petty Engineering. Maurice Petty said that with the small carburetor the hemi 426 wouldn't wind beyond 6000 rpm and didn't produce old-time power until 6500. His engine was giving 410 bhp, he said, which is what they had back in 1963 when they began, and which was a sad contrast with the 620 bhp when the hemi was unrestricted or the 550 it produced with the throttle plates.

But being fair here, hemi production ceased in 1970, and the engine was removed from the catalog in 1971, so considering the three-year eligibility limit, the hemi should have been retired in 1974. The Mopar teams were allowed to keep it because their small-block, the 340-based racing engine, wasn't working at the beginning of the season.

Ford and Mercury had gone to their small-block, the 351 Cleveland-based engine with race-ready block. Pearson and the Wood brothers were supposed to have the best engine in the field and were also happy because the small-block was eighty pounds lighter than the old 427/428/429.

Junior Johnson's Chevy for Cale Yarborough had power but Junior said they weren't sure how long the thing would hold together because they had to wind it into the upper ranges to get competitive power.

Old and not-so-old, Buddy Baker in the big-block Dodge leads Yarborough in the Chevy with the big-block V-8. Bill Warner

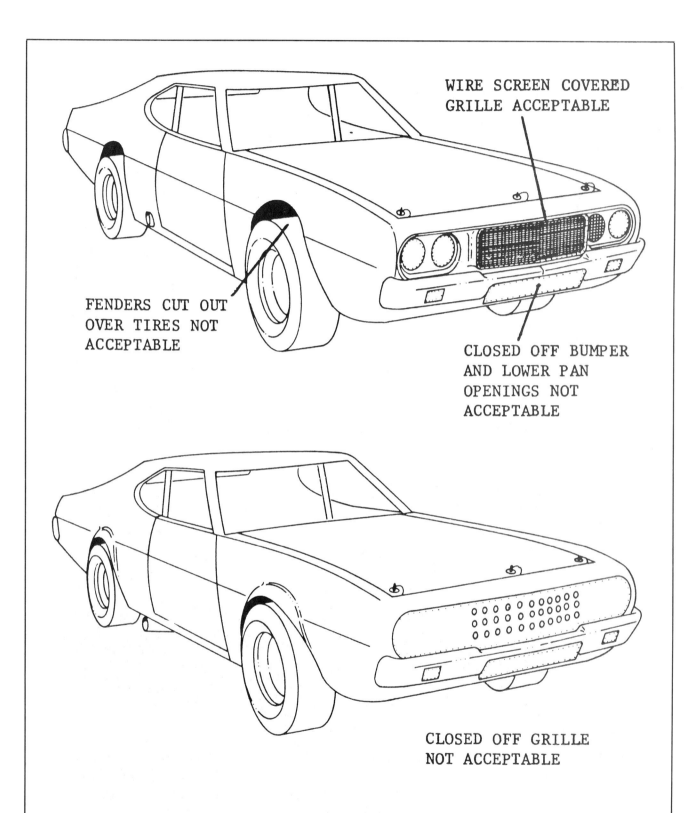

WIRE SCREEN COVERED
GRILLE ACCEPTABLE

FENDERS CUT OUT
OVER TIRES NOT
ACCEPTABLE

CLOSED OFF BUMPER
AND LOWER PAN
OPENINGS NOT
ACCEPTABLE

CLOSED OFF GRILLE
NOT ACCEPTABLE

By 1973 NASCAR's technical committee and inspectors had worked out just how far they wanted the builders to go and in what direction. The rule book was richly detailed: compare these pages with the single sheet of rules used twenty years earlier. They told the new builder and the expert just what he could do, couldn't do and would be expected to do. This made the Grand National sedan the safest racing car in the world. It also meant that a real production passenger car would no longer even be allowed on the track. NASCAR

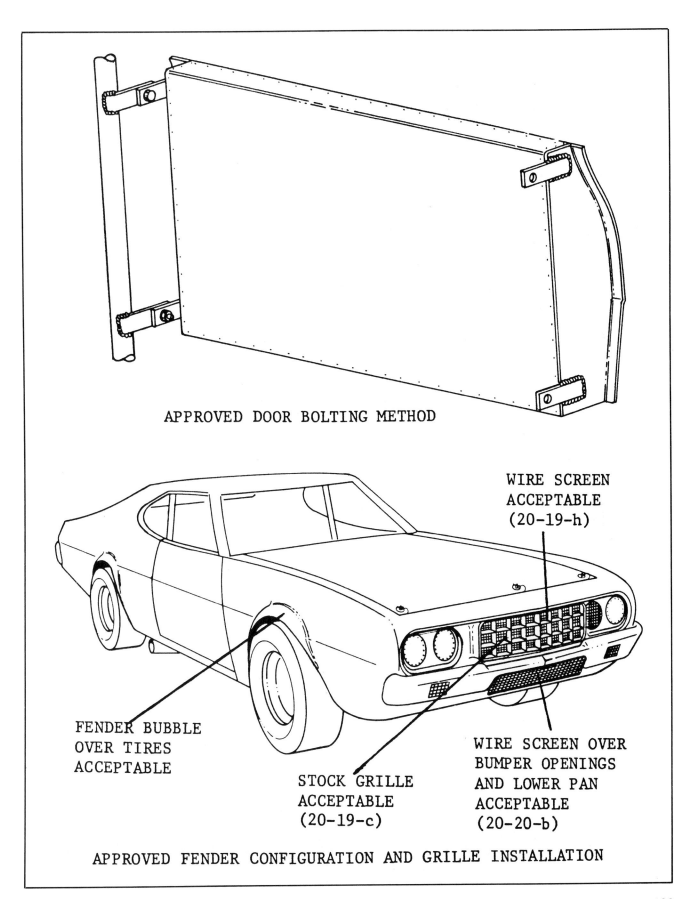

APPROVED DOOR BOLTING METHOD

WIRE SCREEN
ACCEPTABLE
(20-19-h)

FENDER BUBBLE
OVER TIRES
ACCEPTABLE

STOCK GRILLE
ACCEPTABLE
(20-19-c)

WIRE SCREEN OVER
BUMPER OPENINGS
AND LOWER PAN
ACCEPTABLE
(20-20-b)

APPROVED FENDER CONFIGURATION AND GRILLE INSTALLATION

APPROVED FUEL CELL INSTALLATION

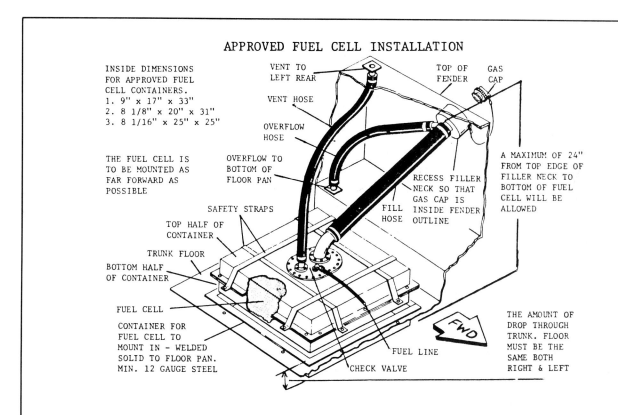

INSIDE DIMENSIONS
FOR APPROVED FUEL
CELL CONTAINERS.
1. 9" x 17" x 33"
2. 8 1/8" x 20" x 31"
3. 8 1/16" x 25" x 25"

THE FUEL CELL IS
TO BE MOUNTED AS
FAR FORWARD AS
POSSIBLE

VENT TO
LEFT REAR

VENT HOSE

OVERFLOW
HOSE

OVERFLOW TO
BOTTOM OF
FLOOR PAN

SAFETY STRAPS

TOP HALF OF
CONTAINER

TRUNK FLOOR

BOTTOM HALF
OF CONTAINER

FUEL CELL

CONTAINER FOR
FUEL CELL TO
MOUNT IN - WELDED
SOLID TO FLOOR PAN.
MIN. 12 GAUGE STEEL

TOP OF
FENDER

GAS
CAP

RECESS FILLER
NECK SO THAT
GAS CAP IS
INSIDE FENDER
OUTLINE

FILL
HOSE

A MAXIMUM OF 24"
FROM TOP EDGE OF
FILLER NECK TO
BOTTOM OF FUEL
CELL WILL BE
ALLOWED

FWD

THE AMOUNT OF
DROP THROUGH
TRUNK. FLOOR
MUST BE THE
SAME BOTH
RIGHT & LEFT

FUEL LINE

CHECK VALVE

APPROVED WINDOW SCREEN INSTALLATION

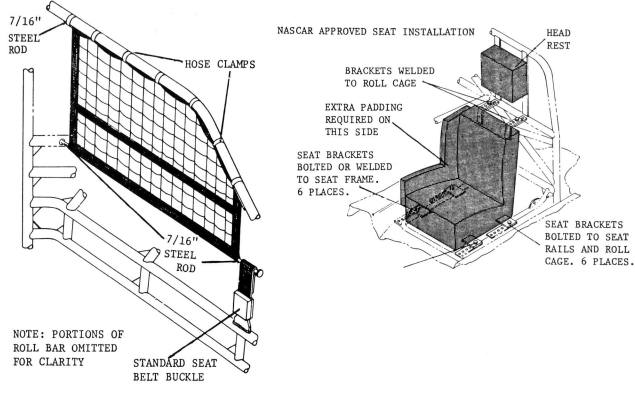

7/16"
STEEL
ROD

HOSE CLAMPS

7/16"
STEEL
ROD

NOTE: PORTIONS OF
ROLL BAR OMITTED
FOR CLARITY

STANDARD SEAT
BELT BUCKLE

NASCAR APPROVED SEAT INSTALLATION

HEAD
REST

BRACKETS WELDED
TO ROLL CAGE

EXTRA PADDING
REQUIRED ON
THIS SIDE

SEAT BRACKETS
BOLTED OR WELDED
TO SEAT FRAME.
6 PLACES.

SEAT BRACKETS
BOLTED TO SEAT
RAILS AND ROLL
CAGE. 6 PLACES.

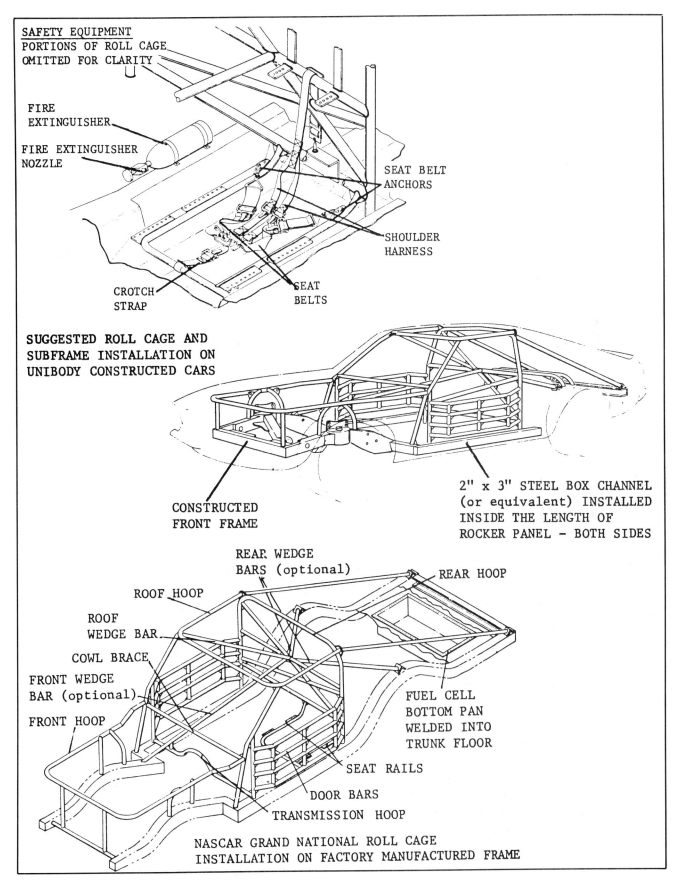

SAFETY EQUIPMENT
PORTIONS OF ROLL CAGE
OMITTED FOR CLARITY

FIRE
EXTINGUISHER

FIRE EXTINGUISHER
NOZZLE

SEAT BELT
ANCHORS

SHOULDER
HARNESS

CROTCH
STRAP

SEAT
BELTS

SUGGESTED ROLL CAGE AND
SUBFRAME INSTALLATION ON
UNIBODY CONSTRUCTED CARS

CONSTRUCTED
FRONT FRAME

2" x 3" STEEL BOX CHANNEL
(or equivalent) INSTALLED
INSIDE THE LENGTH OF
ROCKER PANEL — BOTH SIDES

REAR WEDGE
BARS (optional)

ROOF HOOP

REAR HOOP

ROOF
WEDGE BAR

COWL BRACE

FRONT WEDGE
BAR (optional)

FRONT HOOP

FUEL CELL
BOTTOM PAN
WELDED INTO
TRUNK FLOOR

SEAT RAILS

DOOR BARS

TRANSMISSION HOOP

NASCAR GRAND NATIONAL ROLL CAGE
INSTALLATION ON FACTORY MANUFACTURED FRAME

As one of the forerunners seen early in the year, Donnie Allison was running a Chevelle with a small-block Chevy on a Ford chassis; the rules said the make no longer mattered if the type of suspension was regulation—coil spring, leaf spring or torsion bar.

Another clue was talk that the engine limit might go to 358. By happy coincidence that was the size at which the small-block V-8s from Ford, GM, Mopar and AMC all could be run with close to stock stroke, saving the cost of a stroker crankshaft and letting the engines last longer and saving money, as they always said when announcing new rules.

In the 1974 season, NASCAR officials made an early public relations move as the world suffered under OPEC and the first fuel crisis impelled NASCAR to cut back. The Daytona 500 was the Daytona 450. The parking lot wasn't as full but the grandstands and infield were, as the fans doubled up and shared rides.

Pearson got the pole with his small-block Mercury at 185.017 mph, fractionally slower than the poles of 1973 (185.66) or 1972 (186.63), but not so much slower that anybody noticed. In the race the duel was Petty and his Dodge versus Bobby Allison and his Chevy. Allison suffered a blown tire, went through a lurid slide and then a pit stop, and Petty won, for the fifth time in an event no other driver had managed to win twice.

In the Firecracker 400 Pearson took the pole again but this time won the race by not backing off when he and Petty had one of their famous last laps.

Restrictions or not, Petty won the driving title again, followed by Yarborough, Pearson and Bobby Allison, who had begun the season in his own Chevy but finished the year in the Penske AMC Matador.

The AMC effort had been uphill all the way. Penske's regular driver, Mark Donohue, won the Riverside road race for AMC in 1973 but then retired from driving. Penske then hired Allison, who won another race for the mark in 1974, then got a second checkered flag, at the ill-fated Ontario, California, oval; the run wasn't a win because on inspection the engine was found to contain roller tappets.

This looked rather flagrant to the technical inspectors, because such tappets are specifically prohibited. Penske in turn said he didn't install roller tappets, but had instead affixed rollers to the AMC tappets.

This didn't go over with the inspectors any better. Penske was fined $9100, the largest such penalty levied to that date. Penske didn't like the ruling or the fine, or the resulting flap.

Roger Penske probably coined the phrase, "Don't get mad, get even." He offered to set a new closed course record at Talladega, for a prize of $10,000. Of course, Talladega was owned by the France family, owners of NASCAR, so he'd be getting his money back.

And anyway, Penske wasn't going to drive. Donohue—who'd changed his mind about retirement—was, in an incredibly equipped Porsche 917-30. He ran it at 221 mph around the banked oval holding his breath, collecting the record and—he said later—wishing he'd let Penske get even for himself. But that's another story. The Matador would win three more races, in 1975, and would be retired when AMC decided it wasn't worth the effort.

The other big winner for 1974 was Chevrolet, with twelve Grand National victories. Dodge had ten, all

Move back to 1954 for a minute. This is Ralph Earnhardt, the best and winningest late model sportsman (formerly modified class) driver in NASCAR. He drove hard, built his own machines and had one helper . . .

. . . his son Ralph Dale Earnhardt, who in 1974, after his dad died of a heart attack at age forty-five, was building and racing his own cars. Dale didn't have any money and wasn't one to ask for favors, but his skill and hunger won't go unremarked. Charlotte Motor Speedway

Not terribly subtle, but sponsors outside the normal speed shop and parts house are making themselves known by 1974; witness the Bud Moore-built Ford, George Follmer up, at Daytona in 1974. The television coverage has made the tobacco investment pay off, and vice versa, and the top teams now have enough money to spend making the cars look, well, photogenic, even if the need for speed is making them look a lot alike. Bill Warner

with Petty in control, and Mercury collected seven. Plymouth didn't win any, for the first time since 1959 and Ford was shut out for the third straight year. (Things have changed for Ford, as we'll see, but Plymouth hasn't won a Grand National race since 1973.)

The 1975 rules included the rumored reduction to 358 ci, a limit that's been in effect ever since. The rules included a provision for engines as large as 433 ci if they were standard options in the model to be raced, but by this time the emissions, mileage and safety rules—and even public opinion—had taken the big engines off the market. They weren't raced even if they had been competitive, which they weren't.

The other changes were in details. For instance the minutely described locations for where the bodies would be measured, the angles at which they would be measured and some subtle touches, such as not allowing weight transfer devices to be fitted to the left front, were all altered. The other three corners of the chassis all had manual height adjustments, to be changed only by the crew during pit stops. The left front was ruled out because that's where the static ride height was measured; if the crew could set it at the minimum and then lower it, why, it wouldn't be at legal height any more. By that time the dumb 5 mph bumpers were used on road cars, and the 1974 and 1975 racers got to remove all the mechanisms for such bumpers and mount the bumpers close to the body.

King Richard rules

Richard Petty (and Dodge) ruled the 1975 season. Daytona began the other way, with Donnie Allison and his Chevy on the pole at 185.327 mph: the restrictions were still working. But the winner was unsung Bennie Parsons, who started from thirty-second but got his private Chevrolet working and drove into Petty's draft as the latter stormed through the field after fixing an overheating problem. The two of them caught Pearson and Yarborough and pow! David and Cale whanged each other in their tussle, and Parsons and Petty got past, except that Petty was laps down, in sixth, so Parsons won.

Petty won the Firecracker 400 with more luck or skill. He was racing Buddy Baker in the resurgent Ford of Bud Moore when Baker stopped and got fresh right-side tires, so Petty stopped for left-side tires. He was running high on the track, he said later, and figured his right-sides would be above the traction but his left ones wouldn't be. And when Baker overcooked things getting past, Petty ducked beneath him, got out of the draft and won going away.

The pole for that race was again taken by Donnie Allison for Chevrolet, so the cars were competitive, but Petty had the knack of being in the right place at the right time. He won thirteen more Grand Nationals that year, and his sixth championship. Dodge got fourteen of the thirty races, to six for Chevy, four for Ford, and three each for Mercury and AMC.

The racing wasn't as out of balance as that list appears to make it. Bobby Allison won both Darlington races and the Riverside road race for AMC. Buddy Baker and the Bud Moore Ford got both superspeedway events at Talladega. Pearson and the Wood brothers' Mercury took races at Pocono, Michigan, and Dover, Delaware. Yarborough and Johnson won at North Carolina and Nashville.

If there was an imbalance, it was in the top five. Novelist Kim Chapin figured out that there were 167 Grand National races from 1971 to 1975 and that Petty, Pearson, Bobby Allison, Baker and Yarborough won 140 of them, sometimes all five lined up in the top five places. Because they drove different makes, the rules must have put the basic material at parity, while the best drivers, builders and crews got the top sponsorships and had the money to do it right: Petty, Allison, Pearson and Yarborough had each won more than $1 million by the end of the 1975 season.

This trend has been much the same ever since, in that there have always been a few teams, the best five combinations, who can win. The next echelon behind them are the guys who can survive and inherit a victory while not being fast enough to fight for it. Behind them are the racers who are good enough to make it into Grand National racing, but who for various reasons will never actually win a national championship race, which doesn't mean they lack other talents, but that story won't happen for several years.

There were two milestones in 1976. Neither had to do with the rules (OK, make that NASCAR rules) which remained as they'd been.

The other rules applied overseas, in France, the home of the fabled twenty-four-hour race of Le Mans. By some chance, the 1976 rules permitted full-size—our size—stock sedans, with up to 488 ci. In metric measurement that's eight liters, or larger than anything seen in NASCAR, ever.

The rules were written by the Le Mans home team, the club that ran the track. They did it because they had worked out a deal with Bill France, owner of Daytona, in which he would offer a race for sports cars, the other twenty-four-hour race, you could say. The fix wasn't in, not in any way, but this race was a perfect example of what's now called promoter's option—open the race to entrants whom the crowd will come to see and never mind the other stuff.

At Le Mans in 1976, Dick Hutcherson, the driver turned builder, and co-driver Dick Brooks had a Ford Torino. Hershel McGriff, whom we last saw wearing a funny hat in the Mexican Road Race but who had become one of the best stock car drivers on the West Coast, shared a Dodge Charger with his son Doug.

Neither car had a shot at the pole and both went out with mechanical problems—an oil leak for the Dodge, a gearbox failure for the Ford—well before the finish. But it had been fun. Bill France had waved the starters flag to begin the show and everybody had enjoyed the party.

The other milestone was in exact reverse, a perfect display of competition. The protagonists were our old rivals, Petty and Pearson. They were both good drivers and were a lot alike, and both had good teams behind them. They were close competitors if not always the best of friends and they did, from time to time, become angry—strictly on the track, however, and in front of the cameras. The Daytona Speedway has always had wonderful luck that way.

A. J. Foyt took the pole for the 1976 Daytona 500, driving a Chevrolet to an average of 185.943 mph. The same rules were in effect and they allowed the same speed as for the two previous years. Once again the other cars dropped out or back and when it came to the last lap it was Pearson and Petty, in that order.

Going into the third turn Pearson ducked out of the draft and shot past, into the lead.

A really new combination, as Indy driver Gary Betten-hausen, USAC and SCCA mogul Roger Penske and sensible American Motors have teamed up to run NASCAR. This

Matador finished twelfth at the Daytona 500 in 1974, but the team would go on to win some as well as lose some, and to add some variety to the mix. Bill Warner

Another Chevy, this time for Bobby Allison, and sponsored by a household name. The body is shaped right for speed— Chevrolets finished second through fifth in the Daytona 500 *in 1974 although this car wasn't in the top five—but the brand name doesn't appear here because General Motors isn't in racing.* Bill Warner

Going into the fourth turn Petty ducked out of the draft, at a place on the track and at a speed that nobody else would have even thought about.

There's a dip in the pavement just going into the final chute, the last leg of the tri-oval leading to the grandstands and the finish line. The Mercury and Dodge were side by side, the crowd was on its feet and when Petty's car hit the dip it pitched out, into Pearson's Merc . . . and both cars went out of control.

Petty and his dead machine came to rest 100 yards short of the finish line.

Pearson had the presence of mind to push in the clutch while banging into the wall, so he spun to a halt with the engine running. Urged by his crew he jammed the transmission back into gear and lurched across the finish line in clouds of smoke and steam, while the stunned flagman somehow managed to wave the checkered flag.

The car was dragged to victory circle and Pearson, looking like a hero of a Dead End Kids movie or maybe the crew from a World War II bomber, got the trophy and the kiss, and an apology from Petty. (No, the kiss came from the race queen. Get serious.)

Petty had the last words. The press couldn't hear enough about his daring move, the crash and his loss and what it felt like. The reporters followed him around the track, into the driver's lounge and into the shower, with Petty still wearing his trademark shades. When he emerged, cheerful as ever, he joshed the press with, "You guys are really gluttons, aincha?"

But after all that, the driving title went to Yarborough. He won the Firecracker 400, he won Richmond, twice at Bristol and twice at North Wilkesboro: Cale and Junior grew up on the short tracks. And it was a

bow tie year: thirteen Grand Nationals for Chevy, ten for Mercury, six for Dodge and one for Ford.

That was just the beginning. The world wasn't holding still. The fuel crisis/scare, emissions and social changes were making themselves known and anyway, the car companies kept on making new and different cars.

There's also a hint here that the Chevrolet people, the managers and engineers at least, were doing more for stock car racing than they had done in the past. They came out with a slick 1977 model called the Laguna, which even had a drooped nose from the factory. In the same model year Dodge came out with a new model, but it wasn't as good as the old one had been. Through some sort of political or grandfather clause, with no objections made in public, the three-year rule became a four-year rule, and Petty and Dave Marcis, the only top guys left with Dodge, got another year's lease on racing.

Donnie Allison displayed the improved Chevy with a 188.048 mph pole at Daytona, and Cale won the race in Junior's Chevy. Dodge wasn't through yet; Petty took the Firecracker 400, but that was a slower race, with a winning average of 142 mph, as compared to the 153 Yarborough turned earlier in the year. Cale won the driver's title again, just ahead of Petty, Parsons and a new guy named Darrell Waltrip.

Kim Chapin noticed as he was doing his statistics that the drivers of 1975 were the oldest guys in any sport, with the top stars in their late thirties. NASCAR had become the safest form of motorsport; death and injury rarely took people out, and the feeling of security probably kept drivers from retiring. In single seaters most racers reach a peak, collect the money and begin wondering how many more trips to the well they can risk.

Even so there was natural attrition and there were—and still are—tough young drivers working up through the ranks. There was Waltrip, a brash and outspoken driver from Tennessee. There was Neil Bonnett, an Alabama driver who managed to win with a Dodge in 1976. And there was Ricky Rudd, who began racing with go-carts.

But Yarborough won the 1977 driver's title and Chevrolet took twenty-one of the thirty Grand National races. The only other makes to win were Dodge, with seven, and Mercury with two. That tied with 1949 as the year with the lowest number of winning makes: Plymouth, Olds and Lincoln—and there were only eight 1949 national races to divide.

Something had to be done, and it was.

A lesser imbalance came first. Dodge had been allowed to stay in contention by a rule change letting them run a four-year-old body. But for 1978, they would have to go to the current body style, one that

wasn't as good for racing as the old one. Hinting here, 1976 was the last season in which a Dodge would win a Grand National race.

The universal engine/chassis

The Chevrolet situation was more involved.

Things were tough in 1978, as the US car industry adapted, or tried to adapt, to fuel shortages and imported car surpluses. At General Motors the mood was one of cutting back and rationalizing things, which came to mean making one or two basic models for all the brand names to share.

Ford and Mopar had done this for years but for the same number of years, Chevrolet, Oldsmobile, Pontiac and Buick each made a small-block V-8 and a big-block V-8. They competed within the family as well as against outsiders, and each division had its own engines.

But then the big-blocks were ruled out of road use as well as racing. Next, GM management dictated that

Here begins one of the Great Finishes in Daytona history, where the great is routine. First, Richard Petty (43) and David Pearson have collided in the last turn of the last lap *of the 1976 Daytona 500. Petty's car is sliding along the top of the track while Pearson's grinds to a halt at the entrance to pit road. Daytona International Speedway*

130

there would only be one V-8, the one made by Chevrolet.

This decision wasn't a bad thing in itself. The Mouse Motor, as the engine came to be called, was a classic and a blessing to stock-block racers everywhere. Its adoption by the four divisions—Cadillac later got permission to make its own V-8—hurt some feelings inside the corporation and even generated lawsuits from customers who resented buying an Olds and learning later it came with a Chevy engine.

But it was a wonderful racing engine.

And its adoption by the other divisions put them back into NASCAR racing.

We begin another diversion here. Many people believe that a federal law requires the car companies to make parts for seven years, so the buyer can be sure his or her car will remain in service.

There is no such law. Never has been. Instead, all the makers, domestic and foreign, supply parts for as long as there's demand for them. (One exemption is for emissions-related equipment, which by federal law must remain in service and effective for 50,000 miles.)

In our case, the important part in the equation is that the 1975–1976 Ford intermediate floor pan had become the standard starting point for Grand National cars. Banjo Matthews had become the builder of record, and he used the Ford pan, so all the teams buying cars as kits, which was most of the teams, began with the Ford pan. They still do, by the way, because in one of those odd little sporting gestures one finds in business, the Ford guys have been careful to keep one of their stamping plants ready to whomp out a couple dozen of the pans every year.

And all the makers supply body parts, to be used repairing wrecks. Listed at the dealerships are trunks, roofs, fenders, doors and so on.

Now we come again to 1978. Anybody who wanted to race something other than a Ford, Mercury or Chevrolet could buy the reworked Ford pan with roll cage, the adopted Chevrolet truck suspension in back and Ford parts in front, use the full-race Chevy small-block V-8 from a variety of builders, tack on whatever body parts pleased the sponsor and away they went.

A change in rules for 1978 was designed to keep the Chevys, the real ones that is, from walking away with all the prizes. The Laguna, the one with the slick front, was handicapped with its own carburetor plate to keep the power down and balance out the slicker shape.

For another intricate change, the Chevrolet Monte Carlo lost a stock advantage.

This was another step in philosophical adaptation. We have already seen the progression from weighing what the real car weighed to every car weighing the same, and from each make using its own engine to all the cars having a Ford or Chevy engine of the same size.

The Winaah! with the spoils. The car was demolished and Pearson looks as if he's ready to whup the man who says he hasn't earned this one. Fact beats hell out of fiction. Daytona International Speedway

Petty's car has fallen off the banking and come to rest in the grass, stone cold dead. But Pearson kept his clutch pedal down and his engine running, so his brain-dead Mercury is grinding toward the finish line. The two rivals were so far in front of the field that Pearson won the race. Daytona International Speedway

The Monte Carlo was a personal car, with a longer hood and shorter cab like the original Mustang but bigger, and its engine sat farther back in the wheelbase than the other cars' engines did. That meant more weight on the rear wheels, the driving wheels, and that made the Monte Carlo a better short track car, just as the Laguna was the better speedway car.

For 1978 the rules were changed to force all the other models to keep their engines where they were originally, just as the rules had always said, but the Monte Carlo had to have its engine moved forward 2.5 in., just about where the other cars had their engines anyway.

When they showed up for Daytona practice and qualifying, all the teams obviously had read the rule book. And done their homework.

Yarborough showed up with an Oldsmobile and got the pole at 187.536 mph, fractionally slower than Allison's Laguna the previous year. Right behind Cale was Foyt in a Buick Regal, for heaven's sake.

Even more odd, Bobbie Allison showed up with a Ford Thunderbird. It was a big car, sort of a personal car in the Monte Carlo mode, and had been an accepted model for years. Yet nobody had raced one seriously since maybe 1959.

It was a troubled race. Petty got his Dodge into contention but a tire exploded and in the spin, Petty collected Waltrip and Pearson and all three were out. A second crash among drafting packs took out Foyt.

Then came Buddy Baker in another fast Olds, but his (Chevy) engine blew and Allison was the winner, after starting thirty-third. Behind him were two Oldsmobiles, a Buick and a Mercury.

Cale won at Riverside, the road course, and at Talladega, the super-est speedway. He had a good car and of course was a top driver, and he went on to collect his third title. The 1978 season was a GM, instead of Chevrolet, year as Olds got eleven wins and Chevy ten, against five for Ford, four for Mercury and zip for everybody else.

Some of that was luck; the Buicks were just as powerful as the other GM models and Foyt surely drove his hard. It's just that he didn't win.

Neither did Dodge or Petty. That was a hard one to accept. It was the first season without a Dodge win since 1964 and Petty's first winless season ever! The new Magnum body looked as good as the one they'd had before, and Petty led some races only to have a tire blow at Daytona and a shift linkage fail at Talladega. Harry Hyde, head of the other Dodge team in 1978, said his problem had been that he had been promised durable engine blocks but they hadn't arrived.

The problem, never expressed openly at the time, was that Chrysler Corporation was phasing out its V-8-powered mid-range cars in favor of front-drive and smaller cars, with four-cylinder engines. Congress was imposing new and increasingly silly rules, and the only way Mopar could survive was to downsize, and quickly. So the performance image was scrapped, and with it went NASCAR support.

Betting on the underdog again. Bobby Allison poses with his 1978 mount, a Ford Thunderbird. At the time the 'bird was a big personal car, like the Chevrolet and Buick coupes raced then, but nobody had bothered to race one for several years. This car was built by Bud Moore and was sponsored by Norris Industries. It was finished the day of this photo, which is why it lacks all the secondary decals you'll see on the other cars. Besides, Norris paid for this shot. Road & Track

Daytona Beach, 1980. The lead car is a Buick Regal, pursued by a Chevrolet Monte Carlo. Note first that the cars have the same body style, with minor detail differences; it's a notchback body with fairly large rear spoiler. There was a lot of sheer length to these cars and they were stable at the 200 mph speeds they were running by 1980. Road & Track

Petty was the gentleman, as always, and at the end of the season he and STP went with Oldsmobile, then Chevrolet, Buick and finally Pontiac, where he was in early 1988, popular as ever and still friends with his former factory.

Meanwhile, for 1979 there was a tussle over the rules and their enforcement. The Ford guys said they didn't have as clean a shape as the Chevy had and that some other changes, as in the size of the rear spoiler and the slope of the hood, favored the Chevrolet. They added that the inspectors weren't paying enough attention to the car's static height and angle of attack, which also gave the Chevy an advantage.

It could have been true, because in a dramatic comeback Petty won the driving title for Chevy and for Olds, in 1979. Chevrolet had eighteen wins, against

A variation of the theme was the Oldsmobile Cutlass, with a rear roofline that's nearly horizontal and with what looks like a smaller lip atop the trunk edge. The driver here is Richard Petty and the crew is real busy. Look closely at the man in the right foreground and you'll see that he's delivering the right front tire, chalked RF, and will arrive with the right rear tire about the time the old one is coming off. This is Daytona, 1979, and Petty's crew will have their reward because he's going to win. Road & Track

five for Ford, five for Olds and three for Mercury. The season held lots of excitement, however, and some surprises.

Sticking close to family tradition, Richard Petty put his son Kyle on the Daytona track in the family's second car, the year-old Dodge that had led the race in 1978. Kyle went 184 mph, compared with the 183 that Richard had qualified with the previous year. Richard went out again and turned 190, so Kyle worked up to 187 and dad said that was plenty, son, come on in. Kyle ran the car in the junior varsity race, the ARCA 200 held before the full Grand National race, and won it. It was the first race he had ever entered.

Buddy Baker, also a second-generation racer, took the pole for the Daytona 500 in an Olds at 196.049. The speed was a huge jump from the earlier years; the season had had no major rules changes, so the speed came from the track's new pavement.

Another second-generation man was on his way, but didn't get nearly the attention.

The father, Ralph Earnhardt, was a hard man. His friends used to say that if you walked into Ralph's shop, up the road from the Charlotte track, and Ralph was in the middle of a job, he wouldn't even nod, so he could be sure he'd done the job right. Not until he came to a safe place to pause would he say so much as hello.

Ralph was ahead of his time. When other racers in the fifties used to buy junkers and run them until they broke, Ralph built engines. When the rivals had one car, Ralph had four, which he alternated so no matter what happened or went wrong, he would always have a fresh car ready for the next race.

The big money was in Grand National racing, but the steady money was in late model sportsman racing, where the rules were less restrictive, the cars lasted longer and you could race six nights a week and not be away from home. It was an intense way to earn a living. Banjo Matthews remembers that he and Ralph would race hard and knock each other off the track if they could. Then, after the racing he and Ralph and their families would all go off for dinner together, good friends and no grudges.

His record as a sportsman driver got Ralph some Grand National rides but he wasn't as good there, and never won a major race, to some degree because he wasn't as comfortable with the big teams and the travel. Ralph Earnhardt liked it best close to home, with his only helper his son, named Ralph Dale but called Dale to keep things straight.

Ralph died of a heart attack at forty-five, leaving a devoted family, especially the son who wanted to be a racer like his dad. Dale began on the dirt tracks, in the sportsman classes, and worked his way up to Grand National in 1979 with a good Oldsmobile.

The 1979 Daytona 500 finish was another legend. Donnie Allison and Yarborough were leading, in Oldsmobiles, with Petty in third. The race went to the last lap again, but in this case there was a complication—Bobby Allison. He was laps down but as the leaders came up, he moved out and prepared, or so Cale figured, to block for his brother. Cale made a move out of the draft and down, beneath Donnie, but Donnie moved down too, Cale said, and they collided.

This time there was no save. Both cars were damaged and they were passed by Petty, Waltrip and Foyt. Allison was credited with fourth, Yarborough with

Another view of the fastback Cutlass, this time with Cale Yarborough in 1980. The Olds was one of the fastest cars that year; Yarborough won the pole for the Firecracker 400 *and Foyt for the Daytona 500, but the make didn't have as many wins as the shape and speed implied it should get.* Road & Track

fifth. Not that Cale cared, as he'd jumped out of his car and decked Bobby. Then, when Donnie stopped to be sure his brother was safe, Cale punched Donnie as well. And, he says in his autobiography, he would do it again under those circumstances.

Or maybe not. Yarborough was following the usual career path; one day about this time he was on his way to another business conference when his daughter mentioned he'd been too busy to fix her broken bicycle for weeks. Cale was sorry to hear that but had to admit it was true. He next realized that he'd won millions of dollars and three national championships and didn't have much to prove, except maybe that there was more to life than winning races. So, as had Pearson and a few others before him, Yarborough cut back to running the major races only, and fixed his daughter's bike.

Petty, who didn't cut back despite having won 190 Grand National races by the end of 1979, won his seventh national title. Dale Earnhardt took rookie of the year.

Another identity crisis for "stock" cars

NASCAR was on another edge. Grand National racing was the most popular form of racing in the world, outdrawing not only Indy cars but Formula One as well and beating most of the other American series all lumped together. Record purses were being paid and the television broadcasts pulled in millions of fans and dollars. That was all good news.

The bad news was that the stock car, the kind that people buy and drive on the street and presumably use as a basis for emotional involvement at the races, was changing. Stock cars were becoming smaller, and the cars used as the basis for Grand National racing were being called dinosaurs . . . and worse. NASCAR's management began looking at this and working out what to do next.

There were no major rules changes for 1980. The cars and the tracks, or Daytona at least, stayed the same, as can be seen by Foyt's pole-winning speed of 195.202 mph in an Olds. Baker, also in an Olds, won

By the end of the era—Riverside in 1980—the big coupes were obviously bigger than the cars on the road. But they were fast and made the ground shake. And competition was as close as it looks here, with Dale Waltrip, Cale Yarbo- *rough and Richard Petty nose to tail through turn eight. Waltrip won, Yarborough broke and Petty was third, passed later by Earnhardt.* Road & Track

the 500 with a record average of 177.602 mph. Bobby Allison won the Firecracker 400 with a Mercury. It was, however, a Chevrolet year, as they won twenty-two Grand Nationals, versus three each for Ford and Olds.

The driving title was won under an extraordinary set of circumstances.

Dale Earnhardt is a pleasant man, with a sense of humor, even a taste for cracking jokes when least expected, but he was raised in a hard school and he isn't one to ask for favors. By 1979, Grand National racing required money and help, neither of which Dale had. He was racing in the sportsman classes and doing well, but he was on his own.

Then another driver made a fool of himself in public. The man who owned the car needed a driver and signed Earnhardt on the strength of his reputation and, anyway, the race was at Charlotte; Earnhardt lived five miles up the road, so he could save some money there.

Earnhardt drove hard and fast in the semi-private car and attracted the eye of a businessman putting together a two-car team. Earnhardt was signed as the second driver and was promoted before the 1979 season started because the veteran didn't show up. Next thing everybody knew, Earnhardt was rookie of the year. And in 1980, driving a good Olds

and a better Chevrolet, he won the driver's title. Then the sponsor, having achieved what he'd set out to do, got out of racing and Earnhardt had some lean years. But we will see him again.

(While we're dropping hints, in 1980 a Ford dealer from Dawsonville, Georgia, backed his sons with an old Mercury that managed to come in last in its first race, but the family, named Elliott, didn't let that get them down.)

By 1980 the Grand National cars were fast, the contests were close and the fans were turning out in record numbers. Even so, in the short run it wasn't good to have Chevy winning all the races.

It was even less good that only three models—the big Chevrolet, the Ford and the Mercury—were listed in both production and the NASCAR books as normal stock sedans.

Production cars had changed radically. Chrysler had gone to small cars with front drive, or to a few huge old models. In the fall of 1979 GM introduced the X cars, small front-drivers with nary a V-8 in the bunch. No matter what won on Sunday it was getting harder and harder to buy it on Monday.

Time once again for change and—as it worked out, although nobody mentioned this at the time—it was time for another major rework in what stock cars are supposed to be.

Chapter 8

Modern times: 1981-1987

Chuck Jordan is vice president for styling at General Motors. He's also a car nut and owns a bunch of odd machines, the sort of cars GM would never build. So when GM is criticized in his presence, which happens a lot, Jordan takes a deft tack and defends by turning the thrust in another direction.

When GM went to front drive, Jordan says, it was simply because mass confusion sweeps across the drafting tables of the world on a periodic basis, the way lemmings march into the sea. When all the car makers went front drive, it was one of those mass mistakes, Jordan maintains, done in hopes of making the industry look as if it were worried about improving economy, as indeed the manufacturers may have been.

Front drive, however, is useless when the car gets more than a few horsepower. Front drive works well for economy cars. It doesn't work for sports cars, for performance cars and most of all, it doesn't work on the track, not since the invention of the sticky tire.

When the domestic sedan—formerly on the large side and with a proper V-8 driving the set of wheels best suited to the job—became a small box with a dinky engine set sideways in front and propelling the front wheels, the domestic sedan was no longer a suitable basis on which to build a racing class, never mind a complete multimillion dollar nationwide institution.

Backed by its own tradition, NASCAR redefined the stock car.

The club could do this because the precedents had been set. In the beginning, stock cars had to race with whatever engine, brakes, suspension and weight they came with, wearing the exact body panels and so forth. Stock was what the factories built.

But, as we've seen, shipping weight became minimum weight. All the cars had the same size and type of engine, the same brakes and suspension. If they didn't meet the wheelbase rule, they were required to be changed so they did—likewise for engine location and so on.

It wasn't difficult—once the power to set the rules had been accepted by all parties—for NASCAR to revise the rules. They did, however, have a timetable problem. The first rumors of change surfaced in 1979 and were based on a 1980 timetable, but then the car owners and builders said they had too much invested, and the revisions were postponed until the 1982 season. A few weeks after that official notice, NASCAR made a new final announcement stating

The downsized era begins. This is Earnhardt at Riverside in the fall of 1981, with the Chevy Monte Carlo, the short one.

Earnhardt and team did the best job of making the new car work against the old ones. Road & Track

By Daytona Beach time all the cars had to be short. This is the Buick Regal, which obviously shares the basic body with the Chevy, but the nose gave good downforce and the Buick was faster than anybody expected. Road & Track

The short cars had trouble with the wind; they'd lost two feet in overall length and the airstream was separating and not coming back together, so the back got loose. There was a lot of debate, as seen here, over how big a rear spoiler a given model car could use. Road & Track

that the new system would take effect for the second race of 1981.

The new rules looked like different numbers. There would be the same engine limit of 358 ci and the same minimum weight of 3,700 lb., but the wheelbase would be 110 in., same as the current crop of production cars and a reduction from the 115 in. previously allowed.

(The actual rulebook says that engines can vary from 305 to 430 ci, by the way, except that the racing engine must be a version of an engine in production. Such an engine—that is, the small-block—cannot be larger than 358. Thus, because there were no large engines offered in any of the eligible models, the actual limit was 358 and the 430 class was there because . . . Nobody remembers.)

The second major change was that the 1981 Grand National was open to models made in 1981, 1980 and 1979, a three-year span and one in which most of the models were in the 110 in. size. The two previous years had been open to four model years; that is, in 1980 a driver could run a 1976 body. So the new rules took out the larger, older cars without appearing to do so.

The new rules limited wheel rim width to 9 in., down from 9.5, and reduced the inflated tire diameter from 28.75 in. to 27 or 28, depending on the tire. Tire width went from 12 in. to 11.5.

The final major change came with the list of eligible models. Remember, back a few years, NASCAR had won for itself the right to declare this model in and that one out. For 1981 the eligible models were the Buick Regal and Chevrolet Monte Carlo coupes and the Malibu two-door, the Chrysler Cordoba and Le Baron, the Dodge Diplomat 1980-81 only, the Ford Thunderbird and Granada 1979-80 only, the Mercury Cougar 1980-81 only, and the current Oldsmobile Cutlass Supreme, Pontiac Grand Prix and Pontiac Le Mans.

And then, as they say in the television schedules, the fun began. Having picked cars in the same general size, with small-block V-8s for power, NASCAR's technical experts had to do some figuring of which car would be allowed how much rear spoiler or what roof height or optional (wink, nudge) front panels so they would all be equal.

NASCAR officials could get away with such juggling because they already had, as with the Chevy sedans. They didn't have to worry about some of the cars listed. Nobody would bother with Chrysler or Dodge because the cars were too big and the factory wouldn't provide any help or even advice—and anyway there wasn't a racing version of the block available.

Punchline first: Making them equal didn't work.

The cars did work. Riverside's fall race of 1980 was the first race of the 1981 season and the last race for the long cars. Only five of the new models qualified; mostly, the teams needed to learn how to make them work. Earnhardt got his short Pontiac Grand Prix sorted out and was third.

At Daytona, where the new cars were required, things were shakey. The short cars were loose, as they say, meaning the rear ends were light and tended to get away from the drivers. Two cars literally took off during practice and the qualifying races.

At first there was one clear leader. Bobby Allison put his Pontiac LeMans on the pole at 194.624 mph. His time was a click of the watch slower than the best 1980 time but it was with a completely new car...and it was much faster than the other entries.

This was half a surprise. All the GM cars were built from the same body, the G body in GM parlance. They were all relatively big coupes in the line of that infamous Monte Carlo. But they had different styles, as different as their various designers could make them given the same general profile.

As it happened (and one suspects this wasn't completely by chance) the Le Mans had a rear win-

Richard Petty, in a Buick, on his way to winning the 1981 Daytona 500. The Buick shape worked and the factory had gone to some trouble attracting strong teams and drivers. Road & Track

Smaller wasn't always small. This is the 1982 Thunderbird, built by the Wood brothers and driven here by Neil Bonnett. In size and shape it's like the GM cars except that the front doesn't look nearly as clean, and this body style didn't do well. It may in fact have concealed the promise of the Ford engine and chassis. Road & Track

dow with the most gradual slope, the closest to horizontal, in the group. There had been some flap when Allison showed up with his car and the others realized they didn't have, nor had they seen, Pontiacs quite like that. But the car passed tech inspection and went through the templates, so it ran and took the pole.

But then the fun got even more fun. The two sail-cars proved that there was some basis to the complaints and fears expressed by the other drivers. So the GM and Ford guys were allowed to enlarge their rear spoilers, which put more pressure on the rear tires and kept the car on the track.

The exception was Allison's Pontiac; because it had gone so fast and didn't lose stability, it didn't need any help. Or so the ruling went.

The race was a grand affair. Nine drivers traded the lead forty-nine times. The bigger spoilers had given the new cars the stability they'd lacked at first and the cars were equal, so it came down to the last few laps with Allison and his Pontiac just in front of Petty and his Buick Regal. Allison ran out of gas and coasted into the pits, where he got fuel and tires. But Petty came in, got fuel and didn't wait for tires, and by gosh he won the race, his seventh Daytona 500 and his 193rd Grand National.

And so went the rest of the season. It was close, and for the third consecutive year the title chase went down to the final race. (The schedule was reworked as Ontario had closed, so the second Riverside road race was the last event in the season. For several years before that, Ontario had been the last race of the old year, then the cars went down the road a few miles and ran Riverside as the first race of the new year.)

What wasn't close was the manufacturer's championship. A big chunk of the surprise over the Pontiac's speed came because all the smart money had been on Buick. Johnson, Petty and Yarborough had picked that brand, and so, when the handwriting was plain to all, did Allison. The top teams and the men at Buick had obviously done a lot of research together.

It paid off. Johnson's driver was Darrell Waltrip, who was young, brash and fast. They began calling Waltrip "Jaws," after the movie of that name, because like the monster shark in the movie Waltrip was aggressive and could on occasion be loud about it.

The team had sponsorship from Mountain Dew and Johnson had the money to build eleven Buicks during the season. Waltrip got eleven poles and twelve wins, four of them in a row; Allison won four races, but when he didn't win he was right up there. At the final event, Allison put on a brilliant show on the road course and won handily, while Waltrip relaxed. All he had to do for the championship was finish better than twentieth and he coasted into sixth and got the title.

NASCAR's maturity shows in surprising ways. The car is Richard Petty's 1971 Plymouth Superbird, seen in action earlier, but on this occasion it has been surrounded by a small share of the Petty family trophies and is parked in the trophy room at Petty Engineering. The occasion is the 1983 NASCAR press tour, in which various reporters visited and interviewed the teams, so they would be on familiar terms when the racing and the rudeness began. The Petty family makes the press welcome and is just as friendly when tens of thousands of fans show up for the family's annual open house. Road & Track

Buicks had won twenty-two of the thirty-two races. Ford took seven, Chevy and Pontiac got one each.

Buick was understandably puffed, since in all the previous Grand Nationals, all the way back to 1949, the total for Buick had been two wins, both in 1955. Now, twenty-two out of thirty-two. They were so tickled they came out with the Buick Regal Grand National, even though the engine was a V-6.

This magnificent victory, this stomping into the ground of the other guys, didn't go unnoticed.

The factories return . . . politely

Earlier we saw the various factories slip, sneak or stumble into NASCAR, then get into the sport full time and overtime, then all quit, winners or losers.

This happened again, sort of, but in a different way. Ford management had never been emotional or political about racing. They got into it for business or fun and sporting instincts, then it got too expensive or something and they pulled out.

In 1982 Ford got back into stock car racing as a marketing device. They, the top management that is, knew that racing had the public's attention and affection. Performance had become a dirty word in the environmentalist and consumerist seventies but folks had become bored with that and had begun enjoying their cars again. (We're speaking here of the great mass of people. Most of us real nuts never stopped liking cars.)

Legendary Junior Johnson, who has aged some since we saw him winning at Daytona and before that rolling along the beach. It's the eighties and Johnson is watching qualifying with his driver, Terry (The Iceman) Labonte. Daytona International Speedway

Big Business indeed. This is Johnson's transporter, naturally bearing the names of the sponsors in the biggest letters. The parking area near the pits at any NASCAR track will be packed with rigs like this on race weekend.

Stock cars used drum brakes for years after other forms of racing had switched to disc. They stayed with drums because nobody made disc brakes big enough. Now, thanks to road race influence, they do. And better shock absorbers mean you need fewer of them.

Ford created a subgroup to develop performance cars, sell parts and help the professional racers, NASCAR included.

What they didn't do was form a factory team. Ford developed the parts, the high-level technical knowledge, and the wind tunnel and computer programs none of the teams could do on their own. Ford shared the facts and sold the parts, while they did not actually pay the racers.

General Motors had a more complicated history to undo. There hadn't been an official racing team for twenty-five years, and there had been an official ban since the team was dissolved, while at the same time there had been men in the several divisions doing performance work.

General Motors, the corporation and the men at the top, realized there was a middle ground, so they staked it out: the managers of the separate divisions could, if they chose, support forms of sanctioned competition. By direct order, not to be fooled with and under severe penalty, no division was allowed to own or operate a team. Period.

This change, on the part of both the corporations, although naturally they didn't act together, took place in 1982.

It didn't have an immediate effect.

At Daytona for 1982 . . . Wait, better explain here that in NASCAR, as in any sport, the various members of the various teams seem to stay in the game for years while the combinations swap around overnight. So we will save time and confusion and not list who was driving or building for whom unless it's important.

But in this case, at Daytona for the 500 in 1982, beginning of the season, former Grand National champ Benny Parsons had the Pontiac with which Allison took the pole in 1981. But Allison switched to a Buick and a different team, so Parsons stepped in and here he was, ear-to-ear grin with 196.317 mph, in the car everybody thought they'd taken out of the hunt.

That's racing. And so was the crash that took out Parsons and Petty. There were thirty-one lead changes this time and at the finish it was Allison in a Buick, followed by Yarborough in a Buick, Joe Ruttman in a Buick, Terry Labonte in a Buick and Bill Elliott . . . in a Ford.

In the Firecracker 400 later that year, new kid Geoff Bodine put his Pontiac on the pole with 194.721 mph, but at the finish it was Allison again, then Elliott and his Ford, then three more Buicks.

NASCAR was doing some marketing of its own and had begun creating special events. There was the Busch Clash, backed by the brewing company of that name, a sprint race for earlier winners held as part of the Daytona week. Allison won that and $50,000 as well.

But the year was a repeat of 1981, in that Waltrip won the title again. There were differences, as Waltrip won Riverside this time, Labonte was points leader part of the year and Allison, driving a Pontiac he'd built and sold to his new car owner, led in points late in the year. At the end, Waltrip was top driver and Buick had won twenty-five of the thirty Grand Nationals, to three for Chevrolet and two for Ford.

As usual, this couldn't last and as usual it didn't last.

The first signs of the 1982 factory involvement became visible in 1983. Chevrolet introduced a new version of the Monte Carlo, carrying the initials SS, for Super Sport, a rerun of those initials from the good old supercar days. The SS coupe had a new nose, one that sloped backward, a front spoiler beneath the nose and a rear spoiler. Chevrolet's engineers said the new car had a drag coefficient of 0.375, compared with 0.445 for the old body. (Just in case you've forgotten, the drag numbers begin with 1.0, which is a square, flat surface at right angles to the wind.)

The SS Monte Carlo was a real production model, and came with the Chevy 305 V-8, raised compression ratio and a power rating of 175 bhp. Sure, this was a long way from what supercars had been, but it was a step in the right direction and Chevrolet scheduled production of 6,000 examples, so this wasn't that much of a return to the bad old days.

Ford did even more. The Thunderbird name got a new body, still with small-block V-8 as an option; the complete car was designed to be aerodynamically efficient from the beginning. Next, it was a smaller car than the Monte Carlo. This didn't cause any trouble at the time because Ford hadn't been a threat to the GM cars and by that time the various factories were used to working it out with NASCAR in advance. That is, the division would decide which car the private teams would race, show the car to the technical committee and get an agreement; after that, the NASCAR experts would work out the configuration in which that model would be a fair match with the other models.

Elliott was known as a good Ford man and Dale Earnhardt—remember him?—was driving a Thunderbird for Bud Moore, who was one of the top builders and had an outside line with Ford anyway. Buddy Baker was lined up for a 'bird so it looked as if it would be a fair fight.

It was. Well, after a fashion. The Ford and Chevrolet troops arrived at Daytona and discovered that both the new cars had some trouble with air control, just as they had back in 1981. By race day, negotiations and experiments had given the Monte Carlo a 4.25 in. rear spoiler and a 4.5 in. one for the T-bird. The formal top time of 198.864 mph and pole position went to Ricky Rudd and his Chevy, but the actual best time was turned by Cale and *his* Monte Carlo. First he went 200.503 mph by the official clocks, then he went into the air at turn three and bounced all the way to turn four. The car was written off so the time didn't

count, and Yarborough had to run his back-up car in the race. Bobby Allison, meanwhile, wrote off two new Monte Carlos. Second best at the start was Bodine in a Pontiac Grand Prix; the second row was the 'bird of Earnhardt and the Chevy of Neil Bonnett.

The 500 was the race of the year once again. There were some new factors; CBS put camera and microphone into Cale's car so the home audience got a truly inside look at stock car racing; RJR upped its contribution and NASCAR did the same. It was the twenty-fifth anniversary of the speedway, after all, so the race was for $1 million.

And looked like it. During the first 499 miles the lead changed no fewer than fifty-seven times, among eleven drivers.

Some more words here about drafting. Larry Rathgeb, Chrysler's bright guy during the Mopar years, said they did scientific testing of the draft and its effects. First, as is obvious, two cars close together can go faster than one car by itself. Second, less visible, the car in back is doing less work than the car in front. The lead car is using wide open throttle to hit that 200 mph, but the tucked-in car isn't.

This point leads to the bottom line. When the second car moves over and nails it, not only does it get to go faster, the car in front is slowed down—yes, it is pulled back until the two are side by side and even then the passer has momentum forward and the pas-

An unexpected form of downsizing arrived in 1983, with the really new, aerodynamic and smaller Thunderbird. The new model didn't work out as well as Ford had hoped, nor as well as Earnhardt, in the shot here, had expected.

But the contrast between the 'bird and the Chevy, the Johnson car with Waltrip up, explains why NASCAR had to adjust the rules to keep the two models close to parity. Daytona International Speedway

143

Racing isn't just speed and thrills. This is Bud Moore, who's been a winning constructor and team manager for various Fords for twenty years, deep in thought during practice at Riverside.

see, you could call it, has momentum backward. It happens faster than it can be described but the point is, the car that begins in back is almost guaranteed a place in front and there's nothing the former leader can do.

There was Yarborough when the white flag waved, tucked in behind Buddy Baker and next to Elliott and Joe Ruttman. Down the back stretch he dove to the front. The other guys were slowed and were twenty

yards back when Yarborough took the flag. He'd retired from the full schedule, but he could still cut it when he wanted to. The fans had heard every word because he told everybody, live, what he was going to do next, then he did it. Wonderful show.

The close contest proved the Fords were competitive. So were the Pontiacs. Buick, stung after those years in the spotlight, had some new bodywork on the way and so, not to be left out of the fun, did Oldsmobile. (Wind tunnel tests later in the year, of the new bits for the Buick, showed that the NASCAR version, like the Chevy, had a drag coefficient of 0.375. The basic, stock Regal was 0.440 and the Regal GN, with new grille and front and rear spoilers, was 0.437. Racing doesn't just improve the breed, it also gets you better fuel economy.)

Back on the track, Petty won at Talladega for Pontiac. Cale's Monte Carlo qualified at 202.650 mph, and the first three rows went better than 200.

The year put things into better balance. On the heartfelt side, Bobby Allison won the driving title, edging Waltrip after two years of having Waltrip edge him out in the last race of the season. Chevrolet got the best of the improvements and at the end of the season Chevy had won fifteen Grand Nationals, to six for Buick, five for Pontiac and four for Ford.

That began to set a new stage. Bill Elliott and family sold their team to Harry Melling, an industrialist who had backed teams before with small success. The Elliotts did well enough this time to attract Coors sponsorship for 1984.

Meanwhile, Earnhardt went with Chevrolet and Richard Childress, who'd been a good driver, and worked into the top ten in five seasons, but who'd never won a Grand National in 285 starts. Childress

Aerodynamics has a down side. This is Bobby Allison's Buick Regal, sliding to a stop after it hit everything in sight twice at Daytona in 1983. The best part has to be that the *front has been ripped away and torn to shreds but the rest of the car, especially the central cage, is intact. So is Allison. Daytona International Speedway*

Million Dollar Bill Elliott. Well, he'll earn that title later in the year but here, Daytona Beach 1985, he and his Ford will take the pole, the qualifying race and the main event, the Triple Crown.

was smart and he appreciated how things were done, probably more than he would have if he'd been better at doing them. He was a good salesman and got sponsorship from Wrangler and had an open mind, so he was willing to hire top guys from odd places like Brooklyn and Philadelphia.

The season began on several familiar notes. Cale Yarborough set a new qualifying record, won his qualifying race and went on to win the 500, a feat known in Daytona Beach as the Triple Crown. No one had taken the Triple Crown since Fireball Roberts did it in 1962.

Cale's speed, 201.848 mph, in a Monte Carlo was nearly matched by another Chevy, one driven by Terry Labonte to 200.325 mph. The field averaged nearly 195, and was comprised of twenty-five Chevrolets, six Thunderbirds, five Pontiacs, three Oldsmobiles, two Buicks and a lonely Chrysler Imperial.

Remember the ripple in the pavement that put Petty into Pearson in that epic last lap in 1976? By 1984 it had grown, in fact and legend, into The Hump, a series of ripples in the fourth turn that put cars sideways and into the air when they hit it at 195 mph. This was rediscovered during qualifying but all track officials could do in time for the race was raise the barrier between the track and the garages.

In the race itself it was Chevrolet, Buick and Pontiac as Cale, Allison and Petty swapped the lead, then Earnhardt and Labonte were in front. Then it came down to a trio, Earnhardt, Yarborough and Waltrip, the latter being the poor devil trapped in the lead on the last lap, knowing . . . yup. At the end of the back straight on the last lap, Cale pulled out and away, towing Earnhardt behind him. Two cars are faster than one and they had maybe 200 feet on Waltrip at the finish line. There were four Chevys, then Elliott and his Ford, then Harry Gant in a Chev, then Ricky Rudd in a Bud Moore Thunderbird, then three more Chevys. Score it eight to two, with nobody else in sight.

Things got a bit more even, as Allison won the World 600 for Buick, then back in Daytona Beach ol' Richard got his 200th Grand National victory, watched by tens of thousands of fans, including one Ronald Reagan—yes, the President, there on the Fourth of July to help celebrate a truly American sport and holiday. Petty won in a Pontiac after a banging and shoving match with Cale that had even Reagan (a former sportscaster, don't forget) amazed.

The season came down to a three-way contest in the last race, at Riverside. The leader was Terry Labonte, a quiet Texan (if that's not a contradiction in terms) who got his start in quarter-midgets, then moved to short track and got a job as mechanic—and sort of driver in training—with a Grand National team. The driver quit and Labonte had been in the top ten since 1979; still, in 1984, at twenty-eight he was the second youngest national champ ever. (Petty was twenty-seven when he won the title for the first time.)

Gave away the punch line, eh? Labonte, whose calm under stress had already given him the nickname "The Iceman," played it cool and settled for third. Harry Gant, second in points, was eighth and Elliott, who only had a mathematical chance anyway, finished tenth.

145

Elliott rules at Daytona, 1985. The team was so much faster than the field that they were called in for repairs and made up two lost laps. They also inspired NASCAR to impose some limits. Bill Warner

The door has disappeared in the eighties stocker, and the safety net that keeps the driver's head inside in case of a crash now can be bought over the counter from the racing supply house, complete with lap-belt-style buckles.

It was an odd season, in that Labonte only won two races while bridesmaid Waltrip won seven and Elliott, Geoff Bodine, Cale and Gant won three. But they weren't near the top when they didn't win, and Labonte was.

The legend of Awesome Bill

Here begins one of the best mysteries of NASCAR.

Ford had openly and generously returned to stock car racing and had chosen to promote the Thunderbird as their Grand National star. The 'bird was smaller than the GM coupes, the Monte Carlo/Grand Prix/Regal/Cutlass that General Motor's separate divisions were backing, and it was slicker, at least when it came from the factory, but it hadn't done nearly as well as expected. The 1984 score was twenty-one wins for Chevrolet, to four for Ford, three for Pontiac and two for Buick.

That's a surprise. The other surprise is that nothing was officially done to even things up, to let the other teams catch up with Chevrolet . . . Unless the record doesn't reflect the facts. Unless, as seems to have been the case, the Fords were faster than their finishes indicate, and they had potential not yet exploited; when Daytona's speed week opened for business in 1985, all you could see were 'birds.

All eyes were on the Thunderbird of Cale Yarborough. Yes, the former Chevy pilot. Bill Elliott was noticed because his had been the only competitive Ford in 1984. Also watched were Ricky Rudd in the Bud Moore 'bird, and the Wood brothers with Buddy Baker.

Elliott was incredible. His operation was ostensibly a family one, with Dad the Ford agency owner as the founding father, Bill as driver and chassis man, second son Ernie building the engines and third son Dan on the crew. They had financial backing from Harry Melling, who'd bought the team, and from Coors, the major sponsor. According to public opinion they didn't have scientific help, as in wind tunnel time, the way some of the more established teams did.

So Bill qualified at 205.114 mph, the fastest Grand National time ever recorded, officially or otherwise. Yarborough was second at 203.814, giving Ford its first front row at the speedway. In the qualifying races Yarborough had a tough time beating Pearson, who had a good Chevy, while Elliot walked away from Waltrip, despite the former champ's Johnson-built Monte Carlo having turned 202.584 mph, the third-best time of the year. Elliott won by thirty-seven seconds, almost two miles.

And then came the race. It was Bill and the 'bird, with Elliott and Yarborough together until the second Ford burned a piston, and then the other guys officially led during fuel and pit stops, but Elliott was in charge. He was ready to lap the last two cars still on the same lap, when the officials noticed his headlight cover was loose. They called him in for a fix. It took eight laps for him to get the lead back, and he won virtually without challenge.

OK. The GM guys were furious and demanded changes; one wonders why, seeing that in the previous year there had been eight Chevys and two Fords and nobody got upset then.

More than sportsmanship (or the lack of it) was involved here.

When Petty, Waltrip and Allison had been turning 200 mph laps in their GM cars, they'd been on the edge or beyond it, holding their breath and praying for no wind.

Subsequent research showed that when the downsizing was done, the major change in vehicle dynamics didn't come from the reduced wheelbase. It came instead from the reduced overall length. Nearly two feet had been chopped from between the bumpers.

What this meant at racing speeds was that the air was parted by the front of the car and never came back onto the body sides. The two halves of the airstream did not rejoin, which made the rear of the Chevy/Olds/Pontiac/Buick very light and they re-

Bobby Allison in the old-style, 1985 Buick Regal. This is the notchback body style, as seen for several years and used through 1985, when the Thunderbird was proven clearly better on the speedways. The notchback coupe was a personal car, with the semi-formal roof styled to suggest formality, elegance and so forth. It didn't work at 200 mph, though. Road & Track

quired a lot of rear spoiler. Next, one of the facts people forget in this aerodynamics business is that when you are using engine power to keep the car on the ground, which is what you do when you mount all those wings and spoilers and dams, you are using up power that otherwise would make the car go faster.

Plus, the Thunderbird was a smaller car than the GM coupe. It was allowed a lower static ride height, and it had a narrower tail and a better slope to the

Elegance is the wrong word here. Shown is the instrument panel of Johnson's 1985 Chevy and it's made simply to hold the required instruments. One unexpected item might be the fuel pressure gauge, but NASCAR has used them for years. The pumps are mechanical because two generations back electric pumps were considered dangerous. And a close look here will show a redline of 8100 rpm painted on the tach face. Road & Track

This engine began life as a racing Chevy block. The radiator has been painstakingly shrouded, the catch tank and filler are where they can easily be reached, and the standard-issue NASCAR air cleaner sits atop the carb: the cold-air pressurized cowl intakes were outlawed years before. Road & Track

rear window, which meant it could run a smaller rear spoiler, fifty-two square inches versus fifty-eight for the GM cars. If it had the same power, why, the Thunderbird could go faster with that equal power and would stick to the ground better at that equal speed. (Even later, somebody would work out that the critical speed for the modern Grand National car is 192 mph. Any upset, any sudden disturbance at speed beyond that, and the car is going to turn into a four-wheeled wing.)

Most of this information wasn't known at the time, so while the GM guys griped, and showed up with some strangely narrow and contoured cars in a few cases, NASCAR did some thinking. Just before qualifying for the Winston 500 at Talladega, the tech people announced that all cars could run a roof height of 50 in., rather than 50 for the Thunderbird and 51 for the others.

In reply, Elliott qualified at 209.389 mph, while next to him was Cale, at 205.679. Imagine the feelings of Labonte, who was third, best GM car, with 204.441.

In the race, it was Elliott ahead of Kyle Petty, who had left the family firm in favor of . . . a Thunderbird, prepared by the Wood brothers, no less. In third by two feet came Yarborough, for the first 1–2–3 Ford finish since 1969. There were only two yellow flags and the race average was 186.288 mph, a huge jump in the record: Kyle Petty and Yarborough also finished ahead of the previous Grand National winning average. Oh, and they were the only three cars on the lead lap.

Double-oh, Elliott had stopped in midrace to replace an oil line and lost two laps, which he made up without any trouble.

Well. Superlatives are beginning to pale. Elliott was a lanky, shy country boy, with red hair and a grin and a family just as homespun and folksy as he was. The fans voted Elliott most popular driver in 1984 and 1985 (and 1986, but that comes later). Chevrolet had ruled the roost and here came these new guys, fresh from the farm, and they made their Ford do what nobody else had been able to do.

The next incredible fact came when sponsor R. J. Reynolds, always ready to get the public's attention, posted a million dollar prize for any racer who could win three of the four superspeedway events in a season.

You already guessed it. Elliott won the Daytona 500, and the Winston 500 at Talladega but had mechanical troubles at Charlotte's World 600.

Then came other worries. Effective for the second half of the season all Grand National cars had to use carburetor restrictors, throttle bores reduced to 1.45 from 1.69 in. The officials had noticed that Bill's 'bird was using lots of fuel, which meant he had extra power, so they figured a smaller carburetor would equal less power and even things out.

The smaller bores were expected to reduce power by 30 or 40 bhp, this with some 600 on tap, and to trim 5 to 7 mph from qualifying speed on the faster tracks. Cale did some tests at Daytona and turned 197, so the officials were happy.

So was Elliott. The Southern 500 at Darlington was tougher than the faster races had been but the other just-as-fast guys had trouble and he didn't. He won the third of the four . . . And Awesome Bill from Dawsonville, Georgia, became, inevitably, Million Dollar Bill.

It was an incredible season. Elliott won eleven races, all 500 or 400 miles long, and all major events. He was on television during the races and after, and his natural charm made friends and did racing good. Also, his prize money for the year totalled $2,433,187. Nobody who heard that—and it would have been hard to be in the United States and be awake during 1985 and not have heard that—could doubt that stock car racing was an important sport.

Still to come is the mystery question, and a surprise.

The question is a natural: How did they do it?

When new the Thunderbird wasn't quite up to par. All of a sudden Elliott could run with the Chevys and the other Ford teams couldn't. Then his was the best of the three 'birds that were the fastest cars on the superspeedways. Neither the rules nor the basic machines changed that much during this period, but something must have happened, eh?

We can rule out cheating. Back in the pure stock days, that could have been an answer, but in modern times, when there are so few limits, NASCAR has become nearly infallible at enforcing what few rules

Yes, stock car racing is popular. This is Charlotte, 1985, and that's Elliott in the T-bird leading the bow tie brigade.

Sell-out crowds aren't routine, but neither are they unknown. Road & Track there are. Elliott's car matched the templates, met the weight rules and passed the engine checks race after race, and don't think everybody wasn't watching.

Car and Driver did the best journalistic job, and in their April 1986 issue they asked all the experts. How'd the Elliotts do it? Nobody could really say.

Cumulatively, the experts said the team had worked hard and gotten their act together and if anybody else had a better answer, they would all like to hear it. Charlotte's Humpy Wheeler quipped Black Magic; he meant it partly as a joke, and partly because there sometimes is a mysterious chemistry that lets a team do better than they have a right to do.

The author's guess, posited here several years after that season so it's known that the team wasn't cheating or the wins a fluke, begins with the Elliott's first season, back in 1976.

They started in seven Grand Nationals that first year. They finished thirty-third in one, and in the others the car blew up.

Flip the pages back before that. Richard Petty spent his first season wrecking his dad's cars. It was proof—not that everybody said so then—that when he learned control, young Richard was going to be fast.

Now back to 1986.

Ernie Elliott is famous for building engines that crank out record power, but have a narrow power band and are right on the edge of destruction. My guess is that first, Ernie built powerful engines that were overstressed. He had more power than the experienced builders did, because they knew not to do it.

Then Ford improved the starting points, with special cylinder blocks and cranks from SVO, and the engines met Ernie's demands.

There's also a learning curve. We have in our collective prejudices the belief that anybody from the country is ignorant, and anybody with a Southern accent is stupid. Funny and charming maybe, but still stupid.

The Elliotts run a successful dealership. They are college graduates. They are just as smart as Roger Penske, and more fun besides. The Ford engineers who have worked with Bill and Ernie and Dan say they are quick studies, always ready to learn more and put it to good use.

The Elliotts had Melling and Coors backing them, so they had enough money and skill to bring the 'bird up to its potential, at which point they won the big races.

Which brings us to the surprise.

Bill didn't win the national championship.

Hard to believe, eh? Every time we turned on the television in 1985 there was Awesome Bill, winning another race by what looked like hundreds of miles.

What we forgot was that there were twenty-eight Grand Nationals in 1985, and when Bill didn't win, he was way back there. Bill and the 'bird were tops on the fast tracks and Elliott has displayed a talent for road racing, but he and his car didn't have it on the short tracks. Just why is another puzzle. It could have been Ernie's engines had too much on the top end and not enough off the turns. It could have been that Bill, who tunes his own chassis, didn't have the touch there. (In

The next step, once the little Thunderbird was clearly cleaner than the bigger GM coupe, was improvement to the old car. This is the Monte Carlo Aerocoupe, as accepted in 1986 and raced in 1987 by Darrell Waltrip. Sorry we don't have color film here because Waltrip is backed (you could tell!) by Tide and the car is beautiful, a tasteful blend of yellow, orange and washday white. Seriously, the rear window has been enlarged, extended and blended into the rear deck, and the car works much better at 200-plus.

The Pontiac bubbleback coupe was mostly sold as a kit for the dealer to install if the buyer really and truly wanted one enough to make a fuss. This is Richard Petty and car, at

Riverside in 1987. Along with driving skill, Petty is known for classic cowboy hats and rapport with the fans, both of which he's displaying here.

1987 he added Ivan Baldwin, probably the best short track chassis man on the West Coast, maybe the country, to the team.)

In the event Elliott won eleven races, but was second once and third once. Waltrip, driving a good Chevy, won only three races, but he was second six times, third six times and at the end of the season Waltrip beat Elliott by 101 points and got his third national championship. In the manufacturer's contest, it was fourteen for Ford, fourteen for Chevrolet and zippo for all the others.

Front to back, back to front

While the factories had achieved a sort of parity and the race went to the not-swiftest, NASCAR's planners had been looking at the long run. They made a rules change that may have been the major, most radical revision since the club was founded. Not only that, they did it so smoothly most people never noticed.

In principle, this began way back, when they first allowed stronger hubs and suspension and factory performance kits.

In practice, when the downsizing went into effect in 1981, everybody in NASCAR knew that was the first of several steps. Grand National was committed to remaining the class in which domestic passenger cars (never mind sedans!) were raced, so the class would have to change with actual production.

Ford was the most openly involved, and wanted to use racing to promote certain models, that is, the Thunderbird. Ford was ready to promise that the 'bird, along with the Mustang and Cougar, the other personal cars from that corporation, would stay in production for the next few years.

Chrysler Corporation was out, with some regrets, but still they had withdrawn and had no plans to come back. Likewise AMC and the semidomestics, the foreign-owned plants making cars in the United States, well, they had nothing remotely close and hadn't shown any interest anyway.

At General Motors, the brass had given permission for the several divisions to support racing, if they chose to and could justify it in terms of image or sales. At the same time, GM had committed itself, and its divisions, to wholesale conversions of its product line.

There are those, including the author, who would describe this move as switching from making cars people want, to making cars that people who don't buy cars—that is, Congress, the *Washington Post* and the *New York Times*—think people would buy if they were as smart as the people who don't buy cars. (I know, you may need to read that sentence several times.)

In other words, GM was mandating a switch to front drive and to dumb (sorry, got carried away again) smaller engines. What this switch has done (chuckle, snort) has cost GM market share and bil-

The next step in keeping up with the times was the acceptance of rear-drive, NASCAR-chassis racing cars with front-drive-based bodywork and names. This is the Olds version, although the rules allow such streamlining and closure of the front that it's hard to tell except for the badges.

lions of dollars and what respect they had left. But never mind that.

GM's divisions knew they were going to be forced out of the real car business. Ford had made an earlier, timelier move, from the LTD line to the Thunderbird line and was in good shape.

NASCAR wanted to keep GM in Grand National, obviously.

The first step, the short-term move, was to let Chevrolet and Pontiac fix their aerodynamic problems for 1986.

The long-term move was to allow Oldsmobile and Buick to make Grand National cars out of their new, otherwise hopeless, production cars.

The Chevrolet and Pontiac cars were ramming through the air so hard the air was still split when the back of the car got there. So the slick noses of the Monte Carlo and Grand Prix race versions were matched by bubble backs, extended and sloped rear windows that would guide the air and keep it against the body all the way back. This was still another form of fastback, just like years ago, and it worked.

It was also legal, in no small part because NASCAR required only that Pontiac and Chevrolet allow people to buy the model if they wished to. How hard they'd have to wish depended on the buyer. There were no number requirements, as in the old Daytona 500 or Superbird.

The Oldsmobile is different from the older Chevy and Pontiac and, of course, from the Ford. But because the dimensions and proportions have been subtly altered to fit the front-drive body on the mandated NASCAR pan with cage and rear drive and the V-8 never meant for this body, it doesn't look like the Oldsmobiles in which people came to the race. Nobody seems to mind and Rick Wilson has, as they say, a major sponsor.

So Pontiac scheduled a few hundred versions of the special body to go to selected dealers, with the body parts available as parts, in a kit, for anybody who wasn't on the dealer's good guy list. (The proper name is Pontiac Grand Prix 2+2, in case you read the classified ads.)

Chevrolet was a bit closer to the spirit of the tradition. Their version, the Chevrolet Monte Carlo SS Aerocoupe, was actually produced as an RPO, a regular production option. The Aerocoupe came with stiffened suspension and the five-liter Chevrolet V-8, with fat tires, front dams and rear spoiler. And in model years 1986 and 1987 they made several thousand of them. If you watch traffic in the right places you may even see one in private hands. (The smart man in 1988 would be looking to buy an Aerocoupe today because it's the two-place Thunderbird or 1957 Chevy of tomorrow.)

Over at Buick and Oldsmobile, they were still making rear-drive coupes, the Regal and the Cutlass Surpreme, respectively, for the street.

For the track, the official entries became the Buick LeSabre and the Olds Delta 88.

Mark this well. The LeSabre and Delta 88 are the front-drive coupes that replaced the rear-drive coupes. They have nothing in common, brand names aside, with the other models. They don't have frames and have never had V-8s.

Preparing for the 1986 season meant that the teams working with Buick and Olds, mostly Bobby Allison and Buddy Baker, did a lot of work with the division engineers assigned to help the projects. They took normal Grand National frames, that is the old-time Ford pan cut down and fitted with Ford and Chevy truck suspension. They installed the GM V-8 in racing trim. They got all the body parts, the ones listed for crash repair, one complete set of panels for each car, and put the panels on the framework.

Allison and his guys and the Buick guys made twelve trips to the GM and Lockheed wind tunnels. Or to put it another way, Baker used $65,000 in tunnel time developing the Delta 88.

One other factor in preparing for the season was that the body, name it what you will, had to conform to the regulation wheelbase and it had to cover the mandated wheels and tires. If there was a choice of keeping the panels or covering the tires, the tires won.

Pause here for breath. If we get one step further away from the production car and call it a stock car, our noses will begin to grow.

Speaking technically, these cars were wonderful things. The new Pontiac bodywork added 3 mph to the car, which was equal to getting 36 more bhp from an engine that was already performing miracles.

Oh, but wait. NASCAR has one sort of call that doesn't inspire courage. That's the one involving keep-

Here's the Ford version of the racing production V-8, wearing the required and standard air cleaner. Having all the cars use the same air cleaner and same limited choice of carburetor makes inspection and enforcement a lot easier.

ing the sponsor happy. To that end, NASCAR abandoned the original and wonderful name, Grand National, for its national championship.

R. J. Reynolds must have wanted more splash for its cash, because the useful name—the one that evokes grand for large and impressive, and national for coast to coast, the way Bill France had to do it when he began—was swapped for Winston Cup. One guesses that cup means a trophy, which is fair, but all Winston means is the sponsor gets its name in the headline, or hopes to. Grand National was given to the smaller, older cars raced by the junior varsity, the cars that would formerly have been late model sportsman class. But because Grand National served the top class and the club so well for so long, it has been used here. (Anyway, the abbreviation for Winston Cup is WC and in some English-speaking countries that's where you go when nature calls.)

Back to business. At the opening of the 1986 season Ford had its slick 'bird, and Bill Elliott. Olds and Buick had new, slicker cars and good drivers, and Chevrolet had a surprising new card to play.

Dale Earnhardt, the former Ford driver and national champion back in 1980, who had done well, fallen away and then climbed back, had hit another hot streak in a Chevy. Chemistry is probably a better word for it. Earnhardt was driving for Richard Childress, who'd begun his racing career selling peanuts at the local track, then become a solid driver who made the top ten but never won a Grand National race. The team's engine man was Lou LaRosa, a native of Brooklyn and the man who built engines for Earnhardt's previous title win. All the team members liked each other and could work together, like a family is supposed to do, but doesn't always.

The 1986 preseason favorite naturally was Elliott and he did the expected at Daytona with a 205.039 mph qualifying run, a click off his 1985 record. In the race, Elliott had handling problems and the normal race occurred: twelve drivers swapped the lead twenty-seven times. Earnhardt started fourth and looked the best late in the race, but the crew hadn't done their sums right and Earnhardt ran out of gas, which cost him three laps. He collected a bonus for

The most effective team in 1986 and 1987, in terms of winning races and the championship, was Childress and Earnhardt. Richard Childress, left, was a good but not great driver and learned so much he became a top team owner, manager and builder. Dale Earnhardt, right, hit his stride when he found a team with which he could both talk and listen.

Some thoughts on winning

Probably the easiest question the reporter can ask is the question to which there really doesn't seem to be a good answer: What's the secret of success in racing?

Sure, we know the obvious parts. Some people can drive cars better than other people can. Add bravery to natural ability and give the would-be racer enough hunger to keep him up all night working on the car and enough self-interest to let his mom go hungry so he can buy parts. (Frank Lockhart did just that.)

Put the driver in the right place at the right time, and he wins races. Sounds easy.

But it's complicated first by things like star quality, the mysterious appeal that made Curtis Turner and Fireball Roberts household words while they didn't win the titles their public images suggest. And there's lack of charisma, witness Bill Rexford and Benny Parsons, to name two national champions nobody paid attention to.

There's luck. One man is in the lead and a tire blows. He's passed but just then it begins to rain, the race is stopped and he gets credit and points for second or third. Another man is leading when a tire blows but the race keeps going and he finishes out of points. At the end of the year, the first man wins the series. Things like that have happened, and they had nothing to do with preparation or skill, so we must call it luck.

There are combinations. A good driver who isn't winning teams up with a builder or crew that's merely good and the next thing you know, they're cleaning up. Or, just as common, a team breaks up and neither half wins the way they did together, although on the record both halves can do their share.

Even so, even assuming that not everybody has the same equipment, some guys win and some don't. There has never been proof as to how this works.

Nor is there such proof here. Instead, based on researching fifty years of stock car racing, and on deep discussions with racers who know about this firsthand, and on some peripheral knowledge of the author, some thoughts . . .

We'll deal first with the author's experience. On November 8, 1970, a date I know because the tiny trophy is sitting on my desk this minute, I was in the middle of the pack in a club race, a position I'd held many times before. Some people laugh when they hear about Bobby Isaac hearing the voice during the race. I don't laugh because on that occasion, in the middle of a sweeping hairpin turn, I heard a voice say, "You can beat these guys."

I don't know where the voice came from. I don't care, although I guess it was my subconscious speaking out.

Suddenly, inspired by that voice, I could beat those guys. I charged harder, dove deeper, braked later and surged into the lead. I was so carried away I sailed off the end of the straight and into the weeds. I roared back onto the track, caught the field and worked back into second place at the finish. Not even my loyal crew could believe how fast I'd gone and how well I'd driven.

I never heard that voice again.

I never went that fast again.

But I came away with the sure knowledge that to win, you must believe. You must have that inner confidence. When you believe you can do it, you can.

Next comes something called synergy, the ability to make two and two add up to five. Or you can call it team spirit.

Everybody who has played on a team knows about this spirit. Some days, you don't even have to look. Wherever you throw, the ball is where the other chap will be. The catcher puts his mitt where he wants the ball to arrive and zing! the pitcher puts it precisely there.

Stock car racing isn't like football or baseball, but it is a team effort and the team feeling is vital. The teams are in constant flux, so much so that this book doesn't attempt to chart who drove for whom each and every season. But it's worth wondering, why did Darrell Waltrip and Junior Johnson do so much better together than they have done apart? Why has Dale Earnhardt been so much faster with Richard Childress than with Bud Moore?

There's something about working in harmony that makes everybody work better. How this happens, why engines last longer and give more power when built by guys who like the other men in the room, I don't know. But the record shows it's so, and the constant swapping of team members means people know it, even if they don't know they know.

The final factor has to be concentration and desire. One educated observer reckons that in 1987 there were seventeen teams capable of winning a championship race. They had the power, the knowledge and the skill. They didn't all win.

A study was done some years ago that proved that if you took ten men, same size, age, muscular development, cardiovascular system and so on, and had them run a 100 yard dash, one of them would win every time. Not because he was bigger or stronger or even quicker, but because he wanted to win the most. (The object of that study was a motorcycle racer, an unbeatable, incredible, sensational all-time winner . . . for three seasons. He literally rode his guts out and while he has won since then, he has never been the same.)

I mention that here because one of the puzzles surrounding winning has been, why will a driver win, then fall off the pace even though he has the same backing, the same engine men and so forth?

Racing seldom is listed as one of the arts, but it is creative, and people in the arts do know that most creative people will do all they can do in a set period of time. Musicians reckon their peak to last seven years. Their career will last longer, but that comes from doing what has already been done (witness, oh, the Rolling Stones).

Winning races against the opposition present in the Winston Cup is so demanding, I think, that it takes more sheer effort than a man can deliver for more than a few years. To some degree it's like war, where you can only fly so many missions before thinking about what comes next. At any rate, and meaning no disrespect or offense, the record shows even the very best have a finite time at the top.

That's the author speaking. As counterpoint, Richard Petty says it all comes down to circumstances. "We work hard, we can overcome anything in the world except circumstances. We don't understand it, we don't want to understand it, that's what trust in the Good Lord is.

"This is all part of God's plan. But he doesn't tell you what His plan is, so all you can do is get up in the morning and see what happens next."

Davey Allison, here at the mercy of the press, has the best record to date of the several young drivers whose fathers were Grand National stars before them.

leading the most laps, but it was no consolation. Elliott meanwhile got involved in a wreck and the race went to Geoff Bodine, a short track champion from upstate New York driving a strong bubbleback Chevy.

Earnhardt won three of the normal races, so to speak, and took the points lead while Elliott, who had been working harder than before, but had less to show for it, unleashed an amazing 212.229 mph qualifying run at Talladega, another all-time NASCAR record. In the race the engine blew and he was officially twenty-fourth

Bobby Allison and his new Buick won, with Earnhardt right behind, followed by Buddy Baker (Olds), Bobby Hillen Jr. (Buick), Phil Parsons (Olds), Morgan Shepherd (Buick) and Richard Petty (Pontiac). So the new cars, bodies and rules were fairly close. By midseason twelve different drivers had won at least one of the seventeen races, a record.

But Elliott had a reverse year, in that he was plagued by big troubles, like blown engines, and by little things like a faulty ignition coil and even a stubborn lug nut.

His high point came at The Winston.

Bobby Allison, still racing after all those years. This is his road-race Buick, as shown by the cooling scoop in the central roof pillar. The acceleration and the high power applied at relatively low road speed make the differential more likely to break in road races than on the speedways.

Allison has been competitive even longer than Richard Petty. The theory is that he had to wait twenty years to win his first national title and he worked so hard he still wants another one.

This is an odd event, created as a show. It takes the top drivers at midseason and puts them into a sort of dash for cash: some laps, a stop, more laps, another stop and a final run for the money. Partially this comes from the old bench racing debates about what would have happened if the loser could have fixed his car. Partially it was to fill in time and create a different event.

Anyway, Elliott led all but one of the eighty-three laps, and beat Earnhardt by 2.55 seconds and collected $240,000, the largest payday in NASCAR history.

But for the rest of the season it was Earnhardt, Waltrip and Tim Richmond, who was a sprint car pilot turned stocker, a fast and brash newcomer whose foot often outraced his head. Waltrip was a keen observer and a quick wit, while Earnhardt was more reserved with the press and public. Waltrip at the time drove for the legendary Junior Johnson, while Childress wasn't as well known. Richmond had a strong car from a bright and brash new owner, Rick Hendrick.

Waltrip commented during the season that the equal speeds and the high speeds were getting some drivers into situations they didn't understand, and that the old-time courtesies seemed not be to observed any more.

That probably was true. But in large part because of relative levels of charm, Elliott being due for his third most popular driver award, the burden of the pushing and shoving came down hardest on Earnhardt. It wasn't especially fair. It was strange, and surprised Waltrip most of all because until that time he'd been the other half of the equation, the man in the black hat versus Elliott's white one. Now he found himself moved to the side of the good.

During the season, Earnhardt won five races, to four for Waltrip, seven for Richmond and four for Elliott. But Dale's strong finishes when he didn't win earned him the championship again, nearly 300 points ahead of Waltrip, who in turn edged Richmond by six points. That one wasn't settled until the last race of the year, at Riverside, where Waltrip won by four feet over Richmond but they got equal points for the event because Richmond had led more laps. NASCAR set out years ago to make the finishes tight, and they've done it.

The future postponed

A sidelight during the 1986 season took place at Charlotte, on the infield road course laid out for the occasional sports car event.

The other clubs—CART, IMSA and SCCA—had been running races on city streets in Long Beach, Miami and Detroit, the latter the site of the US Grand Prix. NASCAR didn't want to be left out; road racing could be the venue of the future and anyway, the new

domestic cars were even smaller, so Banjo Matthews was commissioned to build a cut-down chassis, with a 101 in. wheelbase, and Richard Childress finished the job with a GM V-8 and body panels from the Pontiac Sunbird.

The official designation was Left-Right Car, standing for turning in both, well, make that either direction (one at a time). The car came in heavier than hoped, didn't need any ballast and didn't handle all that well because the weight of the engine couldn't be compensated for. But NASCAR announced this would be the next downsize, to be the official racing car of 1988, with V-6 power and with the poor old V-8 outlawed.

Jumping ahead in time, NASCAR's officials then watched a few of the street races, and noticed how

The back of Waltrip's truck looks like . . . a giant box of the sponsor's product! Neat. The team is owned by Rick Hendrick, who has a score of dealerships. Hendrick used to win drag racing and doesn't do all that badly when he drives one of his many stockers in the road races. But he's a sharp businessman and realizes that, as shown, the company that signs the checks gets the credit.

Kyle Petty, NASCAR's sole third-generaton star. Like his father before him, Kyle grew up helping in the family store, but he didn't always have the desire to drive, and in fact also spends time working on his career as a singer.

much money they cost to put on and how little action the poor devils in the stands actually saw. And they may have peeked at the books of the sanctioning bodies, too.

At any rate, it came to pass that nothing more was said about the downsize or the L-R cars, until late in 1987, with most of the 1988 cars already built. At this point NASCAR carefully let it slip during testing that the little cars and the L-R program had been placed on hold indefinitely

Dirty Dale dazzles 'em

Midway through the 1986 season NASCAR officials began to have some concern about speed—where've we heard that before?—and the carburetor bore size was restricted again, with slight effect except on qualifying speeds at the superspeedways. They also had worries about tires. So the 1987 rules began with a de-restriction of bore size, and with a reduction in minimum weight, from 3,700 to 3,500 lb. ready to race: lighter cars exert less pressure, therefore less stress, on tires.

There had also been lots of work behind the rules. Ford had done the most.

Back when the company's engineers developed the first versions of the performance small-block V-8, there was the Windsor version and the Cleveland version, both named for where they were made. Then

Alan Kulwicki's road-race Thunderbird is also his speedway Thunderbird because it's his best car, period. Kulwicki came out of Midwest modifieds and put together a *sustaining deal; he has backing enough to field the car, but if he wants to make a living and put something in the bank, he'll have to do it with winnings.*

Bobby Hillin's Buick bears a reasonable resemblance to the rival Oldsmobiles, even though the GM divisions are as ready to whip their siblings as they are to unite against Ford. Current rules no longer require the body panels to have a seam representing where the door used to be, and the trailing edge of the windshield can be shaped in the wind tunnel. What looks to be a profusion of stickers here actually conforms to an appearance code worked out by NASCAR when television first arrived. Major and supporting sponsors get so many square inches, while companies that support the sport have an allocation, and only a given square footage of the car can carry a commercial message.

Ford phased out the really good one, the Cleveland, and began making the Windsor in Australia (no kidding).

The Windsor engine works fine in normal highway or even police use, but its cylinders are siamesed, with no water passages between them. When the bores are enlarged, as they must be if the 302 is to become a 358, they are too close and the engine has problems with uneven heating.

One of the benefits of Ford's involvement with racing was that for 1987 Ford SVO introduced a new block, for racing only, based on the Windsor but with water passages between the bores. Even cooling equals less stress, which equals more power.

The Thunderbird got new body panels front and rear. Ford's people said there'd been a problem with the back getting loose, so they had reworked the deck to create more downforce, while the front was simply cleaner and had a lower intake.

Pontiac's bubbleback coupe had reworked panels beneath the bumpers but the same nose and deck. Olds and Buick had flush headlights and minor revisions, while Chevrolet's Aerocoupe was virtually unchanged, at least to the outsider's eye. All four makes used the Chevy-derived GM V-8. Pontiac's engine men had developed their own cylinder heads for the Chevy block and had had them accepted, while Buick's similar work was rejected and Chevy's own very latest project was banned.

None of this showed on the surface but the intent obviously was to equal everything out, to let Pontiac have some power while the other GM teams had better aerodynamics.

Daytona 1987 was a lot like 1985. Elliott shattered the record with 210.364 mph. He was followed by two more 'birds, Bobby Allison's son Davey with 209.084, and ex-sprint car star Ken Schrader with 208.227.

Then came Bobby Allison and his Buick, the one that was being mistreated by not getting the Buick heads, with 207.795, then Earnhardt's Chevy at 207.016. Rick Wilson had the best Olds, 206.247.

It was a fast field, which had to be the most important part. Nearly as vital, however, was the virtual equality of the Fords, closely followed by the various General Motors versions, new and old. The juggling of parts and rules was making for good racing, as everybody had hoped.

Next easy pick, Elliott won the Daytona 500, at an average speed of 176.263 mph (second only to Buddy Baker's 177.602 mph in 1980). It wasn't easy. There were nine leaders; Elliott only beat Benny Parsons and his Chevy by five car lengths, the Elliott crew's pit stops being responsible for some of that, but it was plain that the Ford was the best car of the day.

There were also some hints of the future. All the drivers said their aerodynamic cars were a handful in the wind, and in the draft.

But then the rerun of Elliot 1985 turned into an echo of Petty 1967.

Dale Earnhardt, who'd had trouble getting his Monte Carlo right for Daytona, got it right everyplace else. He was fifth at Daytona, first at Rockingham and Richmond. He was sixteenth at Atlanta, then he won Darlington, North Wilkesboro, Bristol and Martinsville, four straight.

It was the most impressive beginning in NASCAR history, Richard Petty's best years notwithstanding. Nobody could explain it except that Earnhardt, Childress, LaRosa and everybody were in harmony, and the car worked better than anybody else's.

Then came a different story.

Elliott and the flying (oh, don't say that) Ford qualified for the Winston 500 at Talladega at 212.809 mph, another all-time, all-track record.

But Bobby Allison, winner in 1986, said "Racing at Talladega is like those fighter plane scenes in *Top Gun*. You don't need a racing uniform here, you need a flight suit."

Earnhardt's speed was 210.360, putting him in the third row. Childress commented, "You don't drive a car here so much as you steer it. The air turbulence generated from the speeds is so great that handling becomes critical."

These comments are most impressive because they were made the day before the race.

In the race, live and on television, Bobby Allison's car jinked sideways coming through the fourth turn, then sailed into the air, spinning all the while, slammed to earth and came apart.

It was a thrilling few seconds for the fans, because thanks to all those years of rules, rule enforcement and engineering, Allison climbed out unhurt.

It was terror for NASCAR and track officials. They knew the car and its parts had been kept from killing the people in the stands only because it hit just where the protection was good, and had just been improved. A few yards either direction and American racing would have had what France had back in 1955—carnage. And in the United States we have hundreds of thousands of lawyers. Racing could have ended right there.

Never had that poor old cliche, Something must be done, been more accurate. And of course something was done as quickly as possible.

Meanwhile, there was a delay and a restart, and the race went to Davey Allison, three quarters of a second ahead of Terry Labonte, with Kyle Petty third and Dale fourth: Ford, Chevy, Ford, Chevy.

Three days later, Les Richter, NASCAR's vice president for competition, announced that smaller carburetors would be required for the two super-tracks, Talladega and Daytona, where speeds had become a problem.

Next, the cars would have side windows on the right, and the right-side body panels would be extended, in sort of a skirt, from front to rear wheelwells.

NASCAR had been testing and observing. They learned that other racing cars, the Indy cars and the prototypes, were going faster and were more dependent on air pressure to keep them on the ground, but that when those cars spun, they spun flat.

The stock car flew because when it was suddenly sideways to the direction of travel, air was rammed into the cockpit and beneath the body, causing lift-off.

The winning team means exactly that. Childress' crew is as fast as any five men in the business and they work— witness this fuel stop—as a team.

Earnhardt's Wrangler-backed bubbleback Aerocoupe was seldom the fastest car in qualifying during 1987, but it won the most races and carried the banner for Chevrolet so well that in 1988 GM's Mister Goodwrench was the major sponsor of the team.

Reduce the size of the openings for the air to use and the speed at which the attack occurs and fewer cars will turn sideways or fly. Or so they hoped, and so it has been since.

The next excitement, other than Earnhardt winning races, came at Charlotte. The management there was working to pull in a weeklong crowd, as they do at Daytona and Indianapolis, so they scheduled The Winston, the showbiz race, one week before the 600.

It worked better than anybody could have hoped. Earnhardt, remember, was known to his detractors as Dirty Dale. Waltrip was the bad boy turned polite, Geoff Bodine was the Northerner, and Elliott was the most popular driver.

The Winston has three segments, with mandatory stops. Elliott won the first two, easily. The pit stops and pauses are there so the crews can make adjustments; it was fun to watch Earnhardt dial his car into contention and Waltrip and crew dial his car out.

Then! In the final segment dust flew going into the first turn and flew again coming out of the fourth. Somehow Earnhardt, in the lead, had been knocked sideways. He came across the grass strip between pit lane and the front kink, doing 170 or so.

Pause for dramatic emphasis. Colin Chapman, the Formula One genius, used to make sure his Grand Prix cars had lots of steering lock. He said one of the ways you can tell great drivers from good ones is that the greats get out of situations where the good are lost. One way they do it is by steering when the car is too sideways to be saved, so Chapman liked to be sure his drivers had the tools for the job.

Curtis Turner was famous for getting sideways, way out of shape and well past the limits, and being in control. So was all-time winning dirt motorcycle racer Jay Springsteen.

So is Earnhardt.

Cocked sideways on grass, headed toward the stands, Earnhardt didn't lift his foot. He steered and fought back and incredibly, impossibly, he not only kept the big Chev in control, he maintained his speed,

The 1988 Daytona 500, the year's biggest race and surely this was one of the most thrilling runs ever. Here is the victor, Bobby Allison's Miller-Buick . . .

. . . and here is Richard Petty's STP-Pontiac. While millions of fans watched in horror, old number 43 crashed in mid-pack, pirouetted four times on its nose and smashed into destruction. When the dust had settled, every- one's hero, the King, limped from the car, shaken but safe. *What a tribute! What a show! Daytona International Speedway*

went into the first turn in the lead and won the final segment of The Winston.

Nor was the fun over yet. Just as Dale took the flag, Bill came out of the pits, where he'd been to have a tire replaced. He roared onto the track and when they reached the back straight Elliott and Bodine both rammed Earnhardt. They hit below the belt, after the bell.

Tempers flared, it comes as no surprise to hear. Earnhardt went to get the trophy and the chit for the $200,000, accompanied by two burly crewmen. There were muttered threats and glares. NASCAR officials called for the tapes, went into an official huddle and had the involved drivers in for a closed-door conference.

They did the right thing. All three drivers, Elliott, Earnhardt and Bodine, were found at fault, fined and put on notice that such behavior would not be tolerated.

Next came some deft moves. Proving something, the governor of Georgia telegrammed Elliott that the people of his state were offering to pay his fine.

No fool, Elliott made a counteroffer. He would pay his own fine but the money donated by fellow Georgians would instead be given to the anti-drug campaign.

Third non-surprise, albeit out of sequence, the fans voted Elliott the most popular driver for 1987, the fourth year in a row.

Back on the track, The Winston had been the perfect race. There had been speed, thrills and chills, hero versus villain. Every fan who'd been in the stands on Sunday spent Monday gloating, telling all the folks who'd missed the show just what a great show they'd missed.

Next week, at 7:00 a.m., the day of the World 600, the highway to Charlotte Motor Speedway was already packed. Nor did it matter that Earnhardt and Elliott both suffered mechanical problems, because the depth of field allowed Kyle Petty, the third generation, to push past second-generation Davey Allison, with dad Richard Petty in second place but one lap down. Davey beat Dale at Dover, then Tim Richmond made a comeback from serious illness and won two straight, then Dale edged Davey at Michigan. Bobby Allison won the Firecracker 400 and made his entertaining speech about how unfair it was for the Buick guys to have to use Chevy heads, after Davey Allison had out-qualified Elliot, 'bird versus 'bird, with the new small carbs and skirts and glass.

Dirty Dale bunted budget-racer Alan Kulwicki out of the win at Pocono, Elliott got his edge back and took Talladega and Michigan, Rusty Wallace won Watkins Glen for Pontiac, Dale won three straight and after twenty-two races for the 1987 title, Earnhardt had won eleven. All he had to do was make one lap of the twenty-fourth race and the title was his for the third time. He did it. Never mind that Elliott won three of the last four events, with Wallace taking the Riverside road race.

The scores were Earnhardt the champ and Elliott second, again. Chevrolet won fifteen of the Winston Cup races, followed by Ford with eleven, Pontiac with two and Buick with one.

The totals are a bit misleading. Chevrolet's score came mostly through Earnhardt, eleven of the fourteen, and one of the others, Waltrip at Martinsville, came because Darrell popped Dale and Terry Labonte out of his way on the last lap. Earnhardt did a lot more of Chevy's winning than did Elliott, who was one of four drivers (the others were Ricky Rudd, Davey Allison and Kyle Petty) who could win with a Thunderbird.

In another sort of contrast, Rusty Wallace was so far in front at Watkins Glen that he came in for a few gallons of gas on the last lap and went back out in time to win. It's the one and only time in NASCAR history that the winner has gotten away with that.

The shape of things to come

To look at the wins and times, especially the qualifying runs for the Daytona 500, and to watch the drivers for 1987, was to come to a welcome if unexpected conclusion.

Forget that the stock car isn't really stock, nor production, nor even out there to prove the best product or improve the breed.

Instead, thanks to all the juggling of the rules and last minute changes and the willingness to make the unpopular call when required, NASCAR has given us racing in which the best men win—just what we asked for back on the beach in 1936.

Chapter 9

Start to finish

We can only understand life backwards, a philosopher once wrote; the problem is, we have to live it forwards.

Today we have an exception. We have looked at stock car racing from its earliest days through the present. So now we can understand it while we go forward, from when a car begins until the race finishes, and we can make some sound guesses as to what will come in the future.

First, the present.

A Grand National or Winston Cup car begins as the gleam in somebody's eye. Who that person will be varies with circumstance. But at some point, some employee or executive of a car maker will suddenly think about racing, and if the company should be in racing, and if so, which model the factory should use.

As we've seen, the model will vary. Ford has gone with its personal car, the Thunderbird, while GM has relied on its family-style coupes and is in the process of changing from the old rear-drive V-8 models to the new, smaller, front-drive cars, the GM-10 bodies. But if Ford had picked its Taurus sedan and GM wanted the Camaro, that could have been done, under the rules in effect since 1986.

This is a cooperative decision. Ford has a Special Vehicle Operation, set up as a marketing arm and

Stock car racing is literally show business; when Oldsmobile officially reentered the sport, they arranged for this show car, to let people know exactly how the Winston Cup car is constructed. From the left, there's precise ductwork inside the outer panels, directing air to the water and oil radiators. The engine is nearly hidden by the fat, slick tire; there are braces for the windshield, from firewall to roof tubes. The driver is surrounded by padding and by braced and crossbraced steel tubing. It's called a cage, for good reason. The driver has a wraparound seat with six straps holding him in. The tank with breather just aft of the left front wheel is the remote oil tank, with three or four gallons of oil. Hanging inside the tubing network that replaces the door is the net that will keep a driver's head inside the car if he hits the wall. (This car actually runs, and attends most national races.) Oldsmobile

apart from the regular passenger car division, although the engineering, styling and marketing staffs work together. At GM it's a divisional specialty, with a performance group inside each of the four divisions that have an involvement in racing.

All the executives in each of the companies or divisions say the choice of racing model is a consensus—that is, somebody proposes this one, another man says use that one, they kick it around until the top guy says OK, we all can live with the Thunderbird/Monte Carlo/Grand Prix/Sable/Firebird, right? And then they begin the actual work.

The cooperation continues because NASCAR has made it perfectly clear first, that NASCAR is running the show and second, the show will be fair. Humpy Wheeler says the deepest and best reason stock car racing is so popular is simply that it's the last form of racing in which the fans come first. The racers are important and so are the sponsors, factories and promoters, but they all line up behind the folks who watch the races, buy the tickets and don't touch those dials.

So just as in life as opposed to what's taught in school, how it's actually done isn't always as clear and impartial as the book says it should be.

How to build a NASCAR car

The rules for Winston Cup cars as of early 1988 say, first, as the rules have since 1949, that this is racing for domestically produced steel-bodied sedans, with production engines.

In working fact, the models that can be used as the basis for Winston Cup cars are those models that have been measured, designated, tested and accepted as being both the cars which the makers want to see raced, and the cars that can be shaped into rough equality on the track with the other accepted models.

In 1988 those models were:

The 1988 versions of the Buick LeSabre and Regal; the Chevrolet Monte Carlo and Monte Carlo SS (but not the Aerocoupe, which is out of production); the Ford Thunderbird, Mercury Cougar, Lincoln Continental Mark VII; Oldsmobile Cutlass Supreme and Delta 88; and the Pontiac Grand Prix.

The 1987 eligibles are the LeSabre and Regal, the Monte Carlo and Monte Carlo SS (but not the bubble-back), the Mark VII, Cougar, Cutlass 442, Delta 88 and Grand Prix.

The 1986 versions can be the LeSabre but not the Regal, all three versions of the Monte Carlo, the Thunderbird, the Cougar and the Lincoln, the 442, the Delta 88 and the Pontiac Grand Prix 2+2.

There's a catch here and although it shouldn't arrive until the end of this chapter, to avoid confusion let the record show that Pontiac (like all manufacturers) uses the old name for new cars. The 1988 Pontiac Grand Prix is built on the GM-10 body, and like the Olds and Buick before it, it's a front driver, and a V-6 is

In the beginning, square tubing and the remains of a floor pan are placed firmly atop the perfectly trued steel plate surface and with the aid of jigs and patterns, are fabri- *cated into a central section, with side and roof panels, a firewall and a front section.* Road & Track

the largest engine offered. The 1986 Grand Prix had the bubbleback option. The guys with factory contacts, such as Petty and Wallace, will use the new version of the model name and sell their old cars to the budget racers, who in turn will fill out the field, gain experience and have better cars than they could have built new or bought. The investment is amortized, to the gain of all parties.

The next step is for the factory racing department and the factory-backed teams—the Johnsons, Moores, Elliotts, Pettys et al.—to spend a lot of time with each other, the styling department and the various wind tunnels.

Some of this is done collectively. The factory guys learn everything they can and pass it along, impartially. The teams are rivals within the structure as well as on the track. They don't have to share and they don't, unless it can be worked as a trade. But when

they begin to develop a new model, they are all in equal need and they work together, for the most part.

They also work with NASCAR. For example, between the 1987 and 1988 seasons, NASCAR wanted to try some restrictor plates. The incoming GM-10 body is smaller, and in theory and street version, it's aerodynamically slicker than the Ford Thunderbird, which is likewise slicker than the older GM coupes. So the brand new Pontiac, the mostly new Buick and Olds, and the old bubbleback Chevy were run at Daytona in December 1987. Petty ran the new Pontiac 200.356 mph unrestricted, with the carburetor that he ran on the speedways in 1987. With a 1.125 in. plate, the car did 192.308 mph, and with a one-inch plate slowed to 190.275. Ricky Rudd in the Bernstein Buick turned 195.185 mph with the 1.125 in. plate and 192.143 with the one-inch plate. Then Terry Labonte in a bubbleback Chevy with 1.125 in. plate turned 197.672, which made the old car look good and made

Another shop, another plate, but the process is the same. This car has roof and front snout with suspension in place, plus roof panels. (It's a car in for revision, rather than *being made as we watch.) Notice the template on the wall.* Road & Track

the proposed limit look too low, and then the Ford guys . . . The point is first, NASCAR gave the teams a chance to see how their engines could work with restrictions and with new bodies. The teams at the same time ran flat out and wide open, in public. (It's also true that if anybody was sandbagging, had more speed than they wanted to let people see, they'd have to show it in races and once that happened NASCAR would get even. At least.)

Another quiet little point here is that when the engineers, stylists and racers are doing the racing version of the production body, that body has to cover a car with the required wheelbase, track, tires and air cleaner. If they have to make new parts to close gaps or cover lumps, they do it. And the templates used to enforce the body rules actually are cut to conform to the NASCAR version of the car, which may or may not be a perfect match for what comes off the assembly line. That's why the racing cars often look more like each other than they look like the car on which they are supposed to be based.

When the design work is done, the actual car is built. Most of the teams use a professionally constructed chassis, from the Matthews shop or the Hutcherson-Pagan shop in most cases. Some of the teams build their own cars. The cars aren't exactly built from scratch because they use the beginning of that Ford floor pan, but the cage, front snout, and rear clip can be what the builder wants instead of what the production version comes with.

There are variations on this method. Junior Johnson, for example, doesn't just build his own cars from scratch; he has engineered his 1988 cars so they won't fatigue until the current rules are outmoded. In

Now the subtle part begins. This is a Matthews car, sent to the owner with rear fender panels in place, including the passage for the fuel filler. But the stock panel isn't wide enough, or deep enough, to do the job . . .

. . . so the builder cuts out the center section of the stock panel and fills it, with some extensions, with rolled sheet. The contours won't be quite the same; the tire will be made legal and stock parts are used, just as the book requires.

Another under-construction Thunderbird, with the stock windshield in place but with new interior panels and the

windshield surround fabricated to give just the right curve and support. Note the cage in place of the right door.

this way, he can keep his cars, he says, because they have secrets that a buyer could find, and put into general circulation.

In the same vein, another team buys the Matthews center section, rear clip and front snout . . . but they buy them in separate pieces. They put the sections together in their own, secret way and they don't want anybody to know how they do it.

A mystery of car building is that some cars turn out better than others, even when the same crew put them together on the same jigs from the same parts. Nobody knows why, although there are as many guesses as there are builders. But some cars are just better than others; some will be best on the miles, when they were built for short track, while a second disappointing car won't work anywhere.

Builders who claim this doesn't happen to them also claim it's just carelessness, but they don't win any more races than do the teams with the occasional dog. One is forced to conclude that there are better

cars, or luckier cars, than can be accounted for by facts.

The bodies are installed over the frame and cage. This also varies with model and team but in general the car arrives from the builder's shop with some panels, usually the rear quarters, trunk and firewall. Each shop has a supply of what the trade calls crash parts—stamped-out panels for doors, hoods, roofs and so on. The factories make sure the racers have a supply of this semifinished metal, although the private owner would have trouble finding the panels at his dealership.

A Matthews Thunderbird, average cost $11,000 delivered, comes with roof, rear deck, quarter panels and firewall. The rear quarters will be trimmed out and replaced with rolled stock that fills the gaps and covers the racing tires; the stock metal can't be stretched that far. Door panels, from the factory, will be welded onto the cage, then front fenders, hood and so forth will be added. The gaps are filled and the

168

panels shaped to match the NASCAR-approved templates.

New cars for old

The 1986 rules, as seen early in 1988, make for some odd stock cars. Back in the first downsize season, in 1981, builders had to make cars with only a few inches shorter wheelbase and a much shorter body. The new (in 1983) Thunderbird was smaller to begin with, the 1986 Buick and Olds were smaller still and so is the 1988 Pontiac Grand Prix.

So the rules get banged into shape as much as the cars do.

Beginning with the obvious, if you or I showed up for a Winston Cup race with a production Thunderbird or Monte Carlo, never mind the front-drive cars, even if we installed full harness, cage, wheels, souped-up engine and racing tires, we'd be thrown out at the gate, never mind not getting into technical inspection.

(In defense of NASCAR here, one major reason would be that the production car is obviously unsafe for racing at 200-plus mph and that the technical people much prefer to see and test frames and equipment which they know will pass all their tests.)

For model year 1988 the eligible models had the following base dimensions:

	Wheelbase	Overall length
Thunderbird	104.2 in.	204.1 in.
Monte Carlo	108.1	200.4
Grand Prix	107.5	193.9
Buick/Olds	110.8	196.1

We are not working here with four cars being converted into one racing car. We are working with one basic car, the certified and approved Winston Cup center section, rear clip and front snout, with a choice of V-8 engines located precisely aft of the front wheels, with a wheelbase of 110 in.

The next step has been to weld in a door panel. The panel is just that, a piece of stamped steel intended for crash repair. But here it's welded into the space where the door should be, while the hole for the handle is covered with a patch of aluminum, and the top edge, where the window was supposed to be, is also filled in with sheet stock. The flat panel for the instruments, where the dashboard was, is a lot plainer than it was in the Holman and Moody days.

This is a new Pontiac and it's a lucky break. Up close, the junction between the windshield frame and top of the front fender needed a bridge; you can just barely see the rear of the air cleaner peeping shyly from under the hood at the base of the windshield. The new car used to be front-drive, so putting a larger engine farther back in the chassis sited the air cleaner where it can get a ram effect—fresh air under some pressure. All Winston Cup cars can do this in 1988, which gives back some of the power taken away by carb restrictions.

Another bridge, this time for an old-style Chevrolet being made into an Aerocoupe. This model gets added wheelbase and some of it will go here, with a longer rear wheelwell and an axle a bit farther aft than the stock one was.

We are using that one basic car beneath a selection of body panels. The overall length can be as the production body was, but the wheelbase must be changed and relocated within the overall length.

And the relationships of engine location to wheelbase, firewall to engine, windshield to firewall and engine, and so on, must be juggled. The front-drivers especially are difficult.

The street versions have engines set sideways within the span of the front wheels, and the firewall and windshield tucked up close behind. The NASCAR racer has the engine mounted longitudinally, aft of the front wheels. So the first thing visible with the Winston Cup version of the Grand Prix Pontiac, the 1988 version, is that many inches have been spliced into the wheelbase, and the windshield and front door seam are much farther aft of the front wheelwell than they used to be.

This is not a stock body, not by eight or ten inches, and don't let anybody kid you about meeting the templates.

Instead, a tip of the hat to NASCAR for using the need for change to balance out the rules.

Back up here to the carburetor plate tests. The 1988 rules first required speedway racers to use a smaller carburetor and right-side window glass and skirts, to slow the cars and keep them on the ground. When the cars still went fast, NASCAR had the teams test restrictor plates. The 1988 rules also increased minimum tread, from 58 to 60 in. The GM cars were that wide already, but the Fords had to be widened.

The new GM cars, the Buicks and Pontiacs, were faster than the new Thunderbirds. The Ford people didn't mention the added width, which had to take off speed. They said their engine had lost 230 bhp, while the GM engine only lost 200 bhp, so the Fords needed less restriction.

The NASCAR technical committee looked elsewhere. They noticed, or more likely they already knew, that the new GM bodies had moved the windshields back so the hood could cover the engine. But the firewall was moved back more than the windshield, and the base of the windshield was just barely aft of the air cleaner.

Years ago, all the cars used the cowl, with high air pressure at speed, to feed intake air to the engine for free power. NASCAR outlawed that. But the new bodies with cowl intake adjacent to the air cleaner had such a power gain, free.

Right. The rules were changed back, all cars were allowed to use cowl, pressure and induction, and the Ford and old GM bodies got the free power, without being exempted from the rules.

No wonder NASCAR is considered the best at that sort of thing.

Horses for courses

The Winston Cup car comes in other varieties. There are four types of race courses: speedway, mile, short track and road circuit, and the demands of each are different. Thus, the best teams build cars matched to each kind of track.

The speedway car needs to be long, smooth and low, because aerodynamics and the banked corners keep the car on the ground.

The short track and road race cars need to be short, wide and lumpy, because they use traction and suspension to keep on the track; cornering power and acceleration are more important than top speed.

The rules spell out wheel, tire, tread and wheelbase dimensions, but beyond that state only that the drivetrain must be centered and the tires must be covered by the body.

The speedway car is as narrow as is legal, with limited suspension and wheel travel and as little extension of fenders as possible. The short track or road race car has flared fenders, and more room beneath them. Oval track cars have their suspension settings biased to the left, the front wheels actually

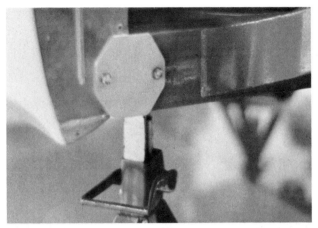

Ballast is legal and expected, provided it's carried in the designated places. This cap covers a long tube, front to rear of the center section. Remove the cap and slide in lead bars or wooden blocks to put weight as low and as useful as it can be.

Rear suspension is an old idea refined to perfection. Here you can see the fabricated frame rails for the rear section. At left is the bracket for the Panhard rod, the tube that goes from the left side of the axle housing to the right side of the frame, and which controls side-to-side motion of the car versus the axle. By changing the heights of the two mounting points, you can vary the roll axis, and the handling, of the car. Inboard of the hub is the chain that limits wheel travel. Unhook the chain and the axle drops low enough for the spring to be changed.

171

tilted into left turns, while the road course cars have their front wheels tilted to the right; the fenders for both are fitted accordingly. Again following rules, oval cars have fuel intake and exhaust on the left side, road cars have them on the right. Cars for the mile tracks, or for tracks longer than the half-mile or with less banking than the speedways, are called intermediates. As the title suggests, they are less extreme in either direction.

The rules require the drivetrain to be centered, but not the car's weight. This rule was created after the Petty family realized that a car with more weight on the left side should go better around a counterclockwise oval, and that the tech inspectors weighed the cars front and back but not side and side. The Pettys built cars with extra weight on the left, other teams figured it out and copied the idea. NASCAR found out and decreed that some weight biasing was OK.

Too much wasn't OK. The rules allow weight shifting, with the limit being a minimum of 1,600 lb. on the right; if the minimum total is 3,700 lb., that puts 2,100 on the left, but when the minimum was reduced to 3,500 lb., the left carried 1,900, and so forth.

This weight shifting is easily done. The completed car, with fuel, oil and water but no driver, will finish out at 3,000 lb. or so, depending mostly on wheels, tires, and so forth. And on preference. Some builders like more beef, others trim wherever they can and ballast up later.

The ballast, permitted by the rules but put only in the center section, is lead bars. Honest. The bars are carried in tubes attached to the platform, and can be on the left or right, in front or in back. Those portions of the tubes not filled with lead are occupied by wood blocks, much in the manner of filling the magazine of an automatic shotgun in states with load limits. Logically, this weight is added, subtracted and shifted according to the car, the track and the needs of the day.

The round black things

Tires are a vital part of NASCAR, as they are in all of racing, but they aren't as important. Tire size and type have been deliberately restricted, to keep teams from depending on their tires for speed to give all teams the same choice of tire and (to some degree) to keep speeds down.

Goodyear has had a virtual monopoly since Firestone withdrew in 1970. (A small company, Hoosier Tire, has been working to supply some teams.) There's nothing in the rules limiting the number of brands; it has simply worked out that most of the majors don't want to spend the money.

What the rules do say is that each and every driver must be allowed the same choice of tire. Next,

Winston Cup cars are literally pieced together, with fabricated panels and crash parts side by side, as seen here. When it's smoothed with Bondo and painted, the car will be seamless. (This is a notchback Chevy, photographed in 1983, hence the lack of streamlined rear.) Road & Track

each car must start the race on the tires used for qualifying. These rules combine to make it impractical for a driver to turn fantastic times with tires that won't last more than a lap or two (gumballs, is what they used to be called).

Goodyear makes different sizes for different tracks. Speedway tires are tall and stiff, short track tires are shorter and more flexible. The tires come in compounds, the chemical mix of material used for the tread, tailored to the track surfaces (tires haven't been made of rubber for decades). Some tracks are more abrasive than others. All the stock car tires come with inner liners, the safety feature invented when the speedways were first built.

Goodyear's racing tires for stock cars are of conventional construction, with the body's cords arranged at crisscrossed angles, or bias ply in the trade term. Most street tires and racing tires now come with radial plies, cords that radiate straight out from the center.

Radials are generally accepted as better but economics have kept Goodyear from shifting over to the better system. Also, the conventional ply tires are made by hand and no two are exactly alike.

This isn't on purpose. It isn't deliberate or even precise. But genius has been defined as the capacity for taking infinite pains to get things perfect. Some unsung genius a few years ago discovered that the tires were of fractionally different diameter, at the same inflation pressure and with the same nominal size. He used this to his advantage, as we'll see shortly.

Setting the chassis

Winston Cup cars use completely conventional suspension. A live (beam) rear axle and independent front suspension with upper and lower A-arms have been used on standard, front-drive American cars for forty years.

The rear axles and differentials used in the cars actually began as truck parts, Fords mostly. They are

No end of care is taken to get the details right; witness the match between the edge of the fenders and the edge of the tires on this new Thunderbird.

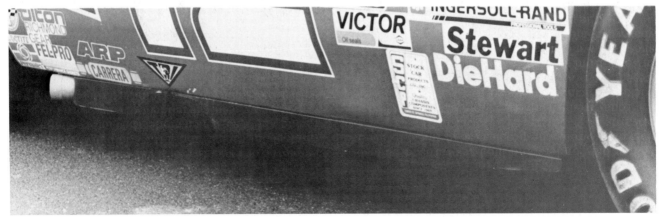

Sometimes the seams show. This Buick was made before the 1987 rule requiring a skirt along the right side of the car's lower center, to keep out air if the car gets sideways. So the

skirt is obvious and the relief for the exhaust is clumsy. Cars built after mid-1987 have lower right panels to begin with.

173

big and strong and can be fitted with a wide variety of gears, from 2:1 through 6:1, for superspeedway to short track or even dirt track. The axles are kept in place with trailing arms, usually from a Chevy truck, and a lateral arm called a Panhard rod. The controls have carefully sited and sometimes adjustable mounting points, so the arc travelled by the car as it moves on its suspension can be predicted and used to improve cornering grip. The springs are coils, set between mounting platforms on the axle and on the rear of the frame.

An odd feature seen when you scrunch down and look at the underside of the Winston Cup car is a chain, from rear floor to axle. That's a travel limiter. Further, if the chain is unhooked and the car raised in the rear, the coil spring can be popped out and replaced—in seconds during a pit stop—with a spring of different stiffness. This isn't done often because a change of spring rate is a drastic step, but it can be done if needed.

The front A-arms are much stronger than those used in passenger cars. They have coil springs backed up by antiroll bars, sort of lever arms that resist roll by transferring the load from the wheel under stress to the other side. These bars can be adjusted or replaced, but not in the pits. There are shock absorbers, one at each wheel. Back when stock shocks were used, they were used in pairs. Current shocks are so much better that fewer are needed.

Here's another controversy, or at least an unsettled debate. Winston Cup cars use standard steering boxes with power assist. Ivan Baldwin, a top chassis man, says the power assist is the single most important change in the past ten years, not because it reduces driver effort, but because the hydraulic booster allows suspension settings so extreme, that put such load and resistance into the front wheels under full engine and cornering power, that a normal man couldn't handle the wheel unaided. (Technically this is known as positive caster, which tips the front wheels into the turn.)

There are ostensibly two kinds of steering in Winston Cup: front steer and rear steer. You hear these terms a lot but they don't mean what they sound like they should mean.

Just as in any car, a Winston Cup car has a linkage from the steering box to the front spindles. In front steer, this linkage is in front of an imaginary line between the spindles; in rear steer, the linkage is behind the line.

Next, the front wheels don't simply go up and down or turn from left to right. They transcribe three-dimensional arcs, and they go back and forth. Suspension geometry means the front wheels shouldn't tip as far as the car does, and the links and arms are designed to keep these motions in predictable control.

In theory, steering linkage is designed so the suspension travel and the steering travel are completely independent of each other. The engineers say correct linkage has no effect on the car's handling, no matter where it's placed.

Speedway cars are easily spotted because they have right-side glass; it's a window in the sense that you can see through it, but it's faired into the body panels for streamlining.

Rear spoilers are allowed on all cars, with size depending on and varying with the model, the track and the conditions. This one is plastic, colored dark green to match the—what else?—lemon yellow of the Country Time Pontiac. The team has a selection of rear panels, in different heights and angles. The smaller and lower the spoiler is, the better the car will go.

The racers don't agree. Ralph Moody says front steer shortens the wheelbase on the inboard side of the car, while rear steer lengthens it. All the Stroh's Light Thunderbirds (driven by Mark Martin in 1988) are rear steer. So are Mike Waltrip's Country Time Pontiacs and Earnhardt's Chevys. Some of the Miller Buicks (Bobby Allison and Bobby Hillin, Jr.) are front steer and some are rear steer, and Ricky Rudd's Quaker State Buicks (actually Chevy chassis with Buick panels) are all front steer. There is great debate about steering—the engineers say it can't matter and drivers switch cars because they can't cope with the wrong system, never mind which system the car has.

Engines

NASCAR engines are part over-the-counter goods, part magic.

Winston Cup cars all use the Ford or GM small-block V-8. Both brands begin with racing parts—engine blocks, crankshafts, cylinder heads and so on—that have been designed and produced for racing, by and at the factory. (You could begin with used passenger car parts if you wanted to, but nobody with any sense does.)

The parts arrive semifinished and the engine builders, in the team or outside, do their own machining, fitting and polishing. Any change can be made provided the piece began as an accepted part, which means the builders get to mount the rocker arms and angle the valves and ports, and so forth.

Displacement is limited to 358 ci, but there's no rule on how that can be achieved and there's a range of bore and stroke—4 to 4.3 in. for the former and 3.5 to 4 in. for the latter—used to reach that limit. Each tuner has his own notions about the perfect ratio of bore to stroke and what he can do with the valve sizes and rev limits that come with these ratios. And in the summer speedway races, when thin air means less

Engines are built by the team, as a rule, from parts designed for racing but made by the factories whose names the racing cars carry. The top teams have engine dynamometers, as shown here, where each engine can be tuned, broken in and measured for output. The exhaust system is convoluted so that all four pipes will be the same length when they reach the collector junction: the resonances of the exhaust pulses at peak power will so perfectly match that they will expel more exhaust and inhale more fresh mixture then the engine displaces at rest. Road & Track

power, sometimes extra horses can be gained with a short-stroke engine with less than maximum displacement, revved higher than the long stroke dares go, fingers crossed lest the engine destroys itself.

The 358 will develop better than 600 bhp in its least-restricted form, with no throttle plates and with the 860 cfm carburetor allowed everywhere but the two fastest tracks, Daytona and Talladega.

Peak power isn't everything, so for short tracks or road courses the engine may carry a 750 cfm carburetor, while the present speedway limit is 390 cfm, along with a one-inch throttle plate.

This astonishing power comes because the engines breathe better than perfect: at peak power, with cam timing, valve size, carburetor, exhaust system and intake manifold all in complete harmony, the engines are so in tune that they inhale and exhale more air and fuel than they have displacement. Sort of a supercharger.

Engines breathe perfectly because incredibly gifted and patient men try new and old ideas for cams, ports and manifolds over and over again. And because no detail is overlooked. You probably think you know how to install a head gasket. One hour in a NASCAR shop will convince you otherwise.

One nearly forgotten component is the gearbox. It has not been mentioned because the transmission isn't a key point in NASCAR races. Most tracks are top gear only, with the intermediate gears used getting out of the pits. For road races, of which there are two per year at present, the drivers do a lot of shifting. The gearbox behind all the engines is the familiar Borg-Warner four-speed, as seen all those years ago in the muscle cars of the sixties.

The Jerico is an improved version of the Borg-Warner gearbox. It has the same case, with four speeds forward and a reverse, but the gear clusters are different and can be removed and replaced with

Preparation is vital. Here, preseason, is a year's supply of differentials and final-drive gears, in a wide selection of ratios. Road & Track

the case attached to the engine, in the car. The Jerico has wide choices of first, second and third gear ratios, so the tuners can have the best gearing for coming out of the various turns of a road course.

The price? A Banjo Matthews rolling chassis, with center section, rear clip and front snout, retails for $11,000. Having them build the rest of the car, another thousand hours of work, adds $14,000, while doing it all in your own shop comes out exactly the same.

An engine, one complete unit ready to go, is also 1,000 hours of skilled hand labor and also costs $25,000.

Team operation

This section could be titled "How the rich get richer," but it's not quite that bad.

We are talking big money, however. Junior Johnson's Budweiser Racing team will begin the season with four or five cars, ready to qualify, and run the preliminary race and then the big race at Daytona, followed by Richmond and so on. The cars are lined up

and ready to go. Johnson's team has thirty-seven full-time employees and a budget of several million dollars annually, which he gets because his team has won eighty Grand National races, six national titles and $10 million during the past twenty years.

The Elliott/Melling/Coors operation has ten cars: three for speedways, three intermediates, four short trackers doubling as road racers. Most of the major teams are equipped this way, with rows of spare engines, gearboxes, suspension parts and body repair kits, so they go to each race with two cars and a couple of engines, all stowed in the eighteen-wheel truck that carries the team, sponsor names and colors.

Maintenance, repair and improvement are constant. As a way to keep things more even, NASCAR decreed in 1987 that there would be a limit on track testing time: four days during the year apart from actual race practice, with a heavy fine against anybody caught exceeding the limit.

Even so, we're looking at four complete cars—that's $200,000—plus four to six $25,000 engines and

Stock car racing tires are bigger than passenger car tires but much smaller, by intent and regulation, than the tires seen on Indy and Formula One cars. This is a race's supply for Rusty Wallace and his number 27 Pontiac. Each tire has been inflated to equal pressure, scrubbed in and measured in fractions of an inch, so if in midrace the team needs a new tire on the right rear, they can be sure it's not going to change the car's balance by being taller or shorter than the tire it replaced. The teams buy their tires, even though the money spent can't come close to matching what Goodyear spends on their design, testing and construction.

A little informal checking here. The inspector is reading a pumper, a device that measures the displacement of a cylinder with the engine intact. It's not perfect, but it may give enough hint to justify a tear-down. And no team knows when the man with the pumper will appear.

the truck, parts, living expenses and salaries for the crew.

Surprising until you think about it, the internal competition these days is for crew chiefs instead of drivers. There are maybe thirty top teams, with fifty to 100 qualified drivers pitching for the job. But there aren't thirty proven crew chiefs in the business, so their salaries have been escalated into six figures.

All that is intimidating, but it doesn't shut the door. Alan Kulwicki is a graduate engineer who came out of the Midwest modified and sportsman ranks. He had one car—a secondhand Thunderbird—and two engines, and he was rookie of the year in 1986. He won enough prize money and support to have the two cars, the good one and a spare, in 1987.

For 1988 he took his '87 winnings of $360,000 and more sponsorship, which came on board because he'd done well without it, true, so he was ready for 1988 with three new cars and his old one in reserve. It's the old-fashioned way, earning it, as the gent on television

This is a formal check, in the inspection garage. The stick measures ground clearance, so all the inspector has to do is try to slide it under the car. No go, no practice or qualifica-

tion or race until it's fixed. This is one of Elliott's road race cars, worth noting here for the size of the cooling intakes for brakes and radiators.

The issue of fuel tank size was settled years ago by the ready expedient of spelling out in the rules the dimensions for the steel box that holds the fuel cell. The car has a cavity of those dimensions in the trunk, so all the inspectors need to do is ask for the tank to be lowered and measured. The plate that bolts to the container carries the filler neck, which can be aimed left or right, for road course or oval, along with the breather and the feed line to the pump.

used to say. It can be done, is the vital part here, and Kulwicki can and has run with the top guys. In fact, it's not that the rich get richer, it's that you do well if you do good.

Rich team or poor, the race begins weeks before the actual start. The crew chief, owner and driver usually have a collective experience for each track that goes back many years, so they have a good idea which final drive gear and suspension settings to start with. The engine, or engines, will be tuned for the course, with camshaft, carburetor, intake and exhaust all tailored to the track—top speed on the speedways, punch out of the turns for short track and so forth.

Running the gauntlet

Rich or poor, ready or not, the team's first job at the track is getting through technical inspection.

Actually, in the late eighties tech inspection isn't nearly the tussle it used to be. For those of us raised on tales of graft and cheating and fistfights, it's almost a disappointment.

But the inspection is done with good humor on both sides. Some of this probably comes from the people involved. Technical director Dick Beaty was a motorcycle racer and then a car racer before signing on with NASCAR. He knows both sides, and has been at pains to ensure a friendly, cooperative atmosphere.

Next, the Winston Cup operation, all involved parties, travels and works as one big circus. NASCAR in effect controls the track for the week, so all the gatekeepers, inspectors and other officials at each Winston Cup race are the same, just as the cars, drivers and crew chiefs are.

But what probably makes the other factors work is that the rules are so loose in general and so detailed in principle. Using stiffer valve springs was one thing. But now, with most of the engine free choice and the limits, as in displacement and carburetor size, so easily and constantly monitored, cheating isn't worth the bother. And if builders do cheat and get caught, the fines—for example, $500 per pound if proven intentionally underweight—are stiff. On top of that, the sponsors of today don't like seeing their guys proven sneaks.

Familiarity means that the same team checks out the same sets of cars, week after week. A new car gets an inspection that lasts an hour or so and involves details like x-raying the frame tubes to be sure they're the legal thickness, and stripping the engine to measure bore and stroke, and so on. Once the car has been certified, it's easier to check next time, and because there's another thorough inspection after a crash or even a bump, the tech crew can keep track of any modifications.

When a known car gets to the track, it's rolled into a shed and measured, at specified points, for height, width, ground clearance and coverage. The tires are marked and the four corners put on certified scales. The car is required to go from the tech shed to the track, and is admitted only if the sticker on the windshield bears the coded marks only the inspectors can interpret.

If the weight isn't right, the crew can add or subtract from any corner they please, and they can

change tires up to the point of qualification. But the car isn't allowed to go from inspection to the garage, and every time it goes onto the track, it's checked again.

If an engine is replaced, the replacement is measured. The inspectors have a useful, fast and informal gadget, called a pumper, that gives a quick and close-enough report on the size of a cylinder. Because the dimensions of the steel box that holds the fuel cell are published and precise, fuel capacity can also be easily watched.

In short, the cars are held close to the mark, while what each team does within the rules is relatively relaxed.

There are interpretations. For example, the rules say the fuel line must be routed from tank to pump to carburetor as directly as possible, and it must be of a specified dimension enclosed in steel tubing of a given size. Longer lines mean more fuel, and on occasion a team hasn't gone as directly as they could have. Or, as has happened, a new man in the engine room did more improvement to an intake manifold, adding

Complete spare engines travel with the teams as a matter of course. This one, a Chevy, came out of the truck with pumps and ignition, ready for plugs and carburetor. Before it goes *into the car, however, the inspectors will give a quick check, just to spare hurt feelings later.*

180

The dreaded templates. This is only part of the collection that goes with the inspection teams to all the races. They check the tops, sides and profiles when the car is new, and usually don't worry about it after that, except for front-to-back profile . . . and again, they have the power to make any test, any time they please.

instead of reshaping material, and the car was in the winner's circle when the change was found. Keep the money and points, the team was told, it was an honest mistake. But we'd better not see that manifold ever again. And they haven't.

Are there fudges and exceptions? Sure, there are probably builders and drivers getting away with stuff here and there. We all slip up. But the impression one gets is that the little tricks that do get through are pulled by teams not quite in the first rows. They need some boosts to keep the pace and it doesn't matter that much because they aren't going to win anyway. This is the impression the asker is left with—which isn't to say anybody admitted anything.

Stagger and wedge

The partnership and working relationship of driver and crew chief begin to pay off—or make trouble—when practice begins. The chief has, or should have, total knowledge of how the engine was set up for this track, and he's got charts to compare carburetor jetting and ignition specs against air temperature, pressure and humidity. Getting the engine just right for the track and the day is tricky, but it's something that can be done by the book.

The suspension, which is where the car wins or loses, can't be done this formally. There are an infinite number of combinations of shock, spring, roll bar, body configuration, tire compound, tire size and pressure, which means it's the work of a minute to make the car hopeless and not even know which direction you went wrong.

The cure is to cut and try. Ivan Baldwin says the first starting point has to be keeping the car as low as the law allows. Next, on the track, the first thing to work on is using all the suspension, all the wheel travel. The lowest part of the car, the bottom of the clutch housing, should just touch down at the heaviest loading on the track, the worst bump or dip. When the car isn't moving on its suspension, Baldwin says, it's sliding or leaping and when it does that, it's not going forward. Going forward is how you win races.

One of the rule book's better loopholes is the clause that allows headlight covers. As Kyle Petty's Thunderbird illustrates, the covers also manage to slick out all the curves, lumps and seams of the production car. Some of the shapes are builder choice; compare this front with the Elliott car.

Each track is different. You can make the car stiffer in roll by setting the antiroll bars, or stiffer straight up and down with the springs, front and back. The shocks can be tuned to be stiffer or softer, while each one of these changes makes the car different in another way.

There's also body tune. Back when stock cars were former passenger cars, when they went fast, they went up. The air being jammed under the body planed the car up for racing cars as well as passenger cars. This consumed power, as the engine had to push the car up against the air and hold it there. When the creative thinkers, guys like Formula One Lotus builder Colin Chapman, began to develop aerodynamic bodies, they made bodies that created enough downforce to keep the car level, freeing the engine's power to make the car go faster.

Then came downforce to keep the car pressed to the track. We're back to using power against air again. The extreme example here is Indianapolis, where they tune the airfoils so the car will go 'round and 'round at wide open throttle and then back off downforce so speed will go up, as high as the driver can keep it under control. (That's why Indy cars spin out in practice so often.)

There's a lot of work done concerning downforce in Winston Cup cars. As noted when the downsized cars arrived in 1981, the racing stock car is big and whams through the air, leaving something of a bow wave. Shaping the body smoothes this wave back together, but to some degree you have a featherless arrow, with a big lump in front and the tail sort of waggling aft. The rear spoiler will keep the tail in line, as it were. It will also consume power and slow down the car. What we want is just enough downforce: just enough to work with the car's static ride height, wheel travel, roll stiffness, roll axis, center of gravity and all the other factors at work at the same time in several directions.

Then we having driving technique.

In the textbook, a car has either understeer, with the front wheels losing grip first, or oversteer, with the rears losing grip first. In the sports car world people

Darrell Waltrip made a breakthrough when he signed up Tide, the washday product, as a sponsor for a racing car. It's been a good deal for all parties, in large degree because the car is such a wonderfully colorful display, with its whites, yellows and oranges. The sight of the car at speed reinforces the familiar image . . . and might even sell the product. This is the 1987 Aerocoupe, which by process of negotiation will carry the Chevy badge while the other GM cars convert to newer and smaller bodies.

say if you leave the road front end first, that's understeer while if you do it back end first, that's oversteer.

In NASCAR, this is called push, with the front sliding, or loose, with the rear trying to hang out and catch the front.

Passenger cars come with understeer. The factories know that the average driver will steer away from the hazard, so they build a chassis that will respond best to normal panic.

Understeer sometimes works in racing, too. A little push lets you keep the power on. So, if you want a good, secure feeling car, dial in the rear spoiler, stiffen up the rear suspension and there it is.

The drawback is obvious. The car is using power to keep the rear wheels nailed to the track and pushing the front tires against it. It's safer, easier and slower.

Another current factor on the speedway is the carburetor plate. The engine produces less power, period. The less power taken up with fighting the air or shoving the tires, the more power available for speed.

Quoting Dale Earnhardt, the restrictors "show us who can drive a loose car."

Against that comes Ricky Rudd: "I like to be bored, driving by myself . . . If you've got your hands full when you're on the track alone, you're going to be in serious trouble when the racing starts."

The key here is balance.

We saw that the tires aren't all the same size. Even when they have the same numbers on the sidewalls, each racing tire is a fraction of an inch taller or narrower than the tire next to it.

The tire crews and the teams measure this very carefully. The exact true size, at the same pressure and down to quarters of an inch, is marked on each tire stacked up in the pits.

The Winston Cup car, as set up for the speedways especially, is an extraordinarily sensitive and difficult machine. Just because it's big doesn't mean it's basic.

At rest the Winston Cup car is a freak, with the body outline offset and the tires tilted.

This takes some thought, but want to guess which side of a speedway car, set for left turns only, is the stiff one? Wrong. You'd think the right side, the outside, should be stiffer and that's how they did it at first. But if you visualize it, if the right side is stiff and the car has that side for a fulcrum, the car will rise up as centrifugal force pushes the car against the springs. Now, if you stiffen the left side, that moves the pivot to the left and the car sinks under centrifugal force.

At rest, the car is tipped this way and stacked that way, with more weight on the inside and the front suspension cranked so far that the driver couldn't handle the wheel without mechanical assistance.

It will never be perfect. But with the springs, shocks, bars, ballast and foils all close to right, we make the final adjustments.

Back in the sixties tuners installed devices to shift weight. NASCAR outlawed the systems with power boost, and those controlled by the driver, but they left legal devices that can be adjusted by the crew, in the shop or the pits. These have evolved into huge threaded rods, topped by bolt (or screw) heads. They are installed through threaded fittings in the frame; the bolt or shaft butts against a plate or other flat surface on the front control arm or rear axle.

This is as simple as it looks and sounds. Crank the shaft down against the suspension, and that corner of the car has more weight on it. (The front left can't be adjusted after tech inspection because that would change ride height and there are rules about that.)

The scientific or magical part comes because the car is wildly out of balance at rest, and the balance

The post-1986 Buick (along with sibling rival Olds) moved into new territory for NASCAR, because the car models recognized were in real life front-drive cars with small V-6 engines that became Winston Cup racers with traditional rear-drive chassis and V-8s. The resulting configuration sort of looks like a Buick (or Olds or Pontiac), but not exactly.

As the sign says, the modern NASCAR team is also a corporation. This is Childress' new shop, actually several new and beautifully equipped buildings. The team's new spon- *sor for 1988 was Mister Goodwrench, a branch of General Motors and an expansion of that corporation's involvement.*

varies with speed, cornering load and application of power.

All four tires are the same size, and the goal is to have equal weight on each tire, under full power, at the place on the track where the going is toughest. The key is balance under full power, at speed.

The crew begins to adjust the suspension with the static suspension settings, as described, and with ballast right and left, fore and aft.

Then come the tires. They aren't exactly alike, so they've been measured, and if the crew wants extra load on the right rear, they'll use a 28 in. tire there, and a 27.75 in. tire on the left rear. The term for this tire adjustment is stagger, which comes from sprint cars, where the rules are less restrictive and all four wheels and tires are of wildly different size.

With the suspension dialed in and the stagger known and allowed for and with weather conditions included—a cool day means cooler pavement and softer springs—the driver and the crew adjust suspension loading in terms of so many clicks (turns) up or down at the three legal corners, and in line with how much push or loose the driver wants the car to have. The term here is wedge.

This adjustment is as delicate, and as vital, as it is simple in concept. There are thirty-five teams making the full national tour. There are twenty good ones, ten who can expect a win during the season and five with a reasonable shot at the national title. Not least among the factors keeping these groups apart is the

art of communicating and making those last, tiny adjustments.

What it's like out there

Readers who have been taking notes may have found themselves wondering if putting the car into balance at full load and full speed hasn't left the car well out of balance when it's not at full load and speed.

The answer is yes. The ideal isn't possible, by the way. The banked ovals will generate better than 2 g centrifugal force and 2 g lateral force, but even then, even with weight bias and spring bias, the outer pair of tires will be carrying more like seventy-five percent of the car's weight (which in turn vectors out to several tons on the tires and the driver) and the inside will have twenty-five percent.

Even so, when the car isn't under full power and load it is way out of balance—which is one way of saying it's damned difficult to drive these cars, no matter how fast they're going.

Flat out isn't always best, for example. Charlotte is a tri-oval; thus, the second and third turns, the ones linked by a straight, are at ninety degrees. But the first and fourth turns are joined by a straight that is not quite straight, with a shallow kink in the middle. No two of the turns are alike, and the heaviest loading comes in and between turns three and four.

Driving wide open down the back straight and into turn three looks good but the car will have too much speed between turns and will drift high and off the best line for the charge down the front kink.

The fastest way is to lift off a fraction at exactly the right spot into turn three, letting the car come down low and then getting back on the power just right. The car then has the short way around the track *and* gets to use all the power to cannonade out of four.

It's just as hard to do as it sounds. That's one track out of thirty, no two are alike, and that's probably why it takes seven years or so for a driver to get as good as he's going to get in these cars.

Drivers from elsewhere, top pilots from Formula One and CART, along with those few journalists who are actually good enough to be allowed a try, report that when they set their borrowed car up to standard standards, so to speak, the car is hopeless. Not until they are convinced and let the crew set the car up to NASCAR's style will it work, and even then, only the few very best visiting drivers, men like Foyt and Andretti, have ever looked good in the big sedans.

Still another example of NASCAR's artful dodging may be that the cars look much more calm and controlled than they are. In truth, from the cockpit,

they don't go straight on the straights and they stop just as strangely. What they do best—go around banked turns at 200 mph—is just about the only thing they do well.

Television is the best place to watch a NASCAR race because you can see all the angles and hear everything happen and if your back is turned when the action takes place, you can see it again on instant replay.

But to watch the cars, as opposed to seeing the race, you really have to get as close to the outside of a first or third turn as the guards will allow. The air blast alone will rock you back from the fence, the noise will literally make your ears ring, and to see the cars rocking and jinking and the drivers making corrections so fast their hands blur, is to give you the closest view you will probably ever get as to what a handful these monsters really are.

Strategy

One of the reasons racing is better than real life is that in racing, the winner is the guy who gets there first.

That isn't always to say the race is to the swiftest. But NASCAR has included several clever techniques

We're talking serious money here. The teams making the full national circuit couldn't do it without at least one big *new semitrailer truck, painted in team scheme and loaded with spares, equipment and tools.*

to ensure suspense, so the drivers and crews needn't be quite as clever as they are in other venues.

Chief among these techniques is the caution flag, the appearance of the yellow flag that means, first, no passing and, second, everybody bunch up behind the leader and the pace car.

Genuine incidents, wrecks or spins always bring out the yellow. But the cautions also appear by remarkable serendipity whenever one car is getting too far ahead of the pack. It makes for thrilling final laps, so nobody bothers to complain.

The caution slows the field, so that's the best time to get fuel and tires, again an obvious thing to do, while it also puts in guesswork. Will I have enough gas to hold out until the next yellow? And teamwork becomes vital, which doesn't hurt crowd appeal either.

There's also the question of where the driver wants to be during the beginning, middle and last laps of the race. There are drivers who say they hold pace and keep something in reserve until the final twenty or so laps, and they may be telling the truth. But the really fast drivers like Elliott and Earnhardt take the lead as quickly as they can, when they can, and stay there until it's over, if they can. It's easier to keep the lead than to take it away, so with no offense intended,

most of the men who say they're waiting until it matters are probably waiting for the breaks.

What of the future?

Early in 1988, at a seminar put on by NASCAR and Charlotte Motor Speedway, Bill France, Jr. (who's been president of NASCAR since his dad officially retired in 1972) said he really wasn't sure what the rules and racing would be like in the year 2000: "We're not smart enough to keep the rules wrapped up for even three years."

He was being too modest. Winston Cup racing's future is taking place right this minute.

NASCAR has, over the years, established the main elements of how to keep things going right:
• NASCAR has the right to make and enforce its own rules.
• Stock car racing is a professional sport.
• The rules keep the competition close and fair.
• Stock car racing isn't supposed to prove who makes the best stock car.
• NASCAR will reflect those parts of motorsports and motor enthusiasm that the paying public wants to see.
• And finally, a stock, American-made passenger sedan is what NASCAR says it is, no more and no less.

What we have at this writing is replica bodies of cars made by several divisions of two of the major American-owned manufacturers. It's hard to imagine the domestic family car getting much smaller than the 110 in. wheelbase, 200 in. overall length cars now being used as the basis of Winston Cup racing.

The next step below Winston Cup is Busch Grand National, the modifieds having been given that wonderful name to please their sponsor. The Grand National cars now use V-6s and V-8s, with limitations imposed on the eights to keep them slightly slower than the sixes.

That also means the sixes are getting more powerful. Earnhardt runs his own Grand National car, just for fun, along with the Childress/Goodwrench Winston Cup effort. His V-6 Chevy is nearly as fast as his restricted V-8 Winston Cup machine.

NASCAR wants to keep superspeedway speeds at 190 mph or so, maybe touching 200 just long enough to make the headlines. The GM cars have V-6s that can do it, or could if allowed. Ford is funding a development program, with help from the Elliotts, so that they, too, can have a competitive six.

Chrysler Corporation's official opinion is that they have thought about getting back into NASCAR, but that the returns don't justify the investment at the present time.

Insiders at NASCAR, protected here because they talked, say huh! Chrysler has been pitching a return, but the Dodge Daytona, the sports coupe that Chrysler would like to promote in Winston Cup, is too small and slick to be allowed into the class with the produc-

Team trailers carry two cars and stacks of parts. This is the Coors/Melling/Elliott operation; there are five times as many cars and workers at home as there are here.

The 1988 Pontiac Grand Prix shares only a name with the conventional big coupe of the past. Pontiac is making a strong effort to improve the brand's visibility. The race car of course is completely different from the road version;

Richard Petty's 43 and STP are as familiar as Mike Waltrip's 30 and Country Time (a product of General Foods and that firm's first venture into motor racing) are new.

tion-based small-block V-8 that Chrysler already makes. Putting that V-8 into the Daytona would of course be legal, just as it's become with the GM cars.

OK, the subject we've been avoiding.

Winston Cup racing is open, as said many times, to American-made passenger sedans. Quoting Bill Jr. again, "We've never said who has to own the companies."

It's virtually certain that the Japanese-owned car companies will reinvent the American sedan, just as they've already reinvented the multi-cylinder motorcycle and the four-valve cylinder head. They will build American-scale sedans in their American plants. (If we're really lucky, they will copy the Germans and use rear drive when the cars are big enough.)

If Ford can make V-8s in Australia and ship them to the United States for assembly, which they do, then Toyota, Nissan and Honda can send V-6s from Japan and qualify them as American-made, when installed in cars assembled here.

NASCAR has the legal and practical power to let Nissan (or the others) fit a Banjo Matthews chassis with a V-6 and Nissan body panels and run it as a Winston Cup car. NASCAR has the technical skill and experience to work out an equivalency formula matching engines, if that's what they want, or even to make the challengers not quite fast enough if that's what they want, and NASCAR can make either choice stick. Watch for it.

NASCAR made stock car racing Grand.

Television made it National.

This will continue for the foreseeable future. The sponsorships will increase and the rules will ensure close racing so the audience will stay tuned and the sponsors will be happy. The junior leagues, the Grand National modifieds and the Daytona Dash compacts below that, and the various regional titles and tracks, will provide a steady supply of good, experienced new drivers. The banked ovals are making money, which will mean new tracks in other parts of the country and that won't hurt, either.

In sum, the rules will change and the show will go on.

Most times the team will haul a race car and a spare car, or perhaps one car to qualify and the other set up for the long haul: the driver qualifies, so he can swap cars if something goes wrong before the start. This is a Road & Track *test at Charlotte Motor Speedway. The car nearest the camera is a road racer, with rear-quarter glass and right-side fuel filler and exhaust; the far side car is for short track, with open sides. Note the squat at the road racer's front, with the right wheel severely decambered.*

Index